# Into the Sun

## Air Force Memories, 1956-1976.
## The Rise to Power.



by
John Womack

Published by
Soliloquy Press

Published by Soliloquy Press
Hickory, NC
http://web.mac.com/fauxtaographer/



Library of Congress Cataloging-in-Publication Data
Womack, John
Into the Sun: Air Force Memories, 1956-1976. The Rise to Power.
p. cm.

1. Air Force – United States 2. Memories 3. History
I. Title

ISBN - 978-0-9655546-5-7 Second Edition, revised

Library of Congress Control Number: 2011914688

Those who travel into the future
are impressed the most by things
they did not go there to find.

**Thanks** to my wife, JoAnn, who proof read and wrestled with misspellings and typos. She suggested the inclusion of some chapters I had thought to discard and suggested the discarding of other chapters. She provided very necessary encouragement during the long period of preparation and particularly the final stages.

Darron Silva was my technical expert on computer and photography issues. He provided advice and assistance in solving problems involving layout and photo placement and presentation.

Four photographs are provided courtesy of the United States Air Force: The schematic of the Titan II missile complex, the photograph of the launch of a Titan II, and the two photographs of the author here in the preface. All other photographs and sketches are the property of the author.

The photograph of the bar background in the chapter about NKP actually was the bar in Udorn RTAFB. College Heights is clearly a fictitious name. The launch messages described here are not those actually used at that time, but are presented to fit the story and avoid any encounter with information which once was classified. It could appear that some Air Force Regulations were not adhered to, and that impression is totally a result of inaccuracies in recollection or facilitation for writing style.

# About the Author

John Womack served in the United States Air Force from 1956 to1976, retiring as a Major, a Master Navigator, Senior Missileer, and a graduate of Air War College. He has a Master's degree in Business Administration and since retirement has taught business-related courses in colleges in three states over twenty-four years. He also worked with the State of Florida as a Budget Director, Auditor, and Supervisor of Accounting Services in the Comptroller's Office.

After moving to North Carolina he has taught photographic art for more than twenty years, presented lectures and art exhibitions throughout western North Carolina. Now he maintains a photographic art studio, an on-line presence with webpage and blogs, and writes. He and his wife have five children and six granddaughters.

The top photo was made in 1956, the bottom one in 1976.

# Other books by John Womack:

Titan Tales - Diary of a Titan II ICBM Crew Commander
Methods and Procedures of Outdoor Photography
Trails in the Southern Mountains
Blue Mountain Kitchen
To Please the Bees

# Table of Contents

# 1
# Reflections

I entered into the Air Force like a young man might fall in love with an enchanting mistress. I was intoxicated by her flash and style. I loved being with her and breathing her breath, and doing daring and crazy things. We reached heights unknown to mere mortals, and sometimes we lay together spent and exhausted, having escaped the very jaws of death with the click of its teeth still ringing in our ears.

No longer was I just a man. Now I was part of a great team. She and I were Valkyrie and Knight. Together we carried our nation's flag into battle, leading Right to triumph over Evil so we might bring that great flag back home again in glory.

Glory however, was not to be our fate. While the Vietnam War slowly became our most important mission it was never to be our nation's great shining hour in history.

Our welcome home from combat was often publicly insulting, sometimes obscene, and then there were devastating private moments alone again with our families that were worse to us than the war itself had been. Now, even that is over and all those sad things have run their course.

Yet dreams of ancient cockpits still recur and images come forth and beckon. Dark aircraft cabins dimly seen are lighted red once more with ember-glowing panel lights.

Would-have-been farmers flew those ancient airplanes. Farmers who were called to serve their country and they served it well and got out. And they were called again and served again and got out again. Now they are called one more time – to fly again with us in these dreams that I know we all still share, and we will sail together one more time above some nameless sea. And in these dreams, we'll fly to and from Bermuda's shores, through wild Azorean winds or assorted crises in Berlin, and yes, we'll cross that other ocean too, where we went so long ago, to – and sometimes from – the land of the Magic Dragon – Vietnam.

I don't know how many times I thought to myself while I was in the Air Force: *I have the best job in the whole world!* I loved the Air Force. You might very well call this a love story. It really *is* about a young man and his mistress, how they lived together in rapture, delighting and enriching each other's dreams and fulfilling the needs of both.

Eventually, a wife became part of the affair and things would never be the same. Oh she understood and the mistress understood, of course they did, and they both sacrificed and looked the other way again and again, but the young man became torn as conflicts arose and persisted and grew, and as both his loves each quietly continued their own claims on him.

Then came both children and war. The ties between the young man and his family threaded, pulled apart and began to break. He and his comrades were stretched too thin again and again by a war that would never end and could not be won. Finally, now no longer young, the man had lost his wife and turned his back upon his mistress, returning to embrace his children and to try to find another life.

When my comrades and I entered the Air Force, *IT* was only seven years old. The officer corps was comprised of two separate groups. The first were patrician gentlemen, those elegantés from the Army, mostly majors, lieutenant colonels and full colonels, those who wore their West Point rings on the same finger as their wedding rings but *above* it to signify that they were married first to the Army (now Air Force), and their families would always come in second. These were the officers who were trained in the art of war and had been to academies to learn those skills. Their idea of a good time was to meet in the evening with martinis at the Officers' Club, then eat a fine steak with good wine, and help the evening slip away as they sipped scotch and soda with a twist, and enjoyed a good cigar while a string quartet played classical music quietly in the background, as they played bridge, or perhaps talked about affairs of the world, or war and peace, or of women they had known.

The other group of officers were men drafted to fight in World War Two, they were the ones who won that war and then got out, glad to go, but were called back in to fight in Korea. They fought *it* to a standstill and got out again, only to be called back again and sometimes again for a Berlin crisis or something else. Now, they seemed like old men, 45 or 50 years old, still captains (even lieutenants!). Old pilots they were, born in 1907 or 1908 or 1909, now with 16 or 17 years total service, frustrated farmers some of them were, some of whom perhaps would have been merchants. They were men who had never seen a college, now had nothing to sell anybody, and who just knew how to fly an airplane by the seat of their pants, and they were worriedly hanging on hoping for twenty years and a retirement. Their idea of a good time was to stay at the Bachelor Officers' Quarters (BOQ) and play an old guitar, drink beer and sing the ballads of Jimmy Rogers, Hank Williams and Oscar Brand, often filled with different words like Chongjin, Dortmund, Kaesong, Heilbronn, Wonsan, Mannheim and many other foreign sounds they had come to know so well.

Into this mix of elegantés and farmers, we entered. Twenty-two years old, most of us were, just out of college with brand new degrees that had kept off the draft. Now we were in for a quick whirl of obligatory fun before we got out to make our fortunes in the civilian world. College football stars we were, some of us, bringing fancy dreams and campus queens, and a sense that we will change the world.

Our degrees were all over the place: physics, English, physical education, math, history, music, engineering, fine art, and on and on. Our idea of a good time was our endless bull sessions. Sparking ideas off of each other's ideas, we were amazed at our collective knowledge and how our diverse clash of facts would bring forth meaningfully obtuse wisdom.

We could sing too. But we sang the popular tunes of the time, songs that heralded the beginning of a new era, and we would dance with the elegantés and their ladies over at the O Club, but insisted on our own show tunes that came in with us: "The Lady is a Tramp," "The Way You Look Tonight," "The Impossible Dream," and so on.

Eventually all those old songs would disappear, the elegantés would fade away, and the old farmer-pilots would be dismissed, finish out their time as sergeants and retire.

We became the Air Force.

The airplanes we flew back in the beginning didn't work well together. Each had its own separate job to do, or else was designed to do a hundred jobs, none of them really well. Our radios would reach across a hundred miles or so, and we flew beyond that in our first half-hour of a ten-hour flight. Weather forecasting was like a game of toss; sometimes it worked but even then was ineffective because we were so surprised that it was really right. Any overall forecast across a continent or an ocean was a hopeless guess.

Our firepower was already devastating, but we learned to concentrate its force and become more accurate and enhance our teamwork and coordination. Under our watch, bombers would take off from Alaska, others from Louisiana, and refuel together with tankers out of Ohio and Florida, then "strike" a common target with precision timing.

New aircraft arrived, new tactics developed, and a new brand of officer and airmen were trained and checked out. Finally, new people came to take our place.

These were not that Happy Band who would never mind, but steely-eyed, sober, staring men of judgment, men without a lot of humor. No barroom singers these young men, not given to bridge or gin - golf perhaps, but not with passion unless it was also played for money. Were they college men? Of course, but business majors mostly, many with MBAs already, some with degrees in engineering. Serious men they were, objective setters, planners, organizers, staffers - executioners. Eventually, we left it all to them.

How did these changes and so many others occur? What would it have been like if you had been there then to see it take place? In part, this book is an account of how some of that change occurred. It tells how the Air Force developed from a stepchild of the Army into the dominant force of modern battle. We who served during that period are the ones who made that change happen, but we didn't know we were doing it.

This book is not fiction. It is history in the sense that it is carries with it those confusing details that are so often lost in the catalogs of historical fact. All of the stories told here are true, to the best of my knowledge and recollection. They took place between 1954 and 1977, or about twenty-five to forty years prior to the writing of the book. Some diary records were available, also a few logbooks and two or three old flight logs along with photographic negatives and some black and white prints. Some color slides have also been found and all of this has shed varying amounts of light and darkness on those events.

The book is also written from memories, so it is not at all like a novel but more like pictures at an exhibition all of which share the same hall and rooms but each with its own story to tell.

They describe events in which I participated, directly observed, or received on a firsthand basis as a reporter might gather information from eyewitnesses who were people I personally knew. I have endeavored to shield the identity of the people who are portrayed, by using obviously assumed names except for historical figures. Some characters might seem to be recognizable, but I did make efforts to protect the privacy of people, most of whom I do not know how to contact today. My intention was to reveal the personalities of the individuals while protecting their identities.

So this book IS a memoir, but the person described as "I," or "me," and which is present in every chapter, is almost never the author - at least not alone. The pronoun "me" could easily have been written as "you," and it is intended that the reader might feel to be actually participating in the related events as they take place.

It is absolutely true that those people identified as "my" wife and "my" children and "my" personal friends are NOT necessarily the same as those in real life; but those depicted in the book, in their composite presence hopefully produce reality, and depict real human beings in the way that I could not portray by a simple recounting of many individual occurrences. They are actually my memories of all the people I ever knew in the Air Force. They are all my friends.

In its highest possible aspiration, the "I" who speaks in this book would be the Air Force itself, telling a small part of its great story. Through the pages of this book the reader can go back in time and walk through those ancient operations shacks, fly in those old aircraft, listen to the sounds of faraway places and smell some of the dust we stirred up.

Everything in the book is a historical occurrence. If you had been there then, you would have seen the same thing. As an enlisted man or a non-rated officer or a pilot, you might have remembered different elements, or seen them from a different point of view, or interpreted, recorded, remembered and reported them differently, but you would have experienced some of the atmosphere which now unfolds before you.

# 2
# The Plain of Jars

February 19, 1970.

Our KC-135 was scheduled to refuel B-52 bombers over the Gulf of Tonkin. But after we were airborne our bombers were sent to strike other targets and would refuel from other tankers far away from  orbit.

We were diverted to the southern part of Vietnam where F-4's were providing close air support to ground forces near the Laos and Vietnam border.

En route to our new orbit area I couldn't help but reflect on the hour and a half we had spent yesterday, carefully planning every second we would fly and every mile we would travel, plotting all the coordinates we would need, when and where we would begin our turns, and selecting altitudes we would fly. Now we are proceeding to a new set of coordinates, in a different part of Vietnam and the actual work we will do still depends upon things that have not yet happened. Air Force crewmembers have a general comment for this type of careful planning and subsequent spontaneous action of a totally different sort which happens altogether too often: "Measure it with a micrometer, mark it with a grease pencil, and cut it with an ax." Chop–chop.

Fighter-bombers were vectored to us for four busy hours and after off-loading most of our fuel we were returning to our home base, U-Tapao (YOU-ta-pow) Royal Thai AFB, in Thailand.

We had just departed our refueling airspace and were climbing to cruise altitude when we heard an emergency radio call from Laos. Two F-4s had been hit by ground fire. One of the aircraft exploded, killing both pilot and navigator, the other aircraft was not able to maintain flight and its crew members ejected over that lonely blue land. They were last seen drifting down in their parachutes, disappearing into the murky haze that covers these grassy ridges known as the "Plain of Jars."

The pilot vanished into the smoky sky and was never heard from again. The navigator began broadcasting on his survival radio saying he had landed OK but was under sporadic enemy fire. He could see enemy forces and they were coming after him. He was running and calling for help.

Air Force and Naval aircraft began congregating over the area although low clouds and the smoke of combat made visual contact with the ground difficult.

All American aircraft in the combat area were under the control and direction of an airborne battlefield command aircraft, which functioned somewhat like an airborne air traffic controller. It's call sign was "Crown" and it began organizing the rescue effort and directing aircraft to the area. Army choppers also reported they were "inbound," requesting headings and directions

The navigator on the ground called in to tell us he was behind a hill and the enemy couldn't see him. "You can get me real easy right now!"

We were the first tanker to reach the area, coming in at 520 knots and 27,000 feet. Crown directed us to assume orbit at 2,500 feet, and we made a rapid descent, our aircraft shuddering and shaking through the aerodynamic forces of its swift drop. Then we leveled off in hot, turbulent air and set up an orbit 1,500 feet over the area of the search.

Immediately an F-4, low on fuel but with ordnance on board, was vectored to us. We made a quick rendezvous and hooked up in moderate to heavy turbulence. He took some fuel and dropped into the murky clouds. Our Boom Operator noticed the receiver aircraft had already been hit by small arms fire.

"I gotta GO!" A disembodied voice broke in over the airwaves. "Dammit! They *found* me! Where *ARE* you guys?"

An Army FAC (Forward Air Controller) was flying his small Cessna aircraft very low over the area trying to mark the enemy location with smoke flares, but was also taking hits from them. The F-4 we had just refueled came over the rescue area low and fast and made two passes but got hit by ground fire. Trailing a heavy, black cloud of smoke he departed for home.

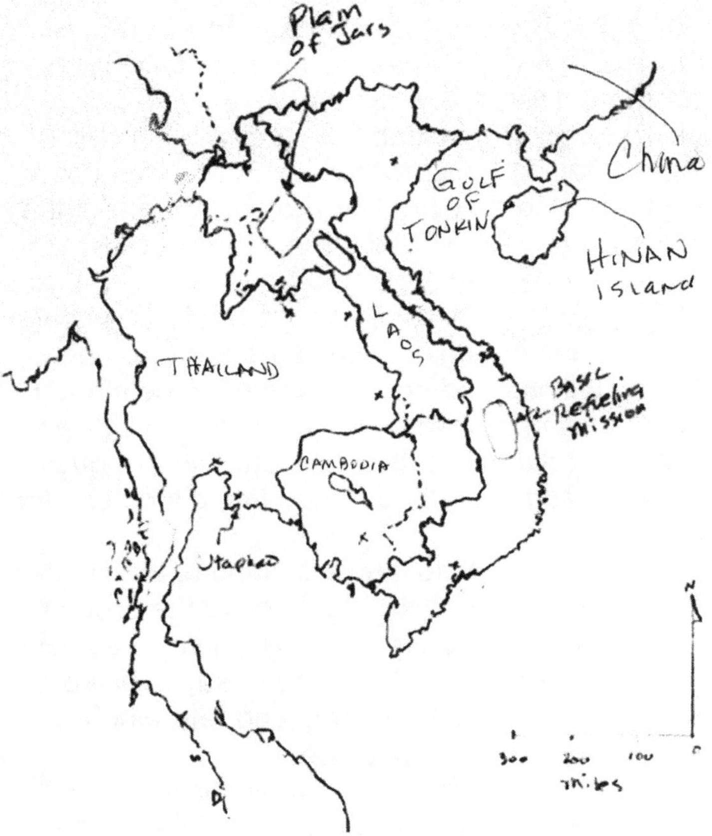


**Plain of Jars**

Another F-4 came in, quickly took fuel then went down for a look. After several low drags through the valley trying to get under the clouds, he found the enemy. He was fired upon at the very end of his run but developed a weapons malfunction. He could not release his bombs and departed for his home base.

Another F-4, "Scarlet Three," came in and joined up with us, took some quick fuel and dropped into the clouds.

"I'm behind a *big black rock*!"

The FAC went in to mark the spot for the F-4 and took several more hits. He finally departed the area, muttering laconically: "I got a real good hosing-down – one of these times those guys are going to have my ass."

A "Jolly Green Giant" was inbound to the area and made radio contact with Crown. The "Jolly Green" is a huge rescue helicopter formidably armed with .50 caliber machine guns, Gatling guns, rockets, etc. They can out-shoot almost anything they are likely to encounter but they fly low and slow, and make good targets themselves.

"They're *shooting* at me!"

Scarlet circled the area where ground fire had been reported but could find nothing. He came back up once more for fuel. This time the hookup was extremely rough. We were all bouncing up and down and skidding sideways, almost out of control in the turbulence, and the F-4 guys were shaky from fatigue – it had turned into a long day for everybody.

The Jolly Green called in the location of the survivor. They were down to less than 100 feet above the ground and had visual contact with him! But the enemy was right there, too. The Jolly Green pilot called to say they were taking small arms fire from the enemy and returning fire themselves and asking for assistance.

Now we knew exactly where the action was and were homing in on radio signals transmitted by the Jolly Green.

"Take me as far north as you can," requested the F-4 pilot.

Our pilot responded: "Roger Scarlet. We're at 'bingo' fuel ourselves."

"I need another minute."

"Scarlet, we'll split our emergency reserves with you - 1,000 pounds each."

"That's all I need!"

Into the forbidden land we carried our receiver, bouncing and skidding, hopping up and down, and sliding from side to side in the turbulence, his great engines burning fuel out of our tanks.

Over the area marked by the Jolly Green Giant we left Scarlet Three. Both the pilot and navigator in that aircraft were obviously exhausted as they went down into the turbulent murk again

We departed the area, now on emergency fuel.

"*They're coming after me*!"

Our radio contact faded as we heard the Jolly Green saying they had both enemy and the survivor in visual contact but were taking heavy fire and abandoning the rescue attempt.

An hour later, we made a straight-in descent and landed on little more than fumes. At debriefing, we asked about the survivor.

"Did we get him?"

"Got him! The enemy had him practically in their hands and an F-4, a 'Scarlet Three,' came in and dropped holy hell on top of them, and a Jolly Green just happened to be in the area and pulled him out before the smoke could clear away."

# 3
# Longbird

For me, this all began in a golden age, back in the time of Kennedy and Camelot and new jet aircraft and a suddenly shrunken world.

Korea was in truce and the American economy was just beginning to boom. We new college graduates were going to see the world for a year or two then go back home and make our fortunes.

The Soviet Union was no military competition for us, even the Bermuda Triangle was a yawn, and we just ignored the awesome Federal Bureaucracy. It didn't seem to know much about us, and we really didn't care much about it.

In 1958, the Tactical Air Command decided to fly a group of F-104s nonstop from Germany to California. In the event of war, it would be important to be able to quickly move these aircraft across the globe into a new combat zone. The 104's are small but they have an enormous thrust-to-weight ratio. They also have astonishing acceleration and are a key element to achieve and maintain air supremacy. But they don't travel well; theoretically, they could just fly on and on with mid-air refueling and go for days. But these airplanes were designed to fly missions lasting about two hours. There was no engineering provision to move flaps to a middle position for refueling, and the pilot fit into the airplane like a foot fits into a shoe. This epic twelve-hour flight would require five midair refuelings, and that's a long time to sit in what a fighter pilot once called "a cross between a sling shot and a jock strap." To assist in the mission, additional KB-50s were deployed to the Azores and Bermuda. For some reason, probably because the headquarters brass were afraid we couldn't do it, the mission was classified "Secret."

My crew was one of three who were chosen to augment our Bermuda detachment for this mission. When we arrived at Kindley AFB, the BOQ was filled to capacity, so we would have to stay off base. Since we would only be on the island for one night we are "assigned" to the nearby Castle Harbor Hotel. This is unusually gracious accommodation by Air Force standards, and it became even better when our early morning flight was canceled about 6:00 that evening. Instead of beginning crew rest at 6:30, we held an impromptu drinking demonstration downstairs at the Castle Harbor bar, but were amazed to find that we Air Force "professional drinkers" were no match for most of the civilian tourists.

Next evening we were in bed by 6:30 and drifted into a fitful sleep only to be awakened about 11:30 by gunshots and horrible screaming!

I raced to the window and watched in amazement as a band of Scotland's Finest marched across the moat with kilts swirling, drumbeats pounding, and bagpipes skreeling to take the Royal and Ancient Fortress in alcoholic victory!

Return to sleep was not easy, and then about 1:00 a.m., the Scottish Expeditionary Force marched down our hallway, with drums and bagpipes shaking the rooms! *Those bastards –- we'll get even!*

Two hours later we got up, making a great deal more noise than we would normally make at 3:20 a.m. in a civilian hotel, but no heads were stuck out to complain. Finally, we stomped down the hallway, reluctantly concluding that our fellow hotel-mates were all still downstairs in the bar.

At 5:00 a.m., after completing our preflight checks we were sitting in front of the aircraft when the operations officer drove by to tell us our mission had been canceled again.

Instead of returning to the Castle Harbor though, we were sent to a dinky hotel in Hamilton. It was a lot farther from the base, but a lot cheaper for the Air Force.

Most of us rented motorized bicycles for the thirty-minute trip into Hamilton, and also for shopping on our newly found day off. We will ride the bikes back out to the base early tomorrow morning to make our flight.

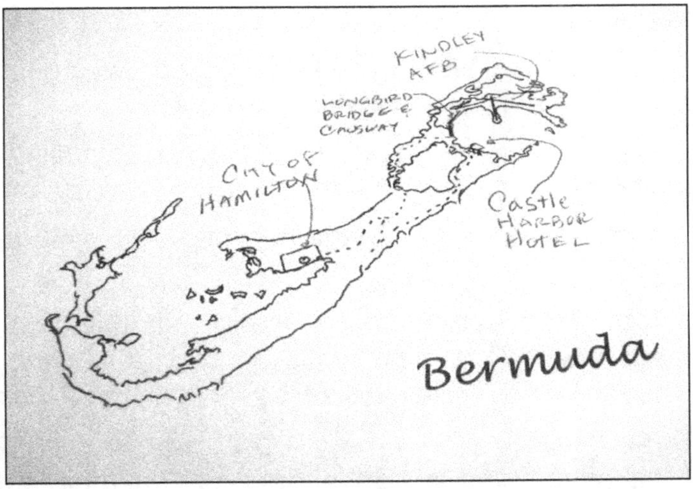


Next morning at 2:30, we woke up to rain pouring down in sheets. It bounced off the road four feet back into the air, and the wind was howling down the dark and empty streets of Hamilton. A telephone call to detachment operations confirmed that our mission was a "GO" and we had to be there in forty-five minutes!

We loaded our luggage and bags on the back of our bikes and took off through the downpour. Two blocks into our mission the leader of our group, Captain Heap, was blown into a ditch and cut his leg. We gathered around and stopped the flow of blood as a Bermuda taxicab pulled up.

"Hi mon, might I be of assistance?"

"You bet yer sweet ass . . ." Heap replied, "I gotta git to Kindley muy prompto!" Then turning to us, with rain pouring down his baldhead, "Get another cab men, we'll leave the bikes here."

"D'yo know yer mission ha' been canceled?" The taxi driver asked.

"*What* mission?" Heap said, his closely set eyes burning into the cab driver's face.

"T'F-104 flight " the driver replied. "H'its been canceled, mon."

"How the hell would *you* know?" Heap was shocked; after all the mission *was* classified "Secret."

"Ah'm ah taxi driver, mon; h'it's my beusiness t'know whut's goin'on."

"Well, thank God!" Said a copilot, "Let's have a party!"

"Wait just a damn *minute*," Heap said, rising on his gimpy leg, "we can't take his word to call off a *mission!* He's not in the Air Force – Hell, he ain't even a damn *Ameri-can!*"

"Hey, mon,' the taxi driver said with an impatient tone to his voice "yer don' need t't'ake my wird fo'rit," He picked up his radio and placed a call.

"Deespotch!" An English voice came over the airways now filled with static as lighting split the night sky.

"This'Abner . . . can yer verify t'F104 mission ha'been canceled?"

"Aye mon, T'Yanks shut it down. T'hy say bod wether ova Germ'ne ." The taxi driver looked at Heap and raised his eyebrows as if to say "*see*?"

"Well, *Hell!*" Heap shouted. "He ain't no damn Ameri-can *either!*" Then turning to us he called out: "No way! This smells of the *KGB!* Get on your bikes men, we gonna *fly!*"

Heap started his motor and took off, and of course we all followed along behind him, as the rain came down harder. We got around two corners before Heap bounced off a curb and slammed into a coral wall. When we caught up with him he was laying on his side, moaning and groaning; his bike was on its side, its rear wheel slowly turning with a wobble-wobble. Lightning struck the ground so close by that everything seemed to bounce, and the sound of the rain falling on our bare heads had become deafening.

As if brought by the storm, the taxi appeared again. Its window partly rolled down and the driver called out: "Hey mon!" He turned the radio volume up and said: "Listen 'ere," then he spoke into the microphone: "Go a'hed, Major . . . " and he handed the microphone to Heap. We could hear a voice over the static.

"Heap? . . . uh . . . what? . . . Oh, yes . . . ***Heap***!"

"This is Captain Heap, here, . . . groan . . . "

"**Heap!** – This is Major Henson here, do you recognize my *voice*, man?

"Roger Major, I recognize your voice, yes *sir, I sure do*."

"Then Heap – *go to bed*!"

"Is the uh . . . you know, ah . . . '*thing*' . . . off , sir?"

"Heap, GO TO BED, and that's a damn order!"

"Then we're not coming out to – ah, you know, '*LOOK*' at the airplanes?"

"Listen Billy Big Deal," the voice hissed back over the static-filled radio using Heap's nickname, "I want your damn ass in bed in ten minutes! And that's a *di-RECT* order! All I want to hear from you is 'Yes Sir!' Is that plain?"

"Yes sir."

There are some who say that was why Heap never made major. But those who knew him well knew there were a lot better reasons.

Next morning we broke ground at 5:48 a.m., lifting quickly into the rose-colored dawn, rising with the sun into a Sargasso summer sky. Climb-out was quick and smooth and we proceeded to the Rendezvous Point thirty minutes away. Radio contact was established with "Bear" flight, identification went smoothly, and the rendezvous was flawless. Eight F-104 fighter jets, gleaming in the morning sunlight, slid up behind our flight of three tankers.

We let our refueling funnels drift backward into the slipstream of our aircraft on long black rubber hoses that unwind from pods on the wing tips of our KB-50 refueling tankers.

The fighters move into pre-contact position.

"Bear flight," the F-104 flight leader calls over the radio, speaking in a snappy Georgia cracker accent, "move flaps to full down . . . NOW!" Then in his best Lawrence Welk imitation, he counts, "Ah wan, nanda two anda circuit breaker – PULL!"

Refueling was perfectly and quickly accomplished, then the F-104's sucked up their flaps, they popped their afterburners and blasted away . . . climbing high . . . into the sun!

**F-104 on KB-50 Drogue**

**F105s in Pre-contact Position with KB-50**

# 4
# Midnight Chow

Yesterday was a big day for me. I was promoted to first lieutenant and also got "checked out", so now I can fly missions without an instructor navigator watching every move I make. Tomorrow I will fly alone – just me and my crew, and my brand new silver bars!

My first flight alone will be an early morning mission out of Lajes Field in the Azores. The briefing will be 0500, which means I have to get up at 0330 if I want to eat breakfast, and I have *got* to have breakfast or the day just won't go right. The flight had originally been scheduled for a 1000 hours briefing, and the fact that it was changed to 0500 was bad enough, but worse than that, was the other notice posted right below it on the bulletin board: "Officers' Club will be closed for maintenance from midnight to 0600 hours on 26 May 1958."

Since I am the youngest navigator in the squadron and am on my first TDY (Temporary Duty away from home station), I asked the pilot and copilot on my crew what they were going to do for breakfast. They said they will get a coke and a candy bar at Base Operations. *Yecch.* I asked my Operations Officer where I could eat breakfast, and he replied that first, I could get up early and eat at the club before it closed at midnight; or second, I could eat breakfast before I went to bed that night; or third, I could go to the Mess Hall and get "midnight chow" since they serve that meal here at Lajes, until 0430. All of these suggestions sounded terrible. I know I will miss the Officers' Club, which is always quiet at that hour. There I would have had a nice breakfast brought to my table while a Mozart melody perhaps, might play softly in the background. Waiters would be standing by my elbow to bring more coffee or butter. Besides, I don't like going in places like mess halls that have a lot of enlisted men because I don't know what to expect from them or how to act around them. I've only been in an operational organization for three weeks and I've spent my entire Air Force career in navigation school surrounded only by other lieutenants. I'm also younger than almost all of the sergeants. I even asked my Flight Engineer if he was going to the mess hall. He is a tech sergeant and could be my guide. He said he would rather sleep than eat any day. Well, there's only one thing left to do.

Ringgggg!

0330 hours. I turn off the clock and hike down the hallway to the latrine and I wash while dreading the ordeal which lies ahead – not the flight, but the mess hall.

After shaving I return to my room, dress and grab my briefcase. Then I leave the Bachelor Officers' Quarters (BOQ), walk past the Officers' Club which has lights on, *people are working in there*, I guess, and proceed to the Mess Hall.

The morning is dark and windy with a sky full of stars. A powerful wind is rushing off the North Atlantic Ocean and shore birds are calling, way off somewhere.

I wonder if somebody will call "Attention!" when I walk in. I hope not – and if they do, what do I do? Now I am at the Mess Hall and grab the door handle. If anybody calls "Attention," I will casually say, "Carry on, men." I pull the door open.

WHAM! I am slapped in the face with the glare of electric bulbs and fluorescent lights all bright and glaring. Music slams against my eardrums as the strains of "Wolverton Mountain" reverberate through the mess hall at full blast. I am transfixed by the smell of onions frying in bacon grease, and hash browns, egg and syrup. A huge sign confronts me immediately. It says: "YOU MESS UP – YOU CLEAN UP!"

I walk toward the line, accidentally stepping in time to the music. I try to break the cadence because I feel every eye in the place is on me. My head is bobbing forward and backward. I *am* the only officer in the mess hall but nobody stands up. Thank God!

I get to the line, pick up a tray and look around for plates – well, forget that – the tray has built up divisions on it to separate one helping from another. I see that everybody is eating right off their tray! God!

They all seem to be looking at me. I ignore them as I drop a spoon that I had tried to put on my tray. It is bigger than I had expected a spoon could ever be. When it hits the floor it sounds like an alarm going off, and then I accidentally kick it under a table. Seems like the entire chow hall is suddenly quiet. I would pick the spoon up except I don't know what I would do with it, so I carefully examine the food that is in front of me. An old sergeant comes over, picks up the spoon, looks at it carefully and puts it in his pocket. Probably an example that he will use later for something. I ignore him and reach for orange juice, but then there is tomato juice too, and pear juice and pineapple juice and grapefruit juice and grape juice. This is confusing, and I dither, but then stick with the orange juice and decisively move on.

A young airman seated near the line stands up as I pass by him. I quietly say "Carry on." He looks at me for a moment, starts to speak, and then goes to refill his milk glass. *Thank God!*

Another huge sign stands before me. It reads: "TAKE ALL YOU WANT – EAT ALL YOU TAKE!"

I look up from the tray at a cook behind the counter, a plump and jovial airman dressed in whites. He smiles broadly: "Good morning, LIEUTENANT, how would you like your eggs, SIR?"

I look over at the griddle and ask "what choices do you have available?"

He grins, "over easy over hard over cooked over sunny, under sunny under cooked, sunny side up sunny side down, rock hard up, rock hard down, scrambled up scratched up screwedup screwed over, cheeseomelet westernomelet hamandsausageomelet, egg-and-egg omelet . . . "

I interrupt, "Cheese omelet, please."

"Yes SIR!" He reaches for a metal water pitcher. "One CHEESEEE coming UP!" He flaps his elbows like wings and cackles like a chicken, as he pours something out of the pitcher onto the griddle – looks like at one time it could have been scrambled eggs.

A small sign over one of the food bowls reads "SOS." Under it is a tray holding several pieces of thick toasted bread slices with some gravy-like stuff in front of it. I pick up the tongs, select a piece of toast and drop it on my tray. It sounds like a brick! I decide to put it back, but I can feel the eyes of all the enlisted men in the mess hall watching me. I scoop up a dipper full of the gravy and pour it over the toast, wondering how any thing short of a grizzly could possibly chew that toast. Connie Francis cries desperately over the loudspeakers "Who's Sorry Now?"

My omelet is served and I select two slices of bacon, a little piece of ham, two sausage links and a sausage patty. I feel a little awkward choosing so many pieces of meat but I've never seen that much served at breakfast before in my life! Everybody watches intently.

Hash brown potatoes are next, and then as I slide my tray along the railing I pass in front of pancakes, waffles, grits, oatmeal, and cereal. Endless servings of white milk and chocolate milk are offered. There is honey, syrup, molasses, jelly and jam.

There's more – the line goes on, now to leftovers from last night. (Maybe before that?) Pieces of fried chicken are in one serving pan, stew in another, and then there are pork chops, mashed potatoes and green beans. Rolls and biscuits are lined up beside bread slices and cornbread.

The end of the line has another huge sign: "YOUR TIME IS THE GOVERNMENT'S MONEY!"

I sit down as Carl Perkins cranks up a high-speed lament about his Blue Suede Shoes, like he's afraid all the people who are shouting at each other in the mess hall are going to make more noise than he is. It's great music to help eat a meal real quick.

I finish eating and scrape the few remaining crumbs into a trash can beside which stands a sergeant who makes sure that enlisted men don't throw away good food. He glances at my tray, which is basically empty, then looks away. I sense that his eyeballs roll up toward the ceiling.

I walk to the door as "Unchained Melody" lends a dimension of immortality to the morning. I get my briefcase and don my cap, then open the door and walk outside. I feel like I've been spray-painted with grease.

The wind rushes up from the sea engulfing me in the smells of salt and wet sand and bringing with it the sounds of the ocean and calls of shore birds. Grass leaves billow in the breeze like so many ribbons blowing in the wind.

The time is now 0445, and I have a five-minute walk to the briefing room.

First light brightens the horizon and splashes a rosy glow across the eastern sky.

The darkest hour of the day has come and now it's gone. It turned out to be delicious.

**KB-50s Flight Line at Lajes Field, Azores**

# 5
# The Lewd Smile

It was always a long ride from Hawaii to California in a KB-50. Today it will take at least eight hours for our trip, maybe even nine to get all the way across but we're going home and that makes it a lot easier.

The day begins with hangovers and improves very slowly. Meanwhile the sun works its way into our flight deck and raises the temperature about one degree every ten minutes. We also have a nagging problem with number four engine, which appears to be slowly getting worse, but since it is not yet a serious problem we will use the engine as long as it is safe to run it.

An hour passes with bright sunlight flooding into the forward cabin. Another hour drags slowly by and the cockpit becomes hot and sleepy. The flight has become too routine, it is tedious, boring - we have become passengers rather than crew.

"BOOM!"

A great explosion rips our plane, and we feel it shudder with the impact. We are slightly over four hours out of Hawaii, half way to California.

"My *GOD!* – What was that?" shouts the pilot. "ENGINEER! What happened? Number four?" And to the copilot, "Stand by to feather number four!"

The engineer answers quickly: "Number four looks OK, sir. "

The pilot again: "Scanners! Are you OK in the back? Are you O.K.? Report! *Report*"

"Roger, this is the left scanner sir; everything's O.K. back here I smell something funny but I can't tell what it is. What the hell *happened* up there?"

"Navigator, Check the bomb bay for fumes."

"Pilot, engineer:  all four engines look good."

"What's the *smell*?"

"I can smell it too, now  – What the hell *is* it?!!!"

"It's *fuel*!"

"Navigator, this is the Pilot, answer me!"

"Pilot, engineer, it wasn't an engine!"

"No . . . it's . . . it's . . . it's . . . is it powder?"

"It's a *FIRE*, somewhere!"

"Where's the damn navigator - did he get lost *inside* the damn airplane?"

"Where the hell is the *FIRE*?"

"It smells like  . . . "

"It's some kind of *gas*!"

"Pilot, this is navigator  . . . what . . ."

"Shutup nav, it smells kinda like . . . a little like. . .

"An electrical FIRE!"

"Beans?"

"Check the crawl-space, navigator!"

"Beans?"

"It's not JP-4, it must be Av gas."

"Where?"

"MY GOD - Where i*s the FIRE*?"

"Beans - it's *beans!*"

"Navigator, check the crawl space for a fire!"

"Oh my ***God!***" The fourth copilot shouts: "I forgot my beans!"

"What the hell is going *ON!*" shouts the pilot.

"Sir, I put a can of bean soup in a hot cup and plugged it in . . . "said the fourth copilot ". . . and forgot it."

FORGOT it? When the hell was *THAT*?"

"About an hour ago – I'm sorry."

"Sorry *HELL*" shouted the pilot. "You *BASTARD!*"

So, now everybody settled back, while the fourth copilot cleaned up a huge mess, and the flight dragged on and on; eventually another hour passed away.

We were returning to the States after three weeks in the Territory of Hawaii, in July of 1957. Hawaii was great, we got to Waikiki and Diamond Head, and Bellows Beach, and Banzai and the Pipeline and all that.

**Waikiki Beach 1957**

Our mission had been to provide aerial tanker support from the Tactical Air Command to help F-104's cross the Pacific Ocean, and we had done all that flawlessly too.

We flew a remarkable aircraft, one that was very familiar to the Pacific: the KB-50K. Similar to the B-29's that dropped the atomic bombs, but with four great big

R4360 reciprocating engines, and out on each wing tip there was a J60 jet engine. The former bomb bay racks had been removed and replaced with two huge fuel tanks; that's where we carry the JP-4 that we transfer in-flight to the fighters. It is an airplane built to do a lot of heavy lifting, and it and we transfer a lot of fuel to a lot of thirsty jet fighter aircraft.

Now our mission has been accomplished and we are homeward bound, heading back to California. We had a rough night at the Hickam AFB Officers' Club last night; partly because we are bringing several other crew members back with us, and what was to have been a simple dinner took on the air of a great party.

Joe Blough, our instructor pilot on this flight, is an old command pilot captain. He's a good man with the throttle or the bottle and he could fly by the seat of his pants whether airborne or not, and regardless of whether he was flying in an airplane or otherwise. He wasn't flying the aircraft on this trip but sat up front to monitor the take off. After watching Hawaii slowly slip away into the morning mist he slowly slipped away into his own misty world, riding gallantly through an apparently rough sea filled with great choppy snores.

About two hours out, the flight engineer alerted us to a possible problem with engine number four; it was losing some oil, and beginning to run rough, and showing early signs of possible overheating. Our engines are numbered, as with all aircraft, from left to right as you face forward, or from port to starboard. Number one is the engine on the farthest left of the aircraft, number two is between it and the fuselage; numbers three and four are on the other wing with three being inside. The jets are numbered separately. The one on the left wing tip is called J1, and J2 is on the right wing tip. We use the jets for take off and refueling, and occasionally other times, but when we are cruising, they are usually shut down to save fuel.

Another hour slowly dragged by and tedium weighed heavily as we approached the halfway point. Capt. Blough was apparently catching up on years of neglected sleep. He was an Instructor Pilot and he knew everything there is to know about this bird. In fact he was *the* recognized expert in the KB-50 with an incredible 15,000 hours at the controls. He would clearly have been far more than a captain if he had spent less time at the Officers' Club bar. Major Post was the pilot behind the controls on this flight, but he was new to the organization and only had twenty hours in the KB-50. He was supposed to be checking-out as an aircraft commander to be assigned to a crew, but it was an open secret that he detested crew duty and hated the aircraft. His checkout proceeded very, very slowly.

Blough's cap had fallen off, revealing his very baldhead. The pilots at the controls joked about the blinding glare coming from his pate. One of the copilots, actually our third copilot on this mission, a young lieutenant who was also a professional artist, joined in merrymaking about the baldness, and then he pulled a magic marker out of his pocket and prepared to draw something on Blough's head.

Major Post held out his hand and chuckled "Awright, Lieutenant, fun is fun, but you don't want to do something you might regret later."

"This is something new," Lt. High said, holding up the tube. "It's called a 'dry erase marker' – see? " and turning it sideways he read from the writing printed on its side: "Dry Erase Marker; wipes off with dry cloth or tissue." He continued: "You can write on a board, like a chalkboard, then when you're through, just wipe it off." He held it up for all to see. "It's brand new - it's great!"

Major Post was surprised and said he would try to find one when we get back home.

Then, quick as a wink, Lt. High made several circles over Capt. Blough's head, and there appeared an incredible drawing of a man's face with an amazingly lewd smile. The mouth of the face was about a hand's width above Blough's eyebrows. Lt. High quickly added a mustache and then a right hand offering a version of a military salute, except with an obscene gesture. What artistic talent! Blough rubbed his face with both hands, stretched, yawned, and settled back for a long nap. Major Post grinned and slipped Blough's cap back on his head.

The sun worked its way into the flight deck and the temperature rose into the Very Sleepy range. An hour later, the Bean Soup Bomb exploded. Then the sun passed behind us and things returned to the normal status of crossing the Pacific at 260 knots.

"Pilot, this is engineer, number four is shorting out." We were now almost six hours into our eight-hour flight. The engineer added, "the oil leak is also getting worse and we may have to think about shutting number four down sometime in the near future."

"Roger, engineer, keep me posted."

"Roger that."

Another hour passed.

Then the pilot screamed "FIRE IN NUMBER ONE! Crew, this is the pilot! We have a *FIRE*!" A second later he called out "Number *one* engine! – Copilot, feather number one!"

"Roger, sir, number one coming to feather!"

"Engineer, shut down number one!"

"Roger, sir, number one is shutting down!"

"Crew, this is the pilot," He was breathing heavily and speaking brokenly " the fire alarm . . . is out - engineer . . . what happened? And how's . . . number four?"

Number four looked about the same as it had been, but the flight became more serious now. Blough, of course awakened during the emergency and he and Post discussed our options. We all know we can lose engine number four at any time. Flying this six-engine beauty on five engines is not necessarily a problem, but when you get down to four, it begins to get a lot more interesting.

We came in through the ADIZ (Air Defense Identification Zone), and flew up a corridor headed for McClellan AFB, California. We were afraid to relax too much though because number four engine was running more roughly than before, and losing a good bit of oil. A little trail of dark smoke now traveled along beside us in our slipstream.

Captain Blough and Major Post discussed problems that could occur during landing, and decided to let the captain take over the controls. Post had not yet landed the aircraft with an engine shut down.

When we pulled back power to begin descent, engine number two did not respond properly. There appeared to be some undetermined problem with it. The pilots and engineer discussed possibilities while everybody cinched up their seat belt and squirmed to make sure they were tight.

We had already declared an emergency, and received priority in our descent.

About four miles from touchdown, we could see eight fire trucks with their red lights flashing lining both sides of the runway.

Then number two engine exploded in a huge ball of fire. The aircraft lurched violently, and was smoothly pulled back into control by Blough.

"Copilot, feather number two; engineer, make sure two is shutdown and isolated," Blough said calmly.

**Fire trucks on Flightline. Hickam Field, Hawaii, 1957**

"Roger sir, number two is feathered!" screamed back the copilot.

"Two is shutdown, but it's on *Fire*! It's really burning - it's burning into the wing!" Shouted the engineer.

"Awright, copilot, let's go ahead and discharge the fire extinguisher on number two," Blough said thoughtfully, like he might be placing a bet on a college football game. And to the crew: "We gonna put'er down boys. this baby's sick - we ain't takin' her 'round."

"Extinguisher Discharged!!" Screamed back the copilot.

Now the aircraft buffeted as it encountered the ground effect, and Blough altered it's heading slightly to align with the runway as the main gear touched down. There was a squeaky "kiss - kiss" as the tires contacted the landing strip, then we could hear the struts rumble as they worked the weight of the aircraft from its wings to the runway. We rolled to the end, and turned off onto the taxiway with two engines smoking, and two feathered, chased by eight wailing and flashing fire trucks.

We parked the aircraft and walked into base operations. It was late now, and we were met by the base commander, Colonel Strong.

The colonel spoke: “Great job of handling the aircraft! Who was flying?”

Captain Blough saluted: “I was flying it, colonel.” And shaking his head, “Yes, it was quite a thrill!”

“What did you think when that engine exploded on final approach?” asked the colonel with a chuckle.

“Well,” replied Captain Blough, whipping off his cap and placing it over his heart, and bowing his head as if to pray – thereby presenting the colonel with a lewd smile and an obscene salute, “It’s not the worst thing I’ve been through.”

The colonel staggered backward as if he had been struck.

“Captain, what’s that on your head?”

Blough looked startled, then with a familiar grin, rubbed his hand over his bald head and says, “Hair, colonel, you gotta look close to get the fine detail.” He lowered his head again.

“Who is your commanding officer?” shouted Strong.

“Lt. Col. Salton, sir.”

“At Langley?”

“Yessir.”

“Captain, I am ordering you to go into the latrine and wash your head clean; either that or cut the damn thing **off!!!** Do you understand?”

Lt. High stepped forward quickly. “Sir, it is a silly joke I played, it is all my fault. I apologize. The face can be easily erased, here let me show you. He rubbed his handkerchief over Blough's head. "See, it's gone now; captain, show the colonel, bow your head."

"What the hell are you talking about?" yelled Blough, turning as if to attack the Lieutenant. Captain Blough was about five feet seven inches tall, and Lt. High was six-foot-four.

"Hey, wait a minute, it's still *there*!" Lt. High said, standing on tiptoe and peering down on Blough's head. "Here, let me get it off." He grabbed Blough's head, pulled it under his arm and started rubbing. Then he began rubbing harder while Blough began kicking and trying to punch.

"What the hell have you done to me?" Blough shouted.

He ran into the latrine to look in the mirror.

"Oh my God!" Blouch came flying back out again before the door could close.

"Did *you* do that to me?" Blough shouted, bowing his head at the copilot, pointing to his head and glaring upwards at Lt. High, with his fists clenched.

Major Post stepped up. "Blough, it will just rub off, don't get bent all out of shape."

"But it won't," Blough shouted. "What the hell is it?"

"It's a 'dry erase' marker" Post said, and pointing to Lt. High. "Show him, Lieutenant."

High pulled the marker out of a pocket on his flight suit and showed it to Blough, and read from the writing on its side: "Dry Erase Marker; wipes off with dry cloth or tissue." He continued to read: "You can write on a board, like a chalkboard, then when you're through, just wipe . . .."

Blough snatched the marker out of High's hand: "Let me see that damn thing!" And holding it up the light he read what High had said. Then he turned it over.

"Dammit, it says *here*," on the other side, "For use on porcelain boards, dry erase surfaces, glass and ceramics, ONLY', and look ***HERE!*** 'Warning: indelible, and may be permanent on clothing, porous material and SKIN!'"

"Oh my God! I didn't see that!"

"How soon can you guys get out of here?" asked the colonel. "Whatever you need just let me know."

# 6
# The Great Pizza Hill

Henry J. Kaiser. What a name!

But our Henry J. was not the "Henry J." of World War II shipbuilding fame, nor the 1940's car that didn't have a trunk door. This Henry J. was a first lieutenant and he was the only officer in our squadron who didn't fly our KB-50 Tactical Air Command aerial refueling tankers. He was neither a pilot nor a navigator but a "ground-pounder" brought in by our Operations Officer who thought we needed an officer to run what he called our Administration Section - in other words, somebody to be the Ops Officer's full-time assistant.

So Henry J. came to work at eight o'clock, went home at five, and seldom came in on Saturdays or Sundays. Consequently he remained pretty much a stranger to us flight crewmembers. We saw him occasionally during the day when we might come in, or for the monthly Commander's Call meeting, or sometimes before or after a daytime flight, but we all got endless messages from him on the bulletin board and in our crew boxes.

We flight crews were often gone from our home station on trips. The Air Force called these short assignments "Temporary Duty Away from Home" or "TDY." As with many things in the military, TDY is either way underdone or way overdone. Some people seem to be gone all the time, while others never get to go anywhere. Eventually, a tension began to develop between Henry J. and the rest of us because of the TDYs. He felt we were paying no attention to him, and we were having all the fun, flying around to Bermuda and places like that.

After he had been assigned to our outfit a little over a year, the squadron commander decided to put him on orders to fly to Bermuda to "inspect detachment files, etc." This way he could fly with us in our airplanes and see the island. Eventually, everything fit together, and we all wound up on the flight line ready for Bermuda. Henry J. was going TDY!

Day 1. December 11. We were part of a six-ship flight leaving Langley at 2 p.m. and landing in Bermuda at 5:00. Take off was normal, the flight was unusually smooth, and after an hour or so Henry J. was yawning and looking for a place to stretch out.

**Approach to Kindley, Bermuda from KB-50**

He got up in time to watch the landing, then took off for the Bachelors' Officers Quarters (which we called "BOQ," or usually just "Q") to check in and change clothes. Then he went to the nearby beach while the rest of us began flight planning for our refueling mission tomorrow and our flight back home. The briefing time for the return trip was two a.m., so our crew rest began at six p.m., which was before we finished mission planning.

When the flight plan was completed we headed to the Officers' Club for supper, and there we found Henry J., perched like a jaybird up at the bar.

"Come over here, and I'll buy you guys a drink for the trip out here!" Henry J. motioned to us.

"We're on crew rest, gotta eat and go to the Q."

"Crew rest? Man, we just got here!"

"Well, you're not on crew rest, Henry J., you can stay here all night, just be at the briefing room, zero two hundred hours – but don't be late. No show, no go!"

DAY 2, December 12. We were supposed to take off at 4:00 a.m., but we were still sprawled out on the ramp near our airplanes at 5:30 when the squadron commander drove by to tell us that the mission had been delayed twenty-four hours.

"Bad weather in Germany kept the fighters on the deck. We'll try again tomorrow; same time, same place, stay tuned."

Henry J. was ecstatic. Two days off in a row, and in Bermuda! And us? Well, we've got twelve hours before crew rest – let's have a party! The only thing Henry J. was worried about was that long flight home – counting the refueling, it would be FIVE hours!

DAY 3, December 13. We were awakened at 1:00 a.m. and told that weather north of the Canary Islands had forced a second twenty-four hour delay. We went back to sleep, and most of us got up about 9:00 a.m. and went shopping again.

DAY 4, December 14. We got up at 1:00 a.m. and went to breakfast in a heavy rain. At briefing we were told that the wind blowing across the runway here in Bermuda was in excess of our allowable crosswind component. So we went out to the flight line where we sat in the dark, damp, leaking aircraft, waiting for the winds to die down. At 4:00 a.m. the mission was canceled because of the weather here in Bermuda.

Henry J. was now beginning to worry about all the paperwork he knew was piling up on his desk back home.

And the long FIVE-hour trip home was clearly a bother to him too. He was not used to flying Air Force.

He also began to worry about getting home in time to do some Christmas shopping. We told him: "Henry J, you've come to the best place in the world to shop - *relax* man!"

We were over at the club that afternoon about 4:00 when our detachment commander came up to us.

"Men, we've got an emergency deployment. Go down to operations, right now for mission planning. We're going to the Azores."

DAY 5, December 15. Four o'clock in the morning. We're at base operations, and we're getting ready to go. Henry J. is trying to get back home.

"We don't have the money in the budget." Colonel Salton said, speaking of a commercial flight. "You'll just have to go with us. We'll get you back home."

"How long is it going to take to get to the Azores?" Henry J. asked.

"About nine and a half hours," came the reply.

"Oh, *my GOD!*" Said Henry J.

The flight to Lajes Field in Tercedia, Azores wasn't really that bad. The ride was a little rough, here and there, with occasional moderate turbulence. Henry J. threw up a couple of times, but lived. He said he was afraid the airplane was going to be torn up by that turbulence and would break into pieces and fall into the frigid seas that he had heard about when he had gone with us to the weather briefing. They had told us that the survival time in the ocean today was less than 30 seconds.

DAY 6, December 16. Next morning was another twenty-four hour delay. Henry J. was now gaunt with worry and concern. He was worried about his wife, worried about his job, worried about his work, and especially he worried and worried and worried about that long, long, long flight home. And then he worried about Christmas getting closer!

DAY 7, December 17. Today, we got diverted to Iceland. There is a difference in December weather between Bermuda and Iceland. Nobody had thought to tell Henry J. about cold weather gear on his one-day trip to Bermuda. Of course we flight crew members carried ours everywhere we went. If we went to Phoenix in August, we took our cold weather gear with us. We found enough stuff for Henry J. but he was starting to look kinda strange.

DAYS 8 & 9, December 18 and 19. Two more days on the ground, sitting in front of the airplanes in Iceland.

DAY 10, December 20. We deployed to Argentia Naval Air Station at Placentia Bay in Newfoundland. Snow was on the ground when we landed, more was falling and it was mixed with rain, sleet, and freezing rain.

DAY 11, December 21. Mission delayed 24 hours. Henry J. complained again and again: "You guys are on flying status, you make enough money to eat off of!"

We would tell him to "Relax, Henry J., you're on per deim, boy!"

He was not happy. "You guys don't do anything – you haven't refueled a damn thing on this whole trip!"

"Well, we've refueled everything that has showed up."

Day 12, December 22. The mission canceled early. The weather here in Newfoundland was deteriorating rapidly and we were grounded. It began with a dense fog, and then a heavy rain fell through the fog all night long. About sunrise it became a freezing rain and that fell until noon. Then it turned to sleet, and the sleet turned into snow flurries, and by sundown, heavy snow was blanketing Newfoundland, covering our aircraft on the flight line, and our individual Christmas spirits. We weren't going to fly on the 23rd, and probably not the 24th either. Word got out that we would probably spend Christmas here, and the Officers' Club would be closed on Christmas Day for the holiday.

Henry J. had just arrived at the bar when we got the word. Nobody wanted to tell him, so Colonel Salton did it himself.

"Henry J., got bad news for all of us. Unless the weather clears up in the next eight hours, we are going to be here for another week."

"I'm going to get drunk." Henry J. said, very unenthusiastically. He was clearly all twisted and torn up inside; he had worried too much for too long, all he wanted was to get home and never go anywhere again.

"Barkeep!" called out Henry J.

"Yessir!" Responded the bartender, wiping his hands on a towel, "What's your pleasure, sir?"

"What's the strongest drink you got here?"

"Oh, gosh, I don't know, sir. "

"Come on, if you don't know, who would?"

The bartender stood for a moment staring off into the distance, holding his towel in both hands. "Stinger, maybe."

"Awright!" Henry J. said, as he slapped both hands hard on the bar and leaned back on his barstool, " Bring me ten stingers!"

"Oooohhh," said the bartender, "Sir, we can only serve one drink at a time. I can get the club officer for you, if you want to talk to him."

"Nah, bring me Number One!"

"Yessir, one stinger coming up!"

After about the third stinger, word began getting around the club.

"Ten stingers?" said Col. Salton. "The world record is twelve, and naturally it was a copilot who did that. Anybody who can drink twelve stingers, I'll buy a pizza for 'em"

So word got back to Henry J. "Twelve is the record, eh?" He took a long pull on his glass. "Bartender, bring me Number FIVE!"

Col. Salton drove down to base operations to check on the weather forecast. He came back with word that the roads were incredibly icy and treacherous, but also, that it looked like maybe, just maybe, there would be a clearing by daybreak, and we had just gotten clearance to go directly home!

"Bart ender! Bringmenum bbber-HAEIGHT!"

"God! Is he still at that?"

"It sure looks like Henry J. is going all the way."

"Yea!" shouted Henry J. "I'mgo naged that PIZZA!"

"What pizza?" Col. Salton asked the Operations Officer.

"The one you promised him," said Major Pound.

"I didn't promise him a damn *pizza*!"

"But he thinks you did." Pound lit his pipe. "He heard that you told somebody that you'd buy a pizza for anybody who could drink twelve stingers." Puff, puff.

"Get him his damn pizza, and give it to him *now*!" Salton said, reaching into his own pocket for some bills. "Here's the money." He handed Pound a couple of dollars. "I'm going back to the Q and get some rest, I'm goin' home tomorrow." Col. Salton left.

When the pizza arrived Major Pound took it to Henry J. "Henry J., here's your pizza! Col. Salton surrenders, and you win!"

He placed the pizza on the bar in front of Henry J.

"So just enjoy the fruits of victory! Eat your pizza and go back to the Q. We're going *HOME* tomorrow."

Henry J. looked suspiciously at the pizza and then at Major Pound.

"NO!" He shouted at the surprised major. "I haven 'tearned t'pizzayet, anIdonwann- hic- nagohic-home!" He swerved around, back to the bar. "Bart-tender! Brinkme-nembe RTIN!"

After that came number eleven, number twelve and finally number thirteen.

But by now the word had gotten about the club that we were going home tomorrow and everybody else had gone to the Q and was already in bed.

"HEY!" shouted Henry J. "Warsherbudy go?" "Hic! I WUN - Hic!."

Well, there was just Henry J. and me left in the club. "Are you going to eat your pizza Henry J?"

"Naw, ImTYRD lesgome - Hic! - I ben wirkin' man! Ha-ha-hic! illea-tit -hic!- t'morrow."

"Good! Let's just leave it here, we can pick it up tomorrow on our way out."

"Naw, i 'SMINE, Hic! iurn-tit."

He picked up a slice of the now cold pizza, smelled it and burped, then put it in the side pocket of his coat. He put another piece in the other side pocket, then one in each inside pocket. He folded another one up and stuffed it in his shirt pocket, then put one in each of his front pants pockets and finally, the last one he shoved down into his back hip pocket.

He patted the hip pocket pizza, burped, smiled and said: "Thasncase iged -Hic!- ungereyon -Hic!- t'way ome - lez gHic!go"

We went outside into a biting wind blowing about 30 to 40 mph. The temperature was about 20 degrees and the ice was so slick we could hardly stand up. We couldn't stand still either because the wind was so strong that we would "sail" along. The BOQ was only about 100 yards from the Officer's Club, but it was all uphill.

I went down first, after climbing about 20 yards up the hill. Henry J. teetered, grinning and pointing at me. I fell again before I could get back to him, but finally caught up. He was down to a deep knee bend position, slapping his legs and roaring with laughter, pointing at me and gibbering and hiccupping. I went down twice more before we got to the top, but not Henry J. He made it all the way.

Then he turned to the hill, arms outwardly spread like an actor receiving applause from an audience. When he tried to bow, he slipped and sat down. He still would have been OK if he hadn't turned to the left when he tried to get up but he slid slightly and then wheeled the wrong way.

Henry J. rolled over and over, again and again, like a rolling pin, all the way to the bottom of the hill. Then he couldn't get up. I had to go back down and get him. He smelled like an old, cold pizza. It had all become pureed by now and pieces of pizza were protruding from his collar and sleeves. He looked like he was covered with blood. We fell eight more times, each of us, before we got back to the top, and finally to his room. I helped him undress and lay out his clothes for the trip home. He threw his suit, pizza and all, into the suitcase and set on it naked, and closed and latched it. Then he went into the bathroom and threw up. He came back and collapsed on his bed.

We got him down to the flight line the next day and he went to sleep in the back end of the aircraft. We got on with the day's work, got airborne and after about five hours came in and landed at Langley in the early darkness of December 24. Christmas Eve – we made it!

What a celebration took place out there on the ramp, bright lights glaring down from the tall light poles, with family and crewmembers embracing one another in great joy! A great crowd composed entirely of our wives and children surrounded us and a festive Christmas atmosphere reigned supreme!

Then somebody noticed Henry J's wife. Patty was a cute little thing and looked like she might be about twenty years old; but right now she looked worried. She asked someone, "Has anybody seen Lt. Kaiser?"

"Who is Lt. Kaiser?" Asked a crew chief.

"Lieutenant Kaiser?" Another crew chief scratched his head

"Henry J.", someone else added.

"Oh, I know!" shouted another crew chief. "He's in my plane, I'll go get him!"

Henry J. was still asleep, back in the far end of aircraft 576. The crew chief woke him up and helped him get to the stairs that led down to the ramp.

Everybody turned to look at him. He looked like he had been run over by a truck. It was Charlie Chaplain gone bad. He slowly came down the ramp in the full glare of the lights and everyone watched as he stood there and swayed.

His sweet little wife ran up to him to hug him. And he said: "Honey, I am so glad to get back, I had a miserable time." He hiccupped twice. "Lesgo'ome."

She leaned over to smell his bag. "Oh Honey, did you bring me a pizza? You're the sweetest thing!"

# 7
# Stead

Some of the worst news anybody in the Air Force ever received was that they had just gotten orders to "go to Stead."

Nobody ever got the news that they were being sent to the Air Force Survival School at Stead AFB, Nevada, in the same spiritual dimension they were in immediately prior to hearing about it. We could all tell you where we were and what we were doing when we got the awful news.

I had just finished my fourth class of karate and was still at the base gym when Major Bigg walked by. He saw me and said: "Hey! – Did you hear you just got orders to go to Stead?"

"Oh, NO!" I cried, "Not *me!*" I clasped my hands and almost sank to a deep knee bend posture.

"Sorry, " the major said, "at least you're the *only* one from *this* base." Adding, "Thank God!"

"Thank God, *hell*!" I replied.

"Well, lieutenant, that's just the way the cookie crumbles; at least you'll probably never have to worry about going out there again." Then he added "That is, if you make it through" – chuckle – "and ever get back" – chuckle, chuckle – "alive, that is" – chuckle, chuckle, chuckle.

Stead was, as they say in the Air Force "Maybe not the end of the world, but you can sure see it from there." It was only a three-week assignment, mainly out in the woods of the Sierra Nevada Mountains but it was no vacation.

It was out near Reno, Nevada. This was where the Air Force taught their combat flight crews how to survive if forced to bail out or crash land in wilderness or hostile territory, and how to escape capture from enemy military forces and theoretically become a one-man army behind enemy lines.

I was an instant celebrity in the squadron for the next two weeks, and regaled with an incredible number of stories about Stead. Most were about how many people had been killed or maimed, or lost and never found again out there. There must have been thousands of people lost to the Air Force. It was also amazing that I couldn't find anyone who had actually ever been there.

"They never come back." I was told. I also heard that February was a great time to go because I probably wouldn't have to worry too much about snakes, and there might even be some snow on the ground.

★ ★ ★

The flight from Virginia in a DC-7 takes about nine hours, and I spend the night in a motel in Reno. There was gambling right across the street. "Bet your life!" A neon sign flashes off and on.

Yeah, you *bet!* The real gamble for me begins tomorrow!

I find the base to be both quaint and rustic. It looks like it is being prepared to be shut down, but I have heard that it has always looked like that. They try to run it a little like boot camp, but there isn't any real zip in that idea. It's a little like sparring with an old prizefighter. About the time you realize you might have your hands full, you can see his attention start wandering.

There's open bunking in an open hooch. Open toilets, too. Real friendly place.

The classes are interesting and the instructors are highly motivated and very good - and they have our complete attention.

There *is* a little snow on the ground, but it's hard to find. We are issued snowshoes and told to practice wearing them about the base. I look for the snow and tramp about in it on the great shoes. This will be fun. Later, we get a two-inch snowfall, and all us newcomers have more fun, and get to be real good in walking about on our snowshoes.

We spend the first week in the classroom, preparing for a Friday evening "orienteering" expedition. "Orienteering" is a map-reading exercise which requires each participant to "navigate" across the woods, fields, streams, etc., and go from a departure point to a destination. Initial practice is accomplished in a very large parking lot where we learn to follow a hand-held compass while walking around with towels over our heads, our eyes fixed on our compasses and our instruction sheet: ". . . walk 48 paces at 318°, then 12 paces at 051° . . ." We are supposed to end up where we began. At first we keep running into each other. Then we get really good.

Next we go into the woods on an isolated part of the base and "navigate" using hand-held compasses and topographic maps. It doesn't work out very good. We navigators have the most problem, mainly because we aren't used to map reading.

Bill, a former Golden Gloves boxer who is a first lieutenant and also an F-104 jock, turns in our group's best performance. He plots a course and goes straight to the end and doesn't allow for any obstacles; when he comes to them, he goes over, under, or through them. Some of them he destroys. Consequently he never gets lost, and he is in such good physical shape, being a world-class athlete, that his body is almost like his own personal F-104! We are all in pretty good condition, but can't hold a candle to him – he would stand out in any group of men.

Unfortunately, Bill seems fascinated by trivial details and is given to argument over minor points. In almost every class, he tries to "catch" an instructor by forcing him into explaining and "justifying" some insignificant detail, about which the instructor is really not very concerned.

"That's not really important . . .." The instructors seem to keep saying to him, over and over.

"Well, why do you *teach* it, then?" Bill will respond, holding his massive arms out, palms upward, mouth open, eyes cocked to one side, eyebrows arched.

The second week ends with us taking part in a "Practice." This "Practice" is designed to give us a "realistic" feeling for crossing enemy lines at night after having been shot down in the bad-guys' territory. There is no real way out. Even when we do make it to the final location, which is a stockade out in the middle of nowhere, we will be treated as prisoners-of-war. The only exception, we are told, will be for the first person to make it in to the camp. He will be treated as an honored guest and will watch the rest of the show as it unfurls through the night. Well, we all know who that "first person" in our group is going to be.

Bill *is* the first one, naturally. He makes it across the fields, gets through the woods, over the ridges and crosses the river. He swiftly penetrates "enemy" lines, and walks into the stockade, which consists of a couple of small wooden structures near a log-building, with a large fire burning in a ring of rocks. He finishes the course in three hours – an all time record!

"Hi guys!" He calls as he walks in out of the darkness. "Am I the first one in?"

A staff sergeant with great red stars on each epaulet, and a nametag signifying that he is playing the role of a colonel in some communist army comes over to him and says, "On your knees, Leftennant!"

"No, now wait a minute, sergeant," Bill replies, very concerned. "Am I or am I not the first one to reach camp?"

"On your *knees*!"

"No! Who got in ahead of me? Tell me!"

"Just means you get to *suffer* longer, leftennant, ha ha ha!" He points to the ground, "On your knees!"

"No! No!" Bill says seriously. "Listen here, that's not what Captain Shafer said yesterday!"

"Get him, men!" The colonel-staff-sergeant shouted to his two helpers.

The young colonel-airmen reach up and take hold of Bill's massive arms as the colonel-staff-sergeant swaggers forward like a great king.

Bill shakes both colonel-airmen loose, sending them staggering backwards. The colonel-staff-sergeant lowers his head and charges Bill. Bill catches him with an easy right to a fairly ample midsection and pokes a left to his right shoulder. That straightens him up, and then he swats a jab with his right palm, fist open, to the colonel-staff-sergeant's left shoulder. This sends him reeling and spinning around in the general direction of the campfire. He trips over a log next to the fire and falls, actually sitting into the fire. He screams, and rolls out of the fire pit, rising to his feet, pounding himself on his rear end sending sparks flying into the night. Heavy smoke rises from the area.

The colonel-staff-sergeant shouts: "School Situation! School Situation! School Situation!"

The two colonel-airmen stand poised like birds caught at the instant of take off, unsure of whether to try to catch the lieutenant again or fly away while they can still get free.

"No!" Bill shouts. "This is *not* a school situation!"

He strides over near the fire. “This is a screwed-up mess that is totally out of control, *sergeant*!” He points his finger at the colonel-staff-sergeant. “You guys can’t get your act together and you don’t know what the hell is going on!” He walks up and puts his face in the face of the colonel-staff-sergeant.

“Call Captain Shafer and tell him to get down here right now!” Then he adds, “Meanwhile, I’m the ranking man present, and until he can get his ass down here I’m taking charge – sit down and *shut up*!”

A little later the next man to complete the course, Captain Heart, walks into the camp. He is aghast at what is happening.

“Sergeant Whyme,” he tells the colonel-staff-sergeant. “Call your headquarters and ask them to send an officer out here.” But the field phones don’t work.

By the time Major Oak arrives out of the dark woods there is a conference of about eight people arguing and trying to figure out what to do.

Oak takes charge immediately. He lines every body up in order of rank and gets a quick and fragmentary briefing from each person, working from the lowest ranking up. He encourages the stories with phrases like “. . . What? You’re *Kidding*! Spit it out! You did *what*? Did you *really* do that?” The entire analysis takes less than two minutes.

Then he addresses the assembly: “You sorry pieces of *junk*!” He glares at both the colonel-staff-sergeant and the lieutenant. “Is this what we flew Tempelhof and Pusan for?” He paused. “Have we turned the corps over to a bunch of twinky-winky-dinky hot-doggies?”

“No We <u>HAVEN’T</u>!”

“Here’s what you’re going to do, *dammit.*” and he gives us our orders. Basically, we are all going to just forget what we have just been through and pretend nothing unusual ever happened.

"If this ever gets out," Oak says, pointing at the colonel-staff-sergeant, and his two assistants, "*all* those stripes are going to go – I'm tempted to rip *half* of 'em off right *now*!"

"And as for you, Lieu-TEN-ant " Oak puts both his fists on his hips, "if there is *ever* a court-martial over this, I'm going to beg to get on it so I can send you to a place that will make Thule Air Force Base look like Times Square!" He glares at Bill for a moment, then pointing his finger at him, he says in very concise, sharp words: "Meanwhile, you are going to suffer through the rest of this night, just like the rest of us!"

So we all arrange everything the way it "should" be and Major Oak turns to the colonel-staff-sergeant, "A'right, sergeant, take it over!"

(And to this day, the Air Force never found out what happened.)

We spend the next day in the Concentration Camp Phase of the class. We live in a cell, of sorts, on a dirt floor with lots of crumbling concrete and rotten wood. Most of the day is spent with us officers sitting around and watching our enlisted people work. They have to sweep and dig, and carry heavy things. It is all part of a plan to try to get the officers to do physical labor to help their men, theoretically breaking down the unofficial chain of command in the camp. But we have all been briefed on this so the enlisted men cheerfully "work," whistling enthusiastically, and we officers stoically watch. It's like watching a real slow, very boring game with no rules and no end anywhere in sight. We spend our second night in the "concentration camp" and wake up the next morning knowing we are going back to the base. Thank God.

The base looks good when we get back, and now we are almost through with the course. The hardest part is well past us now and the only thing left is to spend a week in the woods. Should be a piece of cake.

# 8
# A Piece of Cake

The survival school training at Stead AFB culminates with its last week being spent in the forests of the Sierra Nevada Mountains. When that week is over we will be driven even more deeply into the high mountains and be left to cross about twenty miles of "enemy" territory on foot, using the skills we have learned in the school, all this while being "hunted" in the woods by "Russian" troops!

The appointed day to begin the trek finally arrives. We have completed the classroom teachings and local training part of the course. Now we climb up into the back of a two-and--a-half ton stake-bed truck and drive across the state line into California.

We drive far up into the mountains through a very heavy snowfall area. When we stop, we are told to put our snowshoes on in the truck and then get out. When I step off the truck, I am astonished to find I sink almost to my knees in the soft snow.

"These damn things are no good!" I say, as I take off my left snowshoe. Then, I step forward on my left foot to take off the right snowshoe but fall deep into powdery snow.

"Now you guys wanna be careful!" calls out the instructor. "The snow depth here is about seven feet, and if you take off your snowshoes you can disappear from sight!"

It takes almost ten minutes to recover enough to get my snowshoes set up again, and we are all dismayed at how deeply we sink into the snow with every step. One of us comments about how different this is from walking on the two inch dusting we had back at the base.

Our instructor laughs, "You guys are good - you can do it!"

We spend the first two days at this location in a "base camp" which is so far from civilization that there is no sight or sound of man. We have several parachutes that the school left with us and some rations that are like those in the survival packs that are attached to our parachutes. This is basically what would be available to us if we ever had to parachute out of an airplane.

Our group is composed of six officers and a tech-sergeant. The sergeant claims he is an old hand at hunting and camping in the Minnesota woods, and his actions quickly indicate that he is in familiar territory. In about thirty minutes we are all following his "suggestions," cutting poles, gathering wood, piling snow for windbreaks and snow fences and erecting a pretty nice camp with a good silk tent, a nice fire, and "all the pleasures of home."

On the morning of the third day, a truck from the base arrives and we break camp and climb on board. Then we head deeper into the woods and higher up into the mountains. At one point we stop at a Godforsaken collection of rough buildings where we can see some people in Russian uniforms, complete with fur hats, and AK-47s. They will be "hunting" us in the woods. One of them fires up a monstrous machine called a "weasel" that has a loud diesel engine and which runs easily and quickly over the snow on tank-like tracks.

After changing to another truck with 4-wheel drive and chains, we drive farther into the deep forest and still higher up the mountain. About mid afternoon the truck stops and we are told to get out.

The driver tells us that there will be rescue helicopters out here in five days to get us, but that the weasels will be here tonight. If we are caught, we will have to stay in Stead another three weeks and repeat the entire course. Then he drives off.

In the distance we can faintly hear diesel engines revving.

It soon becomes apparent that we will have to cross the Little Truckee River to reach the relative safety of the deep woods and heavy boulders on the eastern side of that small river.

The western side, where we are, is combed with weasel trails and dangerous drifts. As the sun lowers in the sky we try to find a crossing, but the river lies in a valley about three hundred yards from the woods on both sides of it. The longer we try to find a perfect place to cross the river, the later it gets and the more clearly we can hear the diesel engines.

Sunset comes early, and with it a cursed full moon. Suddenly, the world is very dark and very bright, and we are no longer human beings, but shadows slipping under the great ponderosa pines. We are only dappled points of moonlight fading in and out of forest shadows, pacing back and forth, faster and faster – we are lost . . . trapped . . . and now, soon to be caught!

We will have to make a break and run for it. But in order to cross the small valley, we will have to cross the river. That should not be a problem since it is frozen over. However, we will become visible to anyone who might be in the valley as we cross the river, so we will have to be ready to run as soon as we get on the other side of the river.

We slip out of the forest and start slowly downhill, walking quietly as we can, hardly breathing, hearts pounding, snow crunching loudly beneath our snowshoes.

Then we are caught! A weasel, lying hidden with its engine off, catches us in its piercing searchlight just before we reach the river, so we have to run for it, sinking a foot and a half deep into the snow with every step. Crossing the river, we all break through the ice; not far, only inches, but that's enough to turn our snowshoes into ice-cream dippers. Now every step we take gathers twelve pounds of snow.

The weasel is sweeping the valley with its great searchlight. A bright beam of blinding light passes across us, pauses, then yanks back with a jerk and illuminates us, throwing monstrous shadows of our flailing and thrashing arms and legs far ahead of us as we run through the deep snow. The diesel engine shrieks like a wild beast, and the weasel starts after us.

We race up the far slope of the steep hill, trying to reach the woods before we are headed off. The weasel gains on us, charging at full speed, its engine roaring, its gears whining, its tracks slap-slapping against the ice and snow.

A searchlight lights us up again and we can hear "pops" going off from behind us. Looking back we see what looks like flashbulbs going off from the weasel. "Pop-pop-pop." They are *firing* at us! They are still 300 yards away, but gaining quickly; the forest is still another hundred yards!

"Those are blanks?" Bill gasps out.

"*Blanks hell! What's that whistling over our heads*?"

"Pop-pop-pop! Zing, zing, zing!"

The roaring and whining is closer now, the "slap-slap-slap!" is louder. I look back and see a great black cloud of diesel exhaust pulsing out of the vehicle, rising swiftly into the cold moonlit air. A man with a rifle in his hand and a Russian fur hat is riding on top of the rearing vehicle. A brilliant light sweeps across the snow hitting me in the eyes. It passes on but then jerks back and fixes on me. "Pop-pop-pop-pop!"

Burning lungs, pounding legs – I charge heedlessly into the black forest!

"Yea!!!" Into the dark woods at full tilt, now sinking eighteen inches into powder snow with every stride.

"Safe!"

But then I hear "Varoooommmm! Varooooommmm! Pop-pop-pop-pop-pop!" The weasel is coming into the woods *after* us!

We split into three different directions. I sail over a boulder, falling into whatever lies below – soft snow it turns out. Now I am flat on my back, three feet deep into a snow bank, struggling to climb out and get back on my feet. A rifle shot cracks out from deep in the woods, and another from a different location – they're surrounding us! I go slipping down a steep hill, skiing in a fashion, through the trees. I crawl behind a boulder as I hear snowshoes crunching through the forest floor coming toward me. I actually quit breathing as I hear people stomping around. They come toward my boulder, and then slowly the sounds fade away.

After a long period of time, I cautiously peep over the boulder to see what lies out in the cold dark forest.

I see Colonel Salton. He beckons me to come to him and I head in his direction, sinking deeply into the soft burgundy carpet.

"John is just back from Stead!" says Colonel Salton who is standing at the lectern in the Officers' Club dining room, and turning to me, he begins applauding.

"How was it!" shouts Major Bigg, also applauding. Everyone rises and applauds.

"Well," I say, stepping to the lectern and transferring my martini to my left hand, " it was really easy, just a piece of cake!"

"YEA!" A great roar rises from the assembly.

"I told them at Stead," I continue as I adjust the microphone, "that the TAC tankers could take over their place, and that we were upset that we got so few assignments out there, and we needed more of them!"

"BOOO!" The crowd groaned.

"I told them we have a major, named Bigg, who can blow them away, and we have a colonel, named Salton, who can walk on water – obviously he wouldn't need any snowshoes – and they both dare Stead to invite them out to a winter vacation!"

"YEA!" Applause and cheers rise from the troops.

And I told them, "So can any TAC Tanker Troop!!!"

"BOOO!"

"So I propose a toast!"

"YEA!" from the crowd

"To Stead!" I cry, holding my glass high.
"NOOOOOOO!"

# 9
# Leifur

We fly northward out of Iceland, a single KB-50 sailing quietly through a bright starry night seeking a lone reconnaissance aircraft to refuel. It's late October of 1962.

Looking out across the dark ocean, I think of the Vikings who discovered and claimed the lands that rise out of these great seas and I remember the statute in Reykjavik commemorating Leifur Eiriksson. He stands there tall and brave and looks confident and serene – now representing not only himself but also all his people.

Those who live here call their country the land of fire and ice, and we were able to tour a small part of it on our only day off. The Icelanders arranged the tour and they provided the bus and driver. We Air Force personnel were required to wear our uniforms during the tour.

It was both professional and perfunctory. We saw a glacier and listened to its creakings, and we watched mud bubble and boil, and geysers leap amazingly high. We saw some land that looked like upside down golf tees had been stuck all over the place, and some wild looking horses.

Later we walked through part of downtown Reykjavik. We went to the harbor and saw the great ships, and went into some of the stores. I went to a bookstore and marveled at all the magazines and book titles. Most of them were unreadable (to me).

Next we went to a restaurant. It had been specially reserved just for us and we walked together down the street under the parental-like control of our escorts. Merchants would see us coming and place "Closed" signs (written in English!) in the window as we approached, and then remove them as we walked past. The restaurant that had been reserved for us (by our guides) was also officious. We went in, sat down, and were all delivered the same meal, with the same cup of tea and the same bottle of beer, and that was that. We had time to eat, then the waiters came back and picked up everything, and we left. The food was good. The beer was Carlsberg.

Next morning, as my crew and I prepared to fly the mission we were now flying, we noticed a black woman walking through the terminal with two female Icelandic flight attendants walking beside her. We already knew that no black people were allowed to land in Iceland because we had been forced to leave our black crewmembers behind when we came here. This woman, now walking through the terminal, had been on a commercial airliner that had diverted here and the flight attendants were with her to keep her in sight the entire time she was in Iceland. Incidentally, that may have contributed to an Air Force first, of sorts, since we left a completely black crew at home, and they did fly a couple of missions together. Was that a first of any kind?

Later, when we arrived at our airplane, the aircraft parked across from us was a Soviet Union aircraft with a great big hammer and sickle on it. There were crewmembers around the airplane. One of them waved to us. We all waved back. When we took-off we immediately flew over Soviet "trawlers" which were just off the coast of Iceland.

Now, tonight our refueling is completed and we head south again and it has already become a long night when the first faint flashes of the Reykjavik lighthouse are seen slowly stroking the southern horizon.

When we contact the control tower at Keflavik AFB, they tell us to call our squadron.

Our operations officer, Major Ghon, wants to know the status of our aircraft, and when we tell him we have only one minor write-up, he tells us to taxi to the fuel pits as soon as we land and come immediately into detachment operations.

We land about 0830, just as the sun is rising. Leaving our aircraft at the fuel pits we catch a ride to our ramp area and are astonished to find the other aircraft from our detachment are gone. They were all still there when we took off just eight hours ago, and we were all preparing for a big mission later in the week.

Major Ghon meets us at the door and tells us to go immediately to our quarters.

"Get your clothes and *all* your gear," he says sharply, "and get down to Base Operations fast as you can!"

"Where are we going?" our pilot asks.

"Langley!" came the curt reply. "Get *with* it - *go!"*

"We'll be over our crew rest," the pilot calls back.

"Crew rest has been *waived* lieutenant!" The Major shouts "Go – *go – dammit – GO*!"

At Base Operations, we are handed a flight plan someone else prepared and find it has already even been filed. Weather personnel give us a quick briefing and our aircraft is being towed from the fuel pits to base operations. We never heard of that happening before!

The flight plan back to Langley shows a cruise speed of 420 knots. Wow! Gohn says: "Yep, we're burning the jets all the way; that JP-4 in the bomb-bay is all ours today."

He grabs his bag, "Let's go, I'll fill you in on the way." He shoves the door open with his foot and strides through. We race after him.

It is an hour and a half to Cape Farewell on the southern tip of Greenland, a spike of land rising like the bow of a great ship, lost and motionless, forever gazing down on its flock of endless icebergs. Three more hours take us down to Newfoundland, already dusted with snow, and three more bring us down to Langley.

It is dark again when we touch down, and we taxi in through an incredible maze of aircraft. Never had I ever seen so many aircraft at Langley, and they are all B-47's. There had never been a single B-47 at Langley before. *What's really going on?*

Major Gohn had explained how the Cuban missile situation had reached a serious state, but even he had no idea how serious it really was until now. We were astonished at the number of Strategic Air Command (SAC) bombers at our base, the Headquarters after all, of the Tactical Air Command (TAC)!

We go by our squadron command post to check the bulletin board and crew boxes, but the building is deserted and locked! It has never even been closed before. Major Gohn says we should go home and get crew rest and be ready to fly " Somewhere, maybe anywhere, immediately -- probably early tomorrow."

I throw my bags in my car and head home. On the way I turn on the radio for music, but President Kennedy is talking: " . . . third: It shall be the policy of this Nation to regard any nuclear missile launched from Cuba against any nation in the Western Hemisphere as an attack by the Soviet Union on the United States, requiring a full retaliatory response upon the Soviet Union. Fourth: As a necessary military precaution, I have reinforced our base at Guantanamo, evacuated today the dependents of our personnel there, and ordered additional military units to be on a standby
alert . . ."

So now I knew, too.

Home is pretty quick. I haven't even started to unpack before the phone rings.

It's my pilot: "Be back down here in about seven hours. Get as much crew rest as you can and meet us in base operations at 0500."

# 10
# Slewfoot

October 23, 1962. McCoy AFB in Orlando, Florida, is crammed full of Air Force and Navy aircraft. We taxi through packed apron areas and finally park way out near the end of this great fleet.

A blue Air Force bus takes us to another base on the other side of town where we will have quarters, and as we drive through downtown Orlando people cheer and wave at us. Many of them wave American flags, and others shout, "Go get 'em, Tigers!" We wave back.

Our pilot, copilot and I were assigned a small room with three single beds and one small closet. The only bathroom on the floor was at the end of the hall. We left our bags in our new room and returned to the bus and rode back across Orlando to the other base to our airplane, once again to cheers and flags waving and honking of horns.

Our aircraft has already been refueled and we perform a preflight inspection and prepare it for immediate flight. We call the command post and tell them we are ready to fly and they tell us we are now on alert.

"Alert" is a term which refers to the aircraft, not necessarily to the crew, although we are more than ready to fly anywhere by now. But after we "cock" our aircraft, we sit in front of it all day long.

We spend about sixteen hours each day thereafter, either sitting on the flight line in the sun or under a wing for shade or in the hot aircraft which is still prepared to take-off immediately. When darkness falls we are bused back across town to the other base where we are quartered.

Our main diversion during the day is watching U-2 aircraft take-off several times a day and marveling at the weird looking machines the Navy keeps flying in and out.

By the third day we are driving through the streets of Orlando totally unnoticed by the civilians who are busy again with their workaday worlds. Now we have become just another part of the evening traffic problem.

The following week we develop a staggered schedule providing each crew, officers and enlisted, an hour for lunch at the Officers' Club each day. There seems to be a general understanding that we won't need to fly between the hours of eleven and two. We flight crewmembers wonder if Castro is in on this. Could it be part of some international siesta?

We try to get some "Crew Vehicles" but there are very few available. Finally, we do find some stake-bed trucks. We load up five or six crews in the back of each truck and drive across the base to the Officers' Club for lunch.

Stake-bed Truck

On the fourth day, one of the generals becomes concerned about the aircraft being parked so closely together ready for a quick takeoff. He says that even Cuba could wipe out half the U.S. Air Force and Navy if they were to attack *us*.

We spend the rest of the next day taxiing all over the place to new parking locations so our great armada would be less compacted. Our aircraft winds up way out in the boonies. No more luncheons at the Officers' Club for us!

A week after that, on 4 November 1962, while still sitting out at our aircraft "on alert," we are told that the following day there will be a great exercise of all the crews and aircraft on McCoy AFB. The code name for the exercise will be "Slewfoot," and it promises to be a diversion from our dull routine.

So, we do "Slewfoot." It really isn't much but we get to crank up the aircraft and taxi them around. We can't take-off and fly because then we would compromise the alert status too much. So we taxi to our new parking spot, shut down and refuel the aircraft. Now it's too late for lunch, we can't even get our box lunches, so it will be a really long afternoon.

Then an announcement comes over the aircraft radios from Col. Zeep, our operations officer. He has decided to let us "take a break" from alert and go en-masse, officers and enlisted together, all to the officer's club for "late lunch. " A reward," he says, "boys, for your good work today!"

"Probably because the O Club is losing money with nobody showing up today!" An old sergeant says wryly. We finally wrangle a ride back to the Officers' Club in one of the big stake-bed trucks.

My crew has just made it to the line at the buffet when someone begins making a lot of noise. We all slowly turn to see who is shrieking and screaming, and realize it is none other than Colonel Zeep himself, normally a rather shy and quiet man (for a full colonel), who is shouting and screaming and jumping up and down, shouting something that no one can understand. As we watch, he seems to jump up and down languidly, slipping into a surreal time dimension and he runs like a figure in a dream, dragging himself through the dining room, painfully pulling one foot behind the other, and his words can not be heard, only gibberish seems to be slowly coming out – then slowly we realize he is saying "S L E W F O O T!" Yes – "Slewfoot! Slewfoot! Slewfoot! SLEWFOOT! You bastards! Come ON! Let's GO! Now! Now! Now! Now! NOW! This is

WAR! Now! GO! GO! GO! Get the hell OUT of here! Slewfoot! Slewfoot! SLEWFoot, dammit!"

Deliberately, cautiously, taking great care, we carefully, and slowly, set our trays, carefully down, on the cafeteria rail. Easily, gently, we each turn, to the right, tentatively, we take, a very slow – slow – slow – step, lifting a foot up slowly and slowly moving it slowly forward. Suddenly we are running at full speed out of the club out to the parking lot crawling into the beds of our stake bed trucks and hanging on for dear life, braced against the railings and hoping they do not give way. We race across the base making turns far too fast with crew members falling, sliding and zipping back and forth across the beds of the trucks. We drive at great speed on to the ramp, race toward the aircraft; crewmembers fall and jump off the truck as it passes in front of their airplane. As the truck hurtles on toward the next plane, crewmembers race to their ladder, swarm up into the cockpit, start engines, come up on radios, and begin to taxi.

From here on it is very professional. Communications are calm and insistent.

Now this great armada of aircraft is moving to the only runway. The KB-50's are supposed to be the first aircraft to get airborne in case of war, and we are taxiing at breakneck speed to our end of the runway.

But the control tower is directing some of our airplanes to opposite ends of the runway! We are still puzzling over that when we notice the fire trucks and BULLDOZERS racing out to the edges of the runway. The bulldozers are to shove broken airplanes off the runway so others can take off! WAR! Indeed!

We suddenly become aware of JP4 fumes throughout our aircraft.

"Reel operators, pilot!"

"Go ahead pilot."

"See where the fumes are coming from!"

One of our reel operators is Sgt. Timid. He hates to fly and always tries to find a good reason why we "can't", or "shouldn't," fly.

Sgt. Timid responds: "Pilot – reel operator, the fuel is coming out of the wing tank because of the fast turns we made." He added: "We're O.K., let's go!"

Takeoff is weird. We take the active runway on command from the control tower, in time to watch another aircraft lift up in front of us and roar over our head. We release brakes on command from the control tower and roll down the runway, lifting off as another aircraft takes the active runway heading in our direction. The control tower is launching aircraft in groups depending on which end of the runway has an opening and the other has a line of airplanes ready to go.

Airborne, we join up as we head down the keys. Over Boca Chica Key, we set up orbit and refuel F-105's. The rendezvous and hookup is smooth, professional, calm, quiet, quick. The reel operator said, "These guys have blackened gun ports." That means they have test-fired their guns.

After refueling they disconnect, then ignite their afterburners, and leave at great speed for Cuba and their targets. This is IT!

A radio message comes in loud over Guard channel: It is our collective recall word! What? What?

It is repeated – again and again. The message sent along with it decodes properly and the authentication is valid. We're going back!

"Hell of a way to fight a war!" growls our flight engineer. We return to join in a great mess of aircraft circling McCoy Air Force Base. Eventually, we land. We refuel and finally get back to our quarters about 10:00 p.m.

★ ★ ★

The alert would continue at McCoy AFB for another twenty-one days.

Forty years later, some of us would find out that "Slewfoot 2", or "Son of Slewfoot" was a hassle that erupted when an aerial encounter took place between an unarmed U.S. reconnaissance aircraft and Cuban-based MiG fighters.

# 11

# Echo

I climb onto a barstool at the Officers' Club in the Azores, order a good German beer and spread several blank postcards that I had just bought out in front of me. When the beer comes, I take a deep swig, pull one of the postcards to me and start writing a note to a woman I have never met.

"Dearest Jane," I begin, "How I long to hold you in my arms again and taste the sweet kisses from your lips." I take another sip from my beer.

"The days away from you are torture enough, but the nights out here without you are lonely hours that will never really end until . . ."

Hmmm, now that thought seems drifting away so I take another sip and pull a new postcard to me.

"My Darling Cynthia," I write.

"How I long to hold you in my arms and kiss you again and again . . ." *Hmmmm,* maybe *I should just say 'again' only once*? *Well* . . . I think to myself, t*his is not as easy as I thought it was going to be.*

Ocean Station Vessel Echo,
A tiny ship on an endless sea,
It was hard to find from three miles up,
As it rose and fell
With pelagic swell,
On the grim and gray Atlantic

I check my notes, pull another postcard to me and begin all over again: "Dearest Danielle, We are almost halfway through this tour now, and should be home in about two more months! Everything is OK, I am fine except that I miss you and the boys." That was pretty easy. I finish my beer and after checking my notes carefully, sign the post card, "Love, Bill & Dad."

Another beer and another postcard:

"Hi Mom! It's not bad at all out here. The older guys treat me like one of the men. As long as you can do the job, that's all they want. I'm looking forward to getting back to the east coast in a couple of months and then I'll call home. Love, Darron."

Ocean Station Vessel Echo
Cast its message day and night.
The only human sound around
Except for endless static.
Five hours out, you'd key your mike
And call into the void:
" Ocean Station Echo,
This is Snipe three-five – copy?"
Between the shores, below the scud,
Lifting, falling with the swells,
Echo always had a fix,
They would tell you where you were.

"Hello Mary. I don't know if you remember me or not. My name is Sam. We met in September at the Green Clipper on Cape Cod. You said we might go out sometime and I wanted to let you know I will be back in Boston in late January. I will call you then. Yours truly, Sam Smith. "

I pull Jane's card back to me, and look off over the hills on the other side of the runway, pondering the next entry as I chew on the end of my pen.

"Bartender!" I call, frowning. "What do you say to a woman you love?"

He grins and blushes, and then he speaks rapidly in Portuguese and laughs.

"All these your girlfriends?" he asks in broken English as he points to my stack of postcards.

I nod my head reluctantly and wipe my brow as if overburdened. He calls another Portuguese bartender over and talks to him rapidly in Portuguese and they both laugh.

"Dearest Katherine," I copy from parts of Jane's postcard. "How I long to hold you in my arms again and taste. . . ." *Oh, wait a minute, whose name was I supposed to put on Jane's card – Damn*! - *was that Henry, or Joseph?* I check my notes.

Echo had another job, the really tricky trick.
If you knew you couldn't get across,
You would come to them for help.
You might leave your ship up in the air,
Or ride it down and ditch.
But they would come and get you.
You knew that they would get you.
Because they are the Coast Guard.

"Hello Snipe three-five, this is Ocean Station Vessel Echo– read you 5 by 5, copy?"

"Greetings Echo, Snipe here, copy?"

"Aye aye sir, loud and clear."

Echo would give us their actual position, which was always a little different from their published position. We navigators would plot that point on our charts and take bearings from it. As we passed by them we could get a course line, a speed line and a couple of intermediate cuts. Sometimes that might be the only speed line or course line we would be able to get for several hours on our ten to twelve hour crossing.

We had a checklist to fill out and data to transmit to Echo and they would pass information to us. Sometimes that would be a message left from another aircraft that had experienced bad weather out over the part of the ocean we were headed toward now.

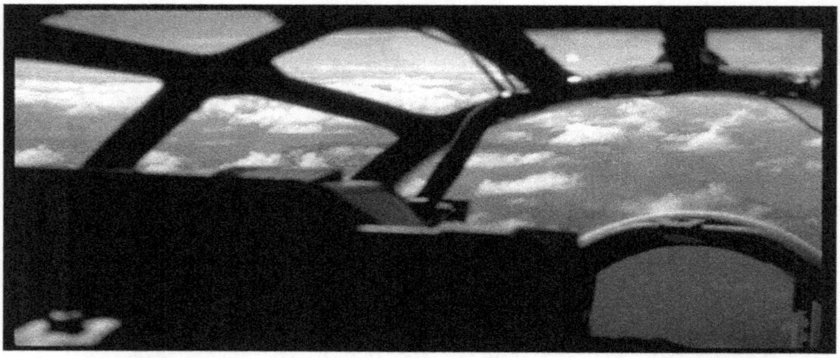

**KB-50 over the Ocean**

We who were flying in the KB-50s rode an aircraft with six engines. We could climb to higher elevations, which many aircraft couldn't easily do. We also had loran for over water navigation and didn't really need Echo's fixes all that much. Sometimes we wouldn't even plot their position.

Occasionally, we would pass on to Echo that the position they had given, the place they said they thought *they* were, seemed to us, to be substantially in error. Sometimes then they would reply, "Thanks, we haven't seen the sky for days, our loran is snarled, and our last position is three days old. We'll use the one you gave us and thanks for your help."

New jet aircraft crews, like those who flew the B-47s, flew seven miles high, and were already talking about the "Atlantic River." These were all signs of things to come.

Every once in a while, after the official business had been taken care of, Echo might call us back.

"Snipe three-five, can you take down some postcards for us?" They wanted to know if we would buy a postcard and stamp for them after we landed and send a few words to someone special. Not all aircrews would do it; many didn't have the time, so when it worked it was always something special.

On board the aircraft the pilot might say: "Nav, Pilot."

"Pilot, Nav"

"Yeah, Nav, can you talk to the man in the boat?"

"Hello Echo, Snipe three-five here, what do I say?"

"You're an officer sir, you been to college, you can write better'n I can. You know what to say to women . . . ."

"Oh sure! Awright, what's her name and address?"

"Her name is Jane Jones, and her address is . . . . "

Some of them would say to tell her they missed being with her, some talked about kisses, others wanted a more formal note, some had names of children. Some wanted post cards to other guys asking them to make a phone call for them, some were to parents. Most commented on how far through they were along on their three-month tour in the middle of the ocean.

The personal messages always began with just one person who wondered if you would mind taking down a message and buying a stamp for him. "If you give me your address sir, I'll mail you the money when I get back to the states." Then, when they were through, they would always say ". . . ah . . . here's Bill? . . . He wants to know if you would do one for him . . .sir?"

It would finally end as the words faded away. It all got lost in the gray clouds, which slowly came in and filled the distance between you and Echo. At 18,000 feet and about 240 mph, you could count on a range of 80 to 90 miles and after official business had been taken care of, that sometimes worked out to about ten minutes.

"Her first name is Susan?"

"Susa. . . .urphy.

"Copy, Susan Murphy. Say address over?"

"17. . . 3 High . . .vnue. . ."

"Roger, copy, in Brookline . . . is that right?"

". . . aye sir . . .ank. . . y. . . ry . . . uch"

"And your name?"

Silence.

"Say again your name, over."

" . . .ich . . . ."

"Say again your name."

The silence is broken only by static.

"Ocean Station Vessel Echo, how copy, over?"

Static-static-static.

Gray sailing clouds have caught another name and taken it away to tease and play with; the Atlantic Ocean will have one more secret to wash tonight. The winds rise, the rain falls, the seas swell and swirl, and so do dreams and fancy tales and very important secrets. Secrets may be hard for people to keep. But the gray Atlantic keeps them well.

# 12

# The Titan

The Air Force had a problem. And it became a big problem real quick. Then it got even worse – a lot worse. Sometime back it had ordered ICBMs with gigantic thermo-nuclear warheads that were now being built and would be shipping to three Air Force bases in less than a year! The problem was that the Air Force didn't have the silos built yet, and nobody knew how to build them, and they didn't have any crews to man the things when they arrived – but the missiles and their thermo-nuclear warheads were already on the way!

I had tried to get an assignment to missiles for several years but had been told by personnel that I could never even be considered for that duty because I did not have a degree in engineering, preferably electrical engineering or aeronautical engineering which the Air Force insisted on for their missile crew officers. They might possibly consider someone who had a degree in science, such as physics, medicine, geology, mathematics, chemistry, or so on but they wouldn't consider anybody else. No way - no how!

Meanwhile, those officers who did have engineering degrees were getting out of the Air Force as quickly as they could. They had big paychecks waiting for them in the civilian world. If they were going to be involved in Air Force missiles, they would be building them for a defense contractor. The officers with scientific degrees were heading out to universities to advance toward their needed PhDs. Others were picking up high paying jobs all over the United States.

The Air Force was finally forced to consider taking aircrew members and transferring them to the missile program. That seemed to be workable because the B-47 bombers were being phased out. The apparent thinking was that B-47 people could trade in their airplanes and go underground and they would be able to make the switch smoothly because they were already crewmembers. Being familiar with the problems of working together as an aircrew, they could obviously make the switch to missiles easily, right? But then the Cuban crisis forced the Air Force to extend the B-47's for another three-year period. So now what?

That is probably why I found myself signing into the Missile Training School at Sheppard AFB, near Wichita Falls, Texas. Wow.

And what about the new soon-to-be missile crew members? Well, we were an interesting group. We had a few flight crewmembers, but we came from all over the Air Force. Most of the flying folk were navigators. Pilots wanted nothing to do with missiles. Many of the pilots we did have in the class had not flown for several years. They had been grounded for various reasons and would probably never fly again. A small number of our class were navigators, mostly from the SAC refueling aircraft, the KC-97, or from Military Air Transport Service (MATS, now the Military Airlift Command) and had flown cargo aircraft. The rest of the students were from all over the Air Force. Many had just reentered the Air Force after a break of several years.

So our new missile officer crew force consisted not of engineers or scientists, but of teachers who were tired of teaching, entrepreneurs who had learned to appreciate a steady paycheck, used-car salesmen who wanted to travel, and a lot of realtors. I remember talking to one returning officer who said selling homes in the southeast Florida market was too strenuous and he wanted to return to the Air Force and have some time off. (Wow!) A couple of other retreads came back in so they and their wives "could afford to have children." When that comment was greeted with astonishment, they would add "Do you know it costs several hundred dollars to have a baby in the civilian world?" Other Air Force people transferred in from Air Police, motor pools, building maintenance, and so on. We had absolutely ZERO engineers or scientists.

The noncommissioned Officers (NCOs) reminded me of many that I had known during my flight crew days. But these guys were an older group and they had a lot of rank. When you saw them walking around together you were reminded of a herd of zebras. These were people who had been around the Air Force a long time and had seen many different problems and were used to having to create brand new solutions for brand new problems. The missile program owed a lot to the fine NCOs who came in there. The ICBM program probably would not have been possible without them.

The school was extremely interesting for me. From time to time I realized that engineers or scientists would probably be bored with all this but we were openmouthed with wonder. Every class was a new revelation of secrets long kept from us. We traced electrical circuitry, and used a lot of colored pencils turning hydraulic piping that had been printed on paper in our notebooks into green lines with right angle twists. Pneumatic connections became yellow squiggles, fuel and oxidizer flow lines had their own colors and it went on and on. The computers were fascinating to all of us and the inertial measurement unit guidance systems were all new tools that we were eager to begin using in earnest.

When we got to our new Air Force Bases we found a few silos that were well started in the construction process and we actually had one missile already in the ground. But we couldn't go see it because there was too much maintenance activity out there on the silo, the launch center and the missile. The complex was a long way from being ready to go "on alert".

New crewmembers continued to pour in for us to form into crews to perform the alert duties. Some of the earlier arrivals who were older men and who also had more time in the Air Force were selected to be instructor crews and we began training the new arrivals.

Crew training began like a pickup game on a sandlot. We had no trainers so we made them. We taped a copy of the Launch Control Console out of our Operations Manual that we called a "Dash One", onto a cardboard box. That box was put on a standard issue Air Force table. The student crew commander set in a chair and "ran" his imaginary complex from there. Other figures were taken from the Operations Manual of the Titan II and pasted on other boxes and placed on other tables. The other three crewmembers would "assume position" in front of their cardboard boxes on which had been taped a paper schematic of that control panel.

One of the classrooms was arbitrarily designated as "The Trainer" and we found ourselves spending hours in that room. My crew would sometimes instruct four or five crews a day and often we spent the entire day there.

We ran checklists. The student crew would take their places sitting or standing in front of their decorated cardboard boxes. The instructor crew stood behind them. The instructor crew commander would speak to the student crew.

"The klaxon is sounding and you have a 'Fuel Vapor in the Launch Duct' indicator flashing red."

The student crew commander would trace his finger along the copy of the Launch Control Console that was taped on a cardboard box until he found the indicator titled "Fuel Vapor Launch Duct". He would then announce to his crew, "Crew, we have a 'Fuel Vapor in the Launch Duct' indicator flashing red. Proceed with the checklist." They would then fumble through their checklists until they found the proper one. The student crew commander would then press the place on the paper figure corresponding to the button on his console that read "CC And Silo Klaxon On/ Off", and say "Klaxon coming off." Well, it wasn't pretty but we all began to learn how to execute checklists as a crew.

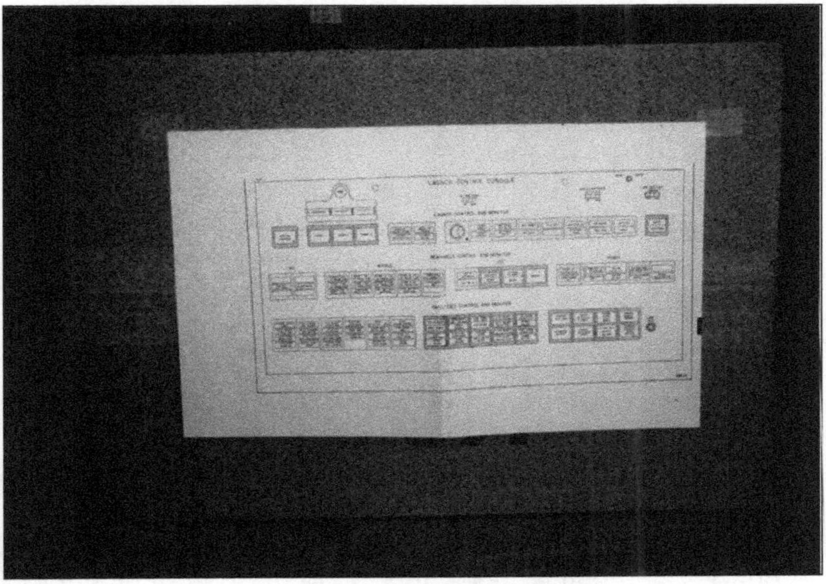

**"Cardboard Trainer"**

The school at Shepherd AFB had taught us how the missile, the silo and all the equipment worked, now we taught ourselves how to run all that, and how to run it the way the Strategic Air Command (SAC) wanted it to go which was using open-faced direct reference to operational and maintenance manuals and checklists.

The Cardboard Trainer continued to improve. Somebody brought in an old electric alarm clock. We used that as a klaxon. Well, the klaxon went off every time there was any emergency in the silo or with the missile and it was often our first notice that there was a serious problem somewhere. So now, the instructor crew commander would turn the alarm clock on: "BZZZZZZZZZZZZZ", and he would say "Crew you have . . ." So you get the idea.

Later, somebody got a real klaxon we could turn on and off. Then we discovered a remarkable thing. A lot of the student crew commanders had come in from the SAC tanker crews as navigators. They flew KC-97 s and had spent many years sitting on alert. That meant they would go to an Alert Facility, out at the end of a runway somewhere, and spend a week sitting "on alert", ready to go fly their airplane on a no-notice basis. There were a number of practice "launches" where the crews would have to run out to their nearby airplanes, start engines and sit and wait until told to shutdown. Those practices were all announced with a klaxon and when the klaxon went off those crewmembers leaped to their feet, raced out of the room and started running for their airplane.

Now, sitting in front of their cardboard Launch Control Console, when this new, real klaxon went off, some of these new student commanders would involuntarily leap to their feet and start to head for the door. Old habits die hard. Embarrassment helps.

A lot of the training we did with the student crews was accomplished on these cardboard trainers. Much more was done at various operational complexes where the buttons actually worked and the environment was the real thing. BUT - we couldn't press these buttons! And this required student crews to drive to various complexes, do the training and return to the base. Some of these trips alone were more than an hour each way.

Within the year we would have a new trainer which was much more interactive and much more realistic. We got a replicia Launch Control Console in the "Training Room", and the following year we received a magnificent Link Trainer that simulated an actual launch complex in every conceivable manner except for the ceiling and the floor. Everything worked exactly the same way as in the silo and the instructor crew pushed buttons from behind one-way windows at another, hidden console. Here you could actually "launch a missile". There was no real missile there of course but everything that would happen during a launch would actually take place.

More importantly, the "problems" that could happen at any time on any actual alert tour could now be simulated on our new trainer, and when we began to get pretty capable at those, we started getting "multiple problems", and that carried on and on. Eventually almost every trainer session wound up with the entire complex collapsing and blowing up - simulated - of course, but we became more and more proficient in handling those real problems that actually did occur from time to time in the real complex with a real ICBM and a real thermo-nuclear weapon there.

# 13
# The Unsolvable Problem

What was it like the first few times we went out to complete a 24-hour tour on a Titan II site with an ICBM loaded and ready to launch?

It was busy. At first, maintenance people were working on many systems simultaneously. It was not unusual to have maintenance in progress the entire twenty-four hour tour.

Almost all the maintenance work was on the silo and complex. The missile mostly just purred away, happy and contented in its nice, cool, dry "gun barrel".

We also had student crews. I was always on an instructor crew so we would sometimes bring a student crew out to spend the entire tour and return with us the next day, but more often we would have student crews drive out in the early afternoon. The mornings were always too busy to do any instruction but we could often teach in the early part of the afternoon. Sometimes, if enough staff cars were available, we would have two different crews come out. One might arrive for a four hour session about noon and then leave, and another would show up to work from four to eight. Maintenance requirements could change all of that very quickly.

Then there was the technical data. The vaunted Operational and Maintenance Manuals always seemed to speak with the authority of Absolute Knowledge, but really – in modern computer terminology – they were "Beta".

That's right, they were basically a good guess. We were reasonably sure when we ran a checklist that was new to us, that those procedures had worked right at least once before. We crews were actually in the process of testing this "Beta" information and rewriting new technological operational and maintenance manuals. We thought we knew what we were doing, but we didn't know what we were doing would really do. It was like getting a new computer, today, and plugging it in, loading software and it didn't work. That's what we had with the Titan II system – at first.

When we had a problem arise at the complex, we would run the available checklists and when none of them worked, we would call the Wing Command Post (WCP). They would then pull out their operational manuals (same ones we had) and tell us what to do step by step. We had already done that and it hadn't worked – that's what we had called to tell them. It took a couple of years before the WCP personnel began to realize we crew members actually knew *more* about the missile and its systems than they did. So in the beginning, they would read the checklists to us and we would do all the steps over again.

When it still wouldn't work, they would call SAC command post. SAC would then pull out their technical data (same one!) and have us run the same checklists again. When it still didn't work, they would contact a commercial Tech Rep - or Technical Representative who worked for Martin Corporation. He would pull out his tech data and have us run it again. When it still didn't work he would usually have some annoyed comment to make and give us a helpful hint. Usually he had experienced that problem a time or two before. The problems got solved and the new tech data changes began to take place when we were finally able to bypass all the colonels and other communicants and get the crew member NCOs to talk directly with the tech reps. Then they could together begin to write new data. But we always had to have the blessings of command and control bestowed on us. It should be remembered that in those very new days in the ICBM program NONE of the high ranking officers or NCOs had any missile experience or background, and those few who did have some experience had that with equipment already obsolete.

There was another problem with all of these telephone conversations. Federal law then required a beeper be attached to any telephone that was recording a conversation. So when you called three or four different organizations on a conference call it could easily get confusing. Each location had a different sounding beeper so a conference call could go something like this:

"Hello, this is the Wing Command Post."

"Hi, this is site 4-7, we've got a problem."

"What's the problem?"

"Well, our doohicky won't conflablabtulate with the loco gomo."

"OK. HaBEEPu run the checklists in 2-11?"

"Yes we have, foBEEP or five times."

"OK. Let's run them again. BEEPthis." After a few minutes, "BEEP this. Now try BEEP else." And, a few minutes later " Hmmmmm. Stand by."

"Ringggg."

"SAC Command Post."

"Roger, this is the Little Rock Wing CoBEEPnd Post."

"What's going on down there"?

"We got a proHEAPm. One of our sites has a doohicky tBEEPon't conflablabtHEAP with their loco gomo."

"TheHEAPs tech data for runninBEEPat. Have you tried that?"

"Yes we HEAP. It didn't work."

"OK, leBEEPo. Set circuit breaker 107 to the off poHEAPn."

"Roger, CB 10BEEPt to "off"."

"OK. Open doHEAP to MGACG paneBEEPlve and access the hurley-burley spinner."

"Roger, door to MGACG panHEAPlve opened and hurBEEPburley spinner accessed."

"OK. Now BEEPess the hippawl HEAP turniBEEPe grimmacemaker to its reseBEEPition and then caliHEAP the itcheypod. BEEP"

"RoBEEPppawl depressed, grimmacemaker set to HEAPt position, itcheypod recalibrBEEP"

When it still didn't work, SAC would call a Technical Representative or two, usually one in California and one in Georgia.

"This' Bill. What's problem?"

"Roger, Mr.HEAP, this is the BEEP supervisor on duty at SAC commend HEAP. The itcheypood on the grimBEEPer at 374-7 won't confabulate with its hurley-burley HEAP."

"Yep, we're gonna have to BEEP that tech data. We gotta work through that,"

"This' BiHEAPhat's yerBEEPblem?"

"RoHEAPMr. Smith, The itcheBEEPon the grimHICmaer at 374-7 woHEAPnflabulate wiBEEPhurley-burley spinHIC."

"YeHEAPt's gonna havBEEPbe changed. WeHICta work throHEAPhat"

Finally, somewhere in all that mess, the tech-rep would get on the line with the Missile Facilities Technician (MFT) or the Ballistic Missile Analyst/Technician (BMAT) on duty as a crew member and begin to work out a new procedure that would permit recovery from the problem. The result of all this effort would be new tech data arriving in the mail sometime in the next week or two. Was there very much of this kind of thing? It happened constantly back in the early days!

Finally there was The Ultimate Problem. The one problem that never could be solved. It was the one that no one had ever thought of before. Standboard crews never encountered the problem. Instructor crews never encountered it either. The WCP never even thought about it and neither did the SAC Command Post. Tech reps would probably just laugh if they ever heard of it. No control center architect had ever dreamed such a problem could occur. In our early days on alert it couldn't happen because we were always swamped with people everywhere. But eventually the unsolvable problem finally got us.

Late one night, a couple of hours after the MFT and deputy commander had gone upstairs to sleep for a three hour stretch, the BMAT told me that he had a problem.

"What is it?" I asked, scanning the consoles, computer and Missile Alignment and Checkout Group (MGACG).

"I gotta go take a leak." The BMAT said, adding in a tense voice, "Pretty quick!"

I looked around the control center. He and I were all alone together here in this area designated by SAC as a "No Lone Zone". Since the control center had access to controls that could launch a nuclear weapon, no less than two people, both knowledgeable to the systems and requirements involved, had to be present at all time.

"Well, you can't *go*." I said, speaking as if the matter were a settled issue.

"I *gotta* go!" He repeated, his voice rising.

"This is a No Lone Zone, sarge."

"I know. But I gotta go potty, sir."

"You can't go potty, sergeant!"

"Sir, I could run upstairs (our single latrine was upstairs, not more than 10 or 12 feet away, almost above our heads) and be back in a minute."

"You can't leave me *alone!* Not down *here*!"

"Maybe we could *both* go?"

I thought about that for about two seconds.

"We can't leave the Control Center with *nobody* down here - it's a NO LONE ZONE!"

"Well sir, what am I going to do?"

"You will just have to tie a knot in it. Wait 'till the Deputy or MFT get up. They've been asleep for almost three hours now, you will somehow have to wait about . . ." as I checked my watch, "forty more minutes."

"Sir?"

"What?"

"How are we going to get them up?"

"Ah . . . well . . .ah . . . hmmmm."

"They won't wake up on their own."

He was right. They were exhausted when they went upstairs. They will sleep for three days.

Silence.

I ventured, "The relief crew will have to get them up"

"Sir. . . ?"

"Yeah, that won't work will it?" The relief crew won't be here for ten more hours.

"Let me think."

"What can we do? I can't wait any longer!"

"Let me think a minute, sarge."

"We could punch on the klaxon, sir. That will get them down here."

"Oh *sure*! They'll come flying down the stairs in their underwear, all blurry-eyed and screaming 'What's the problem?' and I'm goin' to say 'The BMATs got to go take a leak?"

In many respects, working with the ICBM program in the very early days was like exploring a new planet. You constantly needed to invent solutions for problems that had never existed before.

# 14
# CINCSAC

"This is Airman Jones at CBPO (Central Base Personnel Office). Your orders just came in from SAC Headquarters. Can you come by and pick 'em up today?"

My heart falls like a huge rock. Oh *No*! Vietnam!

"Where to?" I ask, my voice trembling.

"Uh . . . can't really tell . . . " he lies, ". . . they're sealed."

*Sealed!* That's worse yet! "I'll be right there!"

I hang up and pause for a moment, heart beating quickly, breathing heavily, still holding the smooth black plastic handle of the telephone.

I hear my dog barking outside and the sounds of my children playing in the next room. The house still smells of bacon, and crumbs from a casual breakfast still lie on my plate. *This is how it happens* . . . I think . . . *this is what it's like*. . . . I wobble into the bedroom on shaking legs and change clothes. This is my day off – it had been, anyway. I hurriedly change into a uniform and race down to CBPO.

I ask for Airman Jones, but he has just left for a detail on the other side of the base. Sergeant Smith says, "Yes sir! I know about *those* orders, I'll get them for you . . . " He reaches into a basket marked "Special Orders" and hands them to me "Congratulations, Captain!"

I glare at him. Then, with my heart pounding, I snatch them out of his hand, rip them open and read:

" . . . The above named personnel are directed to proceed to Offutt AFB, Nebraska, to participate in a three day seminar and to confer with CINCSAC and his staff."

*I am not going to Vietnam, hurrah!* Not today, anyway. I am one of three Missile Crew Commanders who has been selected from our base to go to SAC headquarters and receive a series of briefings from the Commander in Chief of the Strategic Air Command, known by his acronymic nickname CINCSAC (sink-sack). He and his staff are going to entertain us! Wow!

The first evening is auspicious. The Officer's Open Mess at Offutt Air Force Base has a very special presence. Its furniture, wallpaper, carpeting and woodwork are prestigious, confidently hinting of opulence and great power. Bright glints of copper, brass, iron and gold flash from every corner. Chandeliers of pure crystal sweep dancing patterns of colored light across each room, striking sparkles of fire from the fine china and the silverware, and dazzling all the glasses and goblets. Mozart melodies cascade softly from a corner of each room as live string quartets present music suitable for induction into heaven. The Great Wild Blue seems now not quite so way out in a far distant Yonder.

The speakers are all very high-ranking men. Full colonels serve as Masters of Ceremony, transitional narrators and storytellers. Brigadiers and Major Generals, most of whom are of surprising girth and impressive flab, deliver inspirational speeches, reminiscent of a religious revival in a tabernacle tent or an Amway meeting. Tomorrow, we are constantly reminded, we will all see CINCSAC.

The drinks are first class and the food consists of "Steamboat Roast," meaning it has been cooked at least one time before tonight, and "California Golden Chicken", so coated with fat that it keeps slipping out of people's hands, and can not be cut without it skipping off the plate. That's probably why all these Generals have plumped out so nicely.

Next morning we are seated in velvet briefing chairs in front of an incredible stage filled with astonishing and magical projection screens, backlit viewing glass, easels for colored charts, wireless microphones, flood lights and indirect lighting that remotely dims or brightens, and all this controllable by the person at the stand.

Most of the briefings are given by full colonels who are amazingly fit and trim, and move across the stage athletically, each looking younger than the one before (someone comments later they might have been models hired for the occasion).

An old Major General explains why we can expect a surprise attack from "some nation" in the very near future, and that it could come at any time; that "they" might strike this year, maybe even in the next month or two, and that we are within the "envelope of attack" even at this very moment! He glares at us as if he knows something he can't tell us, apparently because we wouldn't believe it.

A bespectacled Lieutenant Colonel points out how we might expect "trouble" with Red China in the near future, and how we can use nuclear weapons to attack them and hold them at bay.

A young captain with a perfect flattop haircut, who looks like he had just graduated from MIT, flings engineering terms about, and we all nod our heads in assumed familiarity. Then he tells us that the United States is developing plans to use our newly emerging space capabilities for war, and someday soon will be able to attach a spaceship onto an asteroid and bring that huge space rock down in the middle of Red China thus ending any dispute with them. One of his briefing charts shows a great splurge of red earth arising from the middle of China and falling to cover that entire country (and only that country) while a streak from an American-directed asteroid still lingers as a trail of dust.

Later the briefings get more monotonous and we get hungrier and hungrier.

Somewhere in this part of the briefing a Major comes running in and excitedly whispers to the brass who are all sitting together. They all get up and leave quickly, except for one lieutenant colonel who steps to the front of the briefing room.

"Gentlemen, " he says, looking at us, "we have just received word of an incoming attack. Enemy missiles have been picked up on NORAD's radar and they are headed in our direction. SAC has launched our own Strategic Alert Force in retaliation."

Needless to say we are shocked, stunned, dumfounded.

Then the brass who had left the room so quickly a moment ago, return with smiles on their faces and the lieutenant colonel explains that the "attack" had been a "training aid" for our edification of course, so now we all can understand better the gravity of the SAC mission.

Next comes The Photograph. All forty or so of our group are to be part of a "class picture" and we assemble outside, squinting in the bright sunlight.

I am one of three captains and all the others are majors, lieutenant colonels and full colonels.

Our photographer is an airman second class, a very young man with two stripes on his sleeves, an Air Force Hasselblad camera and a huge tripod.

"A'right gentlemen!" He calls out in a loud voice of command that seems reserved only for group photographers. "Squeeze closer together!"

He looks through his camera again. "Major!" He points to a guy on his right side, "Get in front of that Colonel. "

He looks back into the camera "a little more to your right . . . " motioning with his hand, "that's good!"

He looks up again. "Colonel, " pointing to a guy on his left "your hat's on crooked . . . can you straighten it up?" Back in the camera again "That's good . . . real good . . . "

We all stand rigidly ". . . hold it . . .  hold it . . . ." We can all hear the "click," and relax and start to move about.

"OK, one more." We all line up again and hold our breath. "Hold it . . . hold it. . . on the count of three now . . . one . . .  two . . .  'click' three!" He folds up his tripod.

"Thank you very much gentlemen." The Airman Second Class leaves in his Air Force station wagon and we all relax.

The colonel who is our guide for the day leads us off to the Officer's Club for a lunch of sandwiches and potato chips. After that we return on buses to another briefing room that is even fancier than our earlier one.

A Lieutenant Colonel introduces the first speaker who is a full Colonel. The colonel speaks for about ten minutes and introduces Brigadier General Davis. Davis speaks for about ten minutes and introduces Major General Smith. Smith speaks for about seven minutes and introduces Lieutenant General Doe. Doe speaks for about six minutes and introduces a four-star general, General Wall. Wall speaks for about three minutes and then, with a grand gesture, introduces CINCSAC, himself!

As CINCSAC walks into the room, no one calls the group to attention but everyone rises as if lifted by magnetism. The lights dim as a tall man, flanked by six aides, walks onto the dark podium. The aides position themselves at either end of the stage at parade rest intently watching us as if looking for some attacker, and the great man turns slowly and dramatically toward us as a single spotlight softly begins illuminating his face. Behind him a magic viewing screen also slowly illuminates and it reads in color: "General Williams – CINCSAC." He motions for us to sit and we all sit down without a sound.

"Good afternoon, gentlemen." His voice reminds me of Charlton Heston's. "You don't know what an honor it is for me to have this opportunity to meet with you."

He adjusts the microphone. "I stand here in the company of a small handful of professional officers who carry the fate of the entire Free World," he points at individuals in the audience "on *your* shoulders."

"The world of tomorrow, will be the world that _you_ have helped create!" He points straight at me!

Now he steps to one side of the lectern. "Someday, all the people of the world will come to recognize their debt to your courage, vision, technical skill and professionalism in the face of grave danger."

He spreads his arms as if to embrace us all. "You are the pioneers of our new future. It is you who will lead the United States of America through a changing world of savage adversaries and move our nation's defenses into space!" He drops his arms and smiles warmly at us.

That evening, back at the Officers' Club, we eat without the presence of CINCSAC.

Later, he arrives in the company of his aides and his aides' aides. He speaks again briefly and then we all form a line and progress through it quickly to shake CINCSAC's hand and have our picture made with him.

I had seen some of these pictures before and CINSAC is always telling the person he is meeting something that looks very confidential. The person who is listening to CICSAC always looks at him in awe. Now it will be my turn.

I proceed through the line with Major Bones who is from my squadron. He whispers to me that CINCSAC looks the perfect picture of a distinguished and famous person of great power.

"How is that?" I ask quietly.

"Because, " Bones whispers back "he has gray hair and hemorrhoids."

"Hmmm . . ." I think for a moment. "Yeah I see the gray hair, but . . . uh . . . how do you know about the other thing?"

"Gray hair gives you that look of distinction and hemorrhoids give you that look of concern."

Suddenly we are next in line. People are stepping up as CINCSAC smiles at them and takes their hand; then they always cock their head as if to listen in amazement to some secret advice while CINCSAC softly speaks to them. The camera flashes and they move on.

Bones steps up and takes CINCSAC's hand, then cocks his head as CINCSAC speaks in confidence to him and Bones is amazed. The camera flashes, and now CINCSAC turns to me with a broad smile and holds out his hand like he is glad to see me again. I catch his hand and look into his face as he starts speaking. I can't hear what he is saying – he is whispering – to me! I cock my head to catch his words – I can hear him!

He is saying " . . . fifteen, twenty, twenty-five, thirty, thirty-five, forty, forty-five, fifty . . . " I am amazed! The flashbulb goes off and CINCSAC turns to the next man and I am swept away by the aides.

A week later, after coming off alert, I find a large manila envelope in my crew box. I open it up and there we are, CINCSAC and me, we're shaking hands and he is speaking confidentially to me as I listen in awe. One of the sergeants on my crew sees it and says: "Wow! That's impressive! What did he say?"

I look at him as I slip the picture back into the envelope. "He was complaining about his hemorrhoids."

# 15
# Liftoff!

The warble-tone shatters the silence in the missile launch control center: "Dee de lee, dee de lee, dee de lee". The Primary Alerting System announces a message: "From The Strategic Air Command Headquarters for Vandenberg AFB, and Site 395 Bravo only."

The Deputy Commander and I copy the message, decode it, verify it is a valid launch message for our site, and I call for the crew to enter the Missile Launch Checklist procedure.

I press The Surface Warning Control pushbutton twice, and above ground a rotating beacon lights bright red and slowly begins spinning around and around, and the sirens begin their loud and eerie scream as they slowly rotate, alerting anyone or any*thing* near the site above ground to run like hell.

I poll the crew, who are now busy scanning their respective equipment panels: "Crew report ready to launch."

"Deputy ready to launch, Sir."

"BMAT ready to launch, sir."

"MFT's ready to launch, sir."

"BMAT, set circuit breaker 104 to on."

"Roger, Commander, circuit breaker 104 — set to 'on'."

Electrical power can now be applied to the missile ordnance items, including the welded-shut fuel and oxidizer valves. I verify we have selected the target that was specified in the launch message, and point to the lighted indicator and announce, "Target 1 is selected."

"Deputy, insert your key, and turn on my count of 'Mark". We both snap the safety seals that secure plastic covers that guard the launch keyholes.

The deputy responds: "Roger, sir, key is inserted." And I continue: " . . . three, two, one, mark."

The Deputy Commander and I turn our launch commit keys. I continue, without pause, now reading from the Launch Control Console as various lights on the console illuminate: "Crew, we have a LAUNCH ENABLE lighted and the Missile Batteries are being activated."

Now there is a long wait. The great batteries out in the missile always sit there dry. A bladder filled with battery acid sits above these dry batteries. During the launch sequence the bladder is punctured and the electrolyte inside drains into the batteries and they become active and come up to power. It's only a 28 second wait but time is different now. The only sounds that can be heard are the calm, monotonous humming of the fans in the control center. It's just like any other morning at 3:00 a.m., on alert, in any other complex — it's calm and quiet in here, almost sleepy.

APS POWER lights. The missile is now operating on its own battery power. Now it's alive - out there in the dark silo.

Another long wait, listening to the humming of the fans again - then SILO SOFT lights: the 750 ton silo door has unlatched and lifted itself up, and is sliding along its railroad tracks, through the swirling fog that has come in from the Pacific Ocean. The "gunbarrel" now lies open to the night sky.

GUIDANCE GO lights – the missile computer has taken over its own control of the missile.

FIRE IN THE ENGINE lights, a steady red.

Still it's very quiet, unreal in an absolute sense, yet it also seems very normal.

Then most of the lights on the Launch Control Console go out.

The klaxon sounds: "UGGGGAAAHHH!". The FIRE IN THE ENGINE indicator begins flashing red. I punch the klaxon off.

The klaxon sounds again: "UGGGGAAAHHH!" The OXIDIZER VAPOR IN LAUNCH DUCT indicator is flashing red. I punch the klaxon off again.

In the upper right hand corner of the console, another indicator lights a steady white, and is almost overlooked. It reads LIFTOFF.

I announce: "Crew, we have Liftoff." The klaxon goes off again. "UGGGGAAAHHH!" The indicator reading FIRE IN THE LAUNCH DUCT is flashing red, and I punch the klaxon off again.

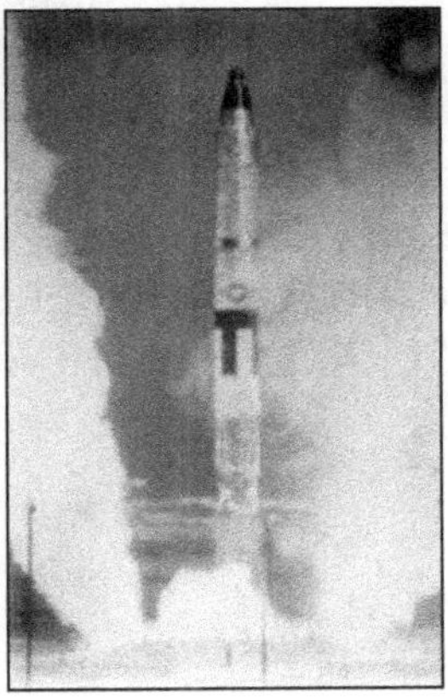

Before dark, we had positioned our topside TV camera so that it faced the silo door. Now we watch the monitor.

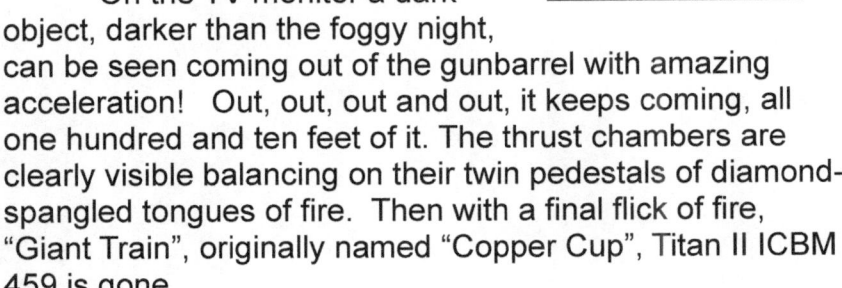

A loud WHOOOOOOOOSH! Is heard. It sounds exactly like air being let out of a huge highly pressurized tire. The sound quickly grows to resemble a near-by freight train at full speed and then vanishes instantly.

On the TV monitor a dark object, darker than the foggy night, can be seen coming out of the gunbarrel with amazing acceleration! Out, out, out and out, it keeps coming, all one hundred and ten feet of it. The thrust chambers are clearly visible balancing on their twin pedestals of diamond-spangled tongues of fire. Then with a final flick of fire, "Giant Train", originally named "Copper Cup", Titan II ICBM 459 is gone.

The penetration team, topside, and two miles away, feel the trademark of the Titan when the engines ignite as the ground pounds up and down like an earthquake. When the missile rises out of the silo they feel the pulse of its sound waves beating against their bodies and faces, then they hear it accelerate into the night sky with the sound of fine silk being torn slowly apart. Finally, that too, is gone, and all that is left is the faint rumble of the second stage climbing into outer space.

We get the silo fires put out and brief the penetration team, who, dressed like spacemen, make a quick tour of the silo and launch duct, and leave.

Then our relief crew arrives. This is a crew who is permanently assigned to Vandenberg and whom we had met once before. We turn the empty hole over to them.

I request permission for my crew to enter the silo, and the new commander agrees.

The cable way, always desert dry and kept at 55°, now is hot and humid, 125° perhaps, and the sound of dripping water is everywhere. As we walk down the cableway, some 6,000 miles away, far over the South Pacific Ocean, a trail of fire and smoke is illuminating the late evening sky there as our re-entry vehicle plunges through the atmosphere of the earth, falling into the target at 18,000 miles per hour — mission accomplished!

# 16
# Changeover

What was it like to spend a day as a crewmember on alert duty in an ICBM complex?

I spent more than missile 600 tours on alert, and did so at 14 different complexes around Little Rock. Here is an example of one those days my crew spent at missile silo 374-5.

It's a Wednesday morning and I'm up at 0615. I shower, shave, eat breakfast; then whisk my bags into the car and I'm off to the briefing room at the Wing Command Post. Our briefing will be at 0730.

I stop at our squadron operations area, a building next to the briefing room which is now filled with sleepy-looking crew-members in their missile white overalls checking crew boxes, bulletin boards and everything else they can find before heading over for the briefing.

Hideous cursing breaks out in a loud and profane voice. Words too vile to place on printed page are shouted. I look in the direction of the noise and see a young second lieutenant staring at the weekly schedule that is tacked to a bulletin board. He looks stunned and his face is red.

"What's your problem, lieutenant?" I ask, heading in his direction.

"I have alert *tomorrow!*" he shouts pressing his finger into a spot on the schedule. "This is my damn day *off!*"

"Well, lieutenant," I say amicably, "that's the way it happens when you're not in command of yourself."

He glares at me "Easy enough for you to say Major, you've got your life all put together, I don't "

"Well, look at it this way, " I say with a smile, you can go out and play a round of golf right now – no waiting. They probably aren't even open – you can play for free!"

"Dressed like *this*?" he shouts, pulling at his overalls. He starts cursing again.

"The world is full of opportunities, Lieutenant, and so is the Air Force, but I think it is time for you to go somewhere else and be quiet" I look directly into his face " Do you know what I am telling you?"

"Yes sir." He picks up his two briefcases and heads over to the administrative office so he can call his wife and have her collect their infant child and come back out and take him home. They will get to do it again tomorrow morning at 0615. Poor wife. Poor child. I will say a word about his behavior to his crew commander. If he were on my crew, I would want to know - not about his coming out a day early, but about his emotional loss of control - I wouldn't want anyone who acts like that to be anywhere near nuclear weapons.

The briefing shows we have thirty-two maintenance personnel scheduled to work at our site today. None of the jobs are important or even significant except in their totality. Often our Maintenance Wing will let minor write-ups accumulate while more serious problems are being fixed, then they will pile all the little work together on one day.

Good news is that we have no students who will be going out with us today, and none are scheduled to show up for training. That's different.

After the briefing, I make a couple of phone calls and get two items rescheduled for a later date. That will help ease the workload today.

The trip to the missile complex takes about an hour. It's an easy ride, keeping just under the speed limit, at first over highways and then the back roads of central Arkansas. Cattle and horses come up to fences along the way and watch us go by. We have become part of their daily routine. Small gardens cluster up close to the roads here and there, and there's always a possum lying dead somewhere on the trip. Old General Stores are located about every 10 miles or so. Most have rusty and dusty pickup trucks gathered around them.

The Missile Facility Technician (MFT), who is a master sergeant, is driving. I'm sitting in the right front seat still reviewing our workload for the day. In the back seat, the deputy commander, a young lieutenant and the Ballistic Missile Analyst Technician (BMAT), a technical sergeant, are sprawled out trying to get a head start on their sleep for the tour.

We'll be in the complex for twenty-four hours; but counting the drive out and back, plus the briefings, we are looking at about twenty-eight to thirty hours from the time we leave our own front doors until we return. We will each probably get about four to six hours sleep – less if there are problems or if we have students show up. I am still trying to figure out how many people we are likely to have in the complex and silo at any given time, what equipment will have to be shut down while maintenance is being performed, and when and how all this will fit together.

When we arrive at the complex, we use a telephone next to the entrance gate to call the underground control center. We identify ourselves and the on-duty crew commander presses a button on the Launch Control Console that unlocks the gate latch.

We enter into the complex area and conduct a brief above ground inspection. Then we head down a short flight of stairs which leads to the entrance to the below ground portion. At the bottom of the stairs is another telephone next to a locked entrance door. One member of our crew, normally the crew commander, calls in again and the crew on duty activates a remote latch that unlocks the door. One of our crew members enters into the place we call the Entrapment

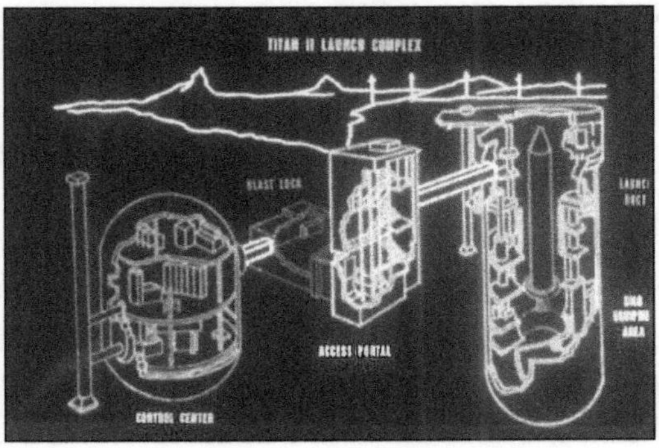

Area. After the entrance door is locked, that crewmember picks up another telephone and tells the crew on duty to let the rest of his crew (the relief crew) in. This "Entrapment Area" is totally safe from any possible coercion or observation. The door to the outside is locked, and the other door that leads into the complex is also locked. The person there has a dedicated line to the Launch Control Center, and there is a TV camera that looks into the Entrapment Area and its screen is in the Launch Control Center.

From there, another flight of stairs leads down to the blast door area. We enter the first one, shut and lock the two-foot thick steel door, then open another blast door, close and lock it, and then open another blast door that enters into the Launch Control Center. Immediately upon opening the last door, the smell of Pine-Sol and coffee wafts over us and we know that we are "home".

Together our crews review the maintenance forms. We discuss current problems with the complex and various issues that may arise today, along with any unresolved problems from yesterday. Then the enlisted men go upstairs to level one of the complex where they usually make coffee and conduct informal briefings among themselves about the complex and its equipment

We four officers gather around the Launch Control Console on level two. I sign documents indicating that I am assuming alert for the complex, for the equipment in the complex, the missile and its warhead.

The off-going commander and deputy hand their top-secret documents to us. We inventory and sign for them. Then they transfer the .38 caliber pistols they were wearing to us. We sign for these too along with their ammunition and strap them around our waist. Then the off-going crew commander and his deputy each remove a dog-tag like chain which contains a single tiny key from around their neck and hand it to me and my deputy, and we place those key chains around our own necks and tuck them in under our uniforms. Those are the missile launch keys.

We call the Wing Command Post and notify them that changeover is complete and that my crew has assumed command of the complex, the missile and its thermonuclear weapon.

The other crew gathers their bags and personal equipment and head back through three heavy blast-lock doors and up the 55 steps to ground level. Our MFT has given the keys to the station wagon to one of their enlisted men and they drive back to the missile wing for debriefing.

The complex is a busy place full of unending sounds. The hum of fans and whistle of servos create a constantly rising and falling background noise. UHF, VHF, and HF radios crackle intermittently. We also have a telephone switchboard and the phones seem to ring constantly. Personnel approach the outside gate, identify themselves, come through the entrapment area, the blast lock area, each step requiring phone calls and coordination with the crew.

As site commander, I brief each maintenance team on conditions in the silo and complex and they brief me on the work they plan to do, what that will require from our operations crew, and how it will affect other equipment. My MFT and BMAT help coordinate with the maintenance teams. We also have a PA system and numerous two-way radio telephones that each crew carries with them when they go into the silo. The Strategic Air Command Primary Alerting System (PAS) intermittently chatters and sometimes sounds with warble tones announcing messages, most are just routine traffic.

Later that afternoon we have twenty-one maintenance personnel in the silo when the lights go out and all the klaxons sound. I am at the Launch Control Console when this occurs and I turn the klaxons off while waiting for the automatic switchgear to changeover to the backup diesel power. It is eerily quiet with no fans or servos humming and the emergency lighting system fills the launch control center and silo with shadows worthy of a Boris Karloff movie. The entire silo and missile are all still fully powered by great battery banks below us on level three, and in the split second between total electrical power loss and the batteries picking up the load, gigantic capacitors carry the full load. About thirty seconds later the diesel is full power and has picked up the electrical load for the complex and the lights cycle back on, servos come back up, fans start up again and everything appears normal. My crew verifies all systems are operating normally and we contact each team in the silo to verify their status and to find out if the power outage affected their work. The Wing Command Post calls to notify that heavy rain and significant air-to-ground lightning is present in our area. I have the MFT isolate the switchgear so we will remain on diesel power for the next two hours.

About thirty minutes later the diesel Start Air Receiver Low light and the Air Pressure Low light comes on and remains on for several minutes. We notify Job Control – *that's all we need* – more maintenance personnel out here today! We transfer back to commercial power about 1700 hours, shut down the diesel and hope we won't have to changeover to diesel power again.

We get the last of the maintenance troops out of the complex about 1930 hours, and are ready to start suppers (Air Force versions of TV dinners) and then begin the sleeping schedule.

Level two of the Launch Control Center is a SAC "No-Lone Zone." There can never be less than two people present on level two at any time. Both of those people must be qualified and knowledgeable of the dangers of access to nuclear weapons and the launching mechanisms of nuclear missiles. Consequently, we can have two people sleeping in the bed area on level one, above the control center, while the other two crewmembers must remain on the second level. We will all have to be up by 0600 tomorrow and the sleeping schedule begins at 2100 tonight, so that's nine hours divided two ways. Tonight, the MFT and deputy will bed down first from 2100 hours until midnight, then the BMAT and I will sleep from midnight till 0400, then the other two go back for two more hours. Not bad as far as missile alert tours go.

At 0230, the Inertial Measurement Unit on the Titan II missile down-modes from Ready Green to Align Mode Six. The deputy and MFT try trouble shooting the problem for about ten minutes then awaken the BMAT and me. Preliminary examination indicates the BMAT will have to run tests to verify alignment procedures, so we notify the Wing Command Post and report that our missile is in a Not-Ready status.

The testing takes about one and a half hours, and is successful. By 0400, we are Ready Green again and notify the command post. I have sent the deputy and MFT back to bed about 0300, and decide to let them continue to get what rest they can. Looks like the MFT will drive the station wagon home tomorrow – or rather, later today.

The rest of the tour passes without further problems. At 0700, the gate telephone rings and we receive the first of our maintenance personnel for the day. They are electricians and diesel people to work on our backup power problem.

At 0800, the gate telephones rings announcing the arrival of civilian tech reps; out to perform some previously scheduled tests on the missile.

At 0830, our relief crew arrives. We clear all personnel out of the control center, perform crew changeover, transfer the pistols, the Top Secret documents and launch keys to the oncoming crew. We sign the necessary forms, notify the Wing Command Post, and then we get our bags and personal gear and head back home.

Back at the squadron area, we check bulletin boards, crew boxes and the all-important schedule. It's almost 1130 hours on Thursday morning and we have the rest of the day off! Friday we will be in class from 0800 until 1200, then Countdown Trainer from 1600 until 1730. Saturday we will be back for another alert tour at complex

374-5 again. That will be our second tour this month. We are scheduled for seven more.

Now I go home for lunch and to play with the kids, then go shopping, and later in the day, maybe some tennis. To bed? Not until at least 10:00 p.m., otherwise, I will introduce "jet lag" into my life.

I have already received orders, effective in sixty days. My missile assignment is now all but over. I will be heading to another base, Minot Air Force Base, North Dakota; and will be going back to flying again.

There will be some "Young Tiger" deployments into Southeast Asia, and I'll be navigating the KC-135. After completing more than six years and almost 700 alert tours in missile crew duty and one launch of a Titan II out of Vandenberg AFB, California, it will be interesting to see how the flying part of the Air Force looks now.

So it's time for another changeover for me and that's a significant part of any Air Force career.

# 17
# Why Not Minot?

The first time I saw Minot, North Dakota, was on a summer day. My family and I had come from KC-135 training school at Merced Air Force Base, California, via Yellowstone National Park and the great American West.

None of that prepared us for what we found. The last towns we drove through looked dirty and unfinished. Each village we reached on our way further north seemed more desolate than the last one.

Still we drove on, still headed north.

Summer sunlight slanted in from a sun that seemed eerily out of place, and strands of wind-chased dirt writhed like snakes down broken streets, swirling around potholes and over crevices.

Finally we pulled into Minot. Two highways cross here in a small strip-mall on a ridge at the south edge of town and the city spreads out to the north, sloping downward toward the Souris River.

The Minot Chamber of Commerce had already told us that "Souris" is French for "smile," yet any Frenchman knows that "smile" is "sourire" (soo-REER), and "souris" (soo-REE) means mouse. The Minot people call it "SOO-whrirs." It splits south of town and the part that runs through Minot disappears into the prairies of Saskatchewan. The rains that fall and the snow that melts in Minot goes neither to the Pacific or Atlantic Oceans nor to the Gulf of Mexico, but northward into those great prairies and eventually on in to Hudson's Bay.

We already knew that North Dakota was different from the rest of the states; now we were discovering that Minot was different from the rest of North Dakota.

The evenings up here were also different. Summer sunset occurs at ten minutes to ten, and the twilight sometimes lingers for 40 minutes or more until after 10:30 p.m. In the years we were there, the aurora was strong and it would fill the northern part of our summer night sky with a pale and wavering greenish light. Twilight could last for hours! Yes, Minot was very different.

Aurora from our backyard

We had heard "Minot Tales" before we left Little Rock AFB. Everybody in the Air Force seemed to know one or two of them although very few people I knew had ever even flown in here.

We heard that it was north of 90% of the Canadian population (a probably false "fact" I never tried to verify). We heard that children's lungs could freeze from breathing the cold air – and many other ridiculous tales that were both frightening and false.

I did not want to come to Minot, and I was glad to leave it, yet I still remember it as a nice town and a good place to be. I will always remember the flat lands of Dakota, and the thrilling wind that raised your spirit to a level you had never known before.

Most of all, I remember Minot as the place I fell in love with the sky.

The sky elsewhere is just something to put over it all but in North Dakota, the sky has a soul that you can see and feel, and resonate with, and your own soul finally finds the place it can learn to fly.

Way up there, the sky is Destiny and Wildness and somehow, it is also "home", and even though I have never been back, and probably never will go back to those plains again, I still miss them and I will always feel incomplete until someday I again become part of the North Dakota sky.

Other than the sky and the wind, how do I remember Minot? Mainly like a series of pictures, snapshots of life, like pictures at an exhibition.

★ ★ ★

The second day there, we move into our house, and after an arduous day of unpacking, I pour myself a martini, and wander out through the garage and around into the back yard where I am hit in the chest with what seems like a plank of wood about a foot wide and four inches thick. But it isn't a plank; it is the North Dakota wind. When I recover my balance, my martini glass is empty, even the olives and toothpick are gone, and the glass is coated with a layer of fine dust.

Electric wires above our house let out a low humming howl that rises in intensity as the wind quickens. The howl finds a harmonic response with something in my spine that makes the hairs rise on the back of my neck. *Well,* I think, *at least the wind doesn't blow this hard in the winter – it can't!* My "reasoning" lay in the understanding that everyone in the world would have heard of it were such a thing true.

In the winter, I would later discover, the Dakota wind does abandon its "harmonic hum" as it crawls up your spine and leaps and soars into the banshee shriek scale.

I remember a weather broadcast one January day: "At Minot Air Force Base currently the temperature is minus 34 degrees, the wind is out of the north, north-west at 45 knots, gusting to 60 knots with peak gusts to 85 knots. The wind chill factor is minus 85 to 100 degrees. Frostbite time is approximately 8 to 15 seconds." It continued. "This is a hazardous condition, and travel should not be attempted."

I also remember my ears popping from the changing air pressure as the windows of our house bow in and out from the wind gusts. *Is that the windows?* Then I wonder if it is the walls of the house!

"Why Not Minot!" reads a billboard just outside town, with a happy, chubby and turban-wrapped fakir holding a crystal ball in his hand. "You can buy it all in the Magic City!"

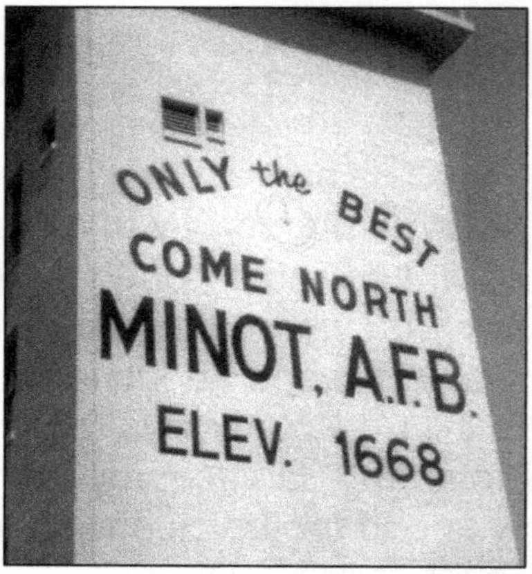


The control tower at the Air Force Base has a sign with another slogan: "Only the Best Come North!"

Some members of the Air Force who are stationed here have been heard to glumly mutter, " . . . and only the lucky ever go south again!"

Electric plugs hang out of the front of the Minot cars; not just one but usually three.

Cars come up here in the summer with only one plug dangling out above or through their grill, and we know they are from Rapid City. That's way down in southern South Dakota, down where we hear that palm trees and bananas grow. These "southern cars" have one plug to heat an immersion heater element, which is thrust down where the oil dipstick normally is placed, and the wire on its other end is plugged into your house circuit to keep the oil warm. Most of those folks pull that thing out in the summer and put the original dipstick back in.

Why do the cars up in Minot all have three plugs? Well, this is Minot, Why Not!

Actually, one plug provides current to an immersion water heater that has been added to the car – we cut the water hose and then attach into that circulation flow a heater, which also has a pump. It not only heats the water up to 140°, but also circulates it from block to radiator and back and forth, all night (or day) long.

A second plug is for the small electric heating blanket that is wrapped around the battery to keep it up to maybe 20° or 30°.

The other plug is for the little one amp battery charger that we keep screwed to the inside of a fender well, or wherever, under the hood so we can hook it to the battery and keep a little trickle charge on it all night (or day). Won't the battery charger be ruined if water is splashed on it? Of course, but there is NO water - anywhere - up here from middle November to middle March.

Can you be reasonably sure that your car will start on a cold morning if it was left in the garage and all three electrical plugs connected? No.

Snowplows come down these streets at 45 to 50 miles per hour, usually late at night or very early in the morning. When the plows get up to speed, they drop their blade to the snow cover and ice pack on the roads and scrape great masses of suddenly melted ice and snow into a huge, frigid rolling mess that spins down the street in front of it. This mess refreezes into a virtually unchoppable wall of black ice as soon as it slides off the snowplow's blade. Great banks of this ice rise on either side of each street and a deposit is left at the end of the street where the plows turn around. These mounds will later become the last ice of the year to melt, sometime in May.

As the winter wears on, the streets come to resemble "rivers" that "don't flow" between great banks of frozen snow and ice piled four to five feet high. Keeping an opening out of your driveway through that rock-hard ice to gain access to the plowed street is the responsibility of each occupant of the government housing.

One picture I remember is a frigid morning, two and a half hours past midnight. I'm flying today and the briefing for this flight is 0300, but since I live on base I have less than a seven-minute drive to my squadron operations building. I go back into the house to finish my coffee and bring my bags out to the car. I've spent the last forty-five minutes chopping and shoveling frozen snow and moving an ice pack out of my driveway. Now I can back my car into the street through the cut I have just made in the five-foot high drifts piled at the curb.

As I lock the door to my house, I hear a great roaring sound begin to rise from the end of the street. *Oh No! The snowplow!*

Here it comes! It lurches and starts down our street like a huge dragster, its rotating beacon on top of the cab slapping flashes of light against the dark houses alongside the street. As its speed increases, the blade falls to the ice pack and instantly a great ball of suddenly melted ice and snow is scraped up, kneaded and churned and scrambled in front of the plow as it charges up the street. Great waves of temporarily melted ice slobbers above the banks on the street like waves at Waikiki. I charge out into my driveway, shouting curses that cannot be heard, shovel in hand and waving it above my head. Then the great blinking, pulsating, snorting beast races past my driveway as great semi-frozen "waves" slosh into the cut I have just made, freezing solid instantly. I charge out upon the quickly freezing mound, slipping, staggering, falling, and sliding down my brand new four-foot high bank of ice and then slip, fall and roll back into my own driveway.

I climb the shovel handle, rising and turning to see the great plow coming back, now down the other side of the street. My curses become distorted into demonic laughter by the wake turbulence of the plow that races past heading out of sight at full speed. It won't come back – not 'till the next time.

★ ★ ★

A Greyhound bus crouches in a narrow alley in downtown Minot, leaning to one side on the icepack, the edge of its roof almost touching one side of a building, and it disappears and reappears as blowing snow rises between us and the bus, whisking the smell of its exhaust and a taste of frozen snow into our mouth and nose. The light gray snow actually brightens the dark world. The bus has a bit of dark blue in its dark gray; the dark alley has a bit of black in it. It's two in the afternoon and already getting dark. The front window of the bus is fogged, and sifted with snow. Great bales of steam puff out of a tail pipe somewhere behind it. A loud speaker crackles. "Now loading for Max, Garrison Dam, Falkirk, Bismarck, and Henley." There are no takers. Eventually, a lone man, hidden in a great fur parka, slips and slides out to the bus, gets in and drives out, heading south in his big bus all alone.

★ ★ ★

There is a picture of an Easter morning. The kids are dressed in their best clothes. The eggs were dyed and carefully placed in the yard last night. Over the night, snow was forecast to fall but none did. And now the kids must have a go at the great search before church. So we go out into the yard. Here we are, twenty-two degrees, out in snow that is waist high in places, on a windy, gusty day hunting Easter eggs that are all snuggled

up against the house. This is Easter? Well, it's a Minot Easter!

★ ★ ★

We sit in the back yard on an August evening, reclining in lawn chairs enjoying our drinks. We flinch every minute or so, every time the rotating sprinkler hits us with icy cold water. We are fully dressed, but stay dry. With zero percent humidity, the precious water evaporates in about one and one-half seconds. The temperature is 110°. Who would have thought North Dakota would ever be so chic?

★ ★ ★

August 24, and we are driving south trying to get into Colorado by nightfall. The temperature is 113° and the wind is out of the south at 60 miles per hour. It is a hot, gusty, miserable trip. Grit is in our teeth every time we close our mouth. We are on a 2400-mile trip to Kentucky for a visit with the grandparents.

We return less than two weeks later, with snow flurries drifting down on September the second. We get home at 3:00 A.M. It is 28°, which is 85° lower than it was when we left only twelve days ago. And when we get out of the car, still in Kentucky shorts and tee shirts, we hear the wind carelessly playing with those wires above our heads.

★ ★ ★

The Minot Zoo is a wonderful place. It has trees! There are no mountains or even hills anywhere around here, but there are some "negative hills," depressions in the land like arroyos or small canyons. The zoo is in one of these, and thus protected from the wind, it has trees.

Every yard on the base also has two trees. They are fir trees and they are all about two to three feet tall and they all lean, pointing to the south. I thought they had been planted just before we moved in. It was quite a shock to find they were each more than 25 years old. It's hard on trees way up here.

★ ★ ★

I take my two-year-old child to the BX on a cold December day. Coming out we can hear a sound: "ding!" . . . "dong!" . . . "wham!" . . . "bam!" The noise is sounding about every 4 to 5 seconds. I can't see what is causing the commotion because of my parka, but it is definitely getting louder with every bang, so I turn around and pull my parka back a bit and then can see a 30 gallon metal trash can coming down the street at about 40 mph, touching down every fifty feet or so. Cars stop to let it go by. The temperature is 22 below zero.

A voice is heard to say, "Somebody ought to stop that thing!"

Someone else says, "Let it go, the poor son-of-a-bitch is going south!"

# 18
# Wrong Side of the Bed

In the 1960's and 1970's the United States and the Soviet Union were locked in a struggle that sometimes seemed destined to climax in nuclear annihilation of each other and the entire world. With both countries willing and eager to poke, provoke and infuriate each other but reluctant to actually attack, we slowly evolved into a "Cold War", resembling an epic water polo match in which the water itself began to assume the proportions of a common bond, and the two antagonists continued to grimly struggle with each other while at the same time beginning to hold on to each other for support. It began to seem likely that some unanticipated and even relatively minor irregularity might eventually ripple across this sea and become the precipitative factor of thermonuclear war that would end life on our planet.

During this period, I was stationed at Minot AFB, North Dakota. The base, which was only 32 miles south of Manitoba, was close enough to Russia that some of our newer B-52 bombers could reach their targets without in-flight refueling. There were KC-135 tankers there to provide these bombers with enough fuel to return to a recovery base after striking their targets, and also to rendezvous with and refuel other bombers that would take off from different bases. We kept a number of B-52's and KC-135's "on alert," parked out at the south end of a runway which faced north; not because it faced Russia, but because the prevailing winds in North Dakota, at least in the winter, were from the north. The airplanes were clustered around an "alert pad," a large building, partly underground, in which some 200 or more men remained "on alert" for seven straight days. Each Thursday there was a changeover and another group of crewmembers and maintenance people assumed the alert. This alert status was maintained unbroken for some 40 years.

President Nixon found himself in confrontation with Congress over a problem which became known as the "Watergate" affair, and this began to draw attention away from the great Cold War. Slowly the awareness was dawning upon the rest of the world that Nixon was becoming unable to serve effectively as president, and eventually only two choices would remain to him: to resign, or be removed from office. However, many of us who were involved with the nuclear weapons delivery program worried quietly that there might be a third option that could "save" his presidency – a major confrontation with Russia would change everything – overnight, he would become a great national hero!

On one alert tour I was studying an AF correspondence course and was writing late into the evening in the alert pad dining room. Two or three crewmembers were sleeping in the TV room under a gray unblinking buzz from the set which was still on although the two television broadcasting stations that we could receive here had signed off for the night. The other 200 or so crewmembers and maintenance personnel were asleep in their beds in the rooms beneath us and most of them had been there for an hour or more. Finally I too went down the steps into the sleeping area which was quiet, still and peaceful.

I washed my face in the latrine, walked down a hallway that led out toward the parked aircraft to the room I shared with my pilot & co pilot, who were already asleep. I paused outside the door to the room and quietly hung my flight jacket on one of many pegs there. I glanced at my watch, which read 1:10 a.m., recalling that I had to get up at 6:30. Slowly I opened the door and quietly, very quietly closed it behind me as I stepped into the dark room. I sneaked over to my bed, tiptoeing carefully through the darkness and sat down cautiously so I would not make any noise. The bed squeaked a little and I stopped for a moment and then slowly sank down.

I reached down and quietly unzipped my right flight boot, very slowly as not to make any noise with the zipper, even holding my left hand over the zipper for added quietness. When I reached the bottom of the zipper, the klaxon in every room in the alert pad went off. Sound waves reverberated throughout my body. I could feel the bed vibrate with the ten second long "UGAAAAAAAAAAAH!" of the klaxon. I felt as if a huge ice pick had been rammed straight through my head into my body and then connected to an electric current. I could neither breathe nor think. I immediately pulled the zipper back up as if in an apology for causing all that noise and then realizing what the noise was, and what it meant, I reached to find the light at the end of my bed to turn it on, but knocked the lamp over on the floor.

BANG! – BANG! – BANG!

That was the copilot running into a wooden closet, falling back on his bed, leaping up and running into the closet again, and again. Finally he rolled over the bed to the other side. He stepped into his flight suit, squirming it up over his shoulders and as he dragged the zipper up, all the klaxons went off again "UGAAAAAAAAAAAH!"

I walked out of the door, casually pulled down my flight jacket and then started a slow dogtrot out to the planes.

"HALT!" a guard called with an M-16 pointed at my stomach.

"EPIX!" I yelled, shouting the new day's password.

"PASS!" he responded.

I reached the nose gear of our aircraft at the same time as the crew chief. I noticed he was missing his cap and one boot. I reached for the ladder to climb up to the flight deck.

POW! A B-52 fired up the starter cartridge in its number four engine. This controlled explosion provided hot gasses at high velocity to start the jet engine turning over.

Fuel was added and it was operating in a second or two. There followed a great shrieking whine as the engine was brought up to full throttle so it could provide electrical and hydraulic power to start the other engines. It all sounded like a great beast had just been shot and was screaming with rage!

POW! Whine! Another B-52 fired up with black smoke rising high up above it like a black tornado!

POW! Whine! Another B-52 fired up and black smoke drifted through the parked aircraft turning the flight line into an unreal world of light and darkness with great belches of dark red flame from the full running engines.

POW! Whine! Our own engines were starting.

Relays clicked on, generators wound up, intercom and radios came on line.

"Crew - this is the pilot, intercom check!"

I started to answer, but instead, heard over the radios:

"I repeat, this is SAC Headquarters with a Message for all SAC Aircraft; all aircraft taxi immediately to your active runway and standby to implement immediate takeoff using MITO (Minimum Interval Take Off) procedures."

"My God!" I thought, and in fact said aloud over the aircraft intercom, "Nixon has blown it!"

"What's your problem, Nav?" the pilot asked tersely as he taxied between two aircraft that were lost in smoke as they fired up their engines.

"We're going," I answered.

"You gotta be kidding!" The pilot exclaimed. "Nixon, you bastard! "

"We gotta copy!" I said, needlessly as the message was repeated again and again.

"That SOB!" The copilot screamed.

The copilot and I copied the message and began decoding it. We taxied in a quickly moving line of aircraft to the runway while a warble tone sounded over the radios to announce that a new message was coming in from SAC Headquarters. We copied it, and as we decoded it realized it was a recall message! The authentication was valid! The Alert Force was NOT to launch!

The first B-52 was already rolling down the runway with a huge cloud of black smoke following behind it.

Fifteen seconds later the second B-52 started down the runway with a huge cloud of black smoke following behind it.

The warble tone sounded over the radios and another message began being broadcast.

The third B-52 started down the runway with a huge cloud of black smoke following behind it.

I copied the message and began decoding it.

The fourth B-52 started down the runway with a huge cloud of black smoke.

I completed decoding the message and began to authenticate it.

The fifth B-52 started down the runway with a huge cloud of black smoke.

This message was a verification of the earlier recall message!! We were downgraded.

Fifteen seconds later the sixth B-52 started down the runway with a huge cloud of black smoke as the first bomber lifted into the dark night sky at the far end of the runway. Five B-52's all loaded with nuclear weapons were still on takeoff roll, one behind the other on the same runway. My watch read 1:19 a.m.

We were the first tanker ready to take off after the bombers were gone, and we rolled into takeoff position but waited as the pilot called our Wing Command Post and asked for a rebroadcast of the last message.

We all copied it down again, decoded and verified it to make certain. Then we taxied to the far end of the runway along with all of the other tankers. At the end of the runway, we turned off the active runway and headed back to our refueling area. The entire base was lit up like a carnival. Cars and trucks were racing all over the place. Flashing red lights and flashing blue lights and flashing amber lights and flashing white lights were all over the taxiways and ramp. The trip back to the refueling pits was a long and slow process. It was a journey through a land where time had ceased to exist; we felt drained, as if all of our energies had roared down the runway and taken off without us and were now far away racing together with destiny through a dark night sky. The world now moved slowly as time averaged itself out. The lights were too bright, all sounds seemed to echo; we kept jerking and straightening up as if hearing the first notes of another warble tone announcing a new message that would bring the world to an end.

We refueled our aircraft, went through our normal post-flight check and spent two hours on the flight line cocking the aircraft back on alert status. Finally, about three hours after the first B-52 had taken off, we got back to the alert pad. Our Bomber compatriots were now headed back from over the north pole after an airborne abort, and they would not get back until later this morning.

As we walked back into the alert pad, since it was just after 5:00 a.m., somebody asked about sleep and someone else was heard to say that he would never sleep again. Our pilot glanced at the copilot, and said: “God, Ken! What the hell happened to your face?”

Ken put his hand to his right temple and winced. Then he turned his head. Bruises were looming all over his head and face, and dried blood ran down just in front of his right ear.

“Yeah,” he said, “I guess I got up on the wrong side of the bed today.”

# 19
# The Wondrous Toy

Way back on December 18, 1959, my crew landed our KB-50 at Westover AFB, Massachusetts, en route from Newfoundland to Langley AFB in Virginia.

Base Operations was a bustling and active place filled with busy people. There was a gift shop with books and handy things to take on trips. A tiny cafeteria and grill sent the sizzle of hamburgers and the smell of French fries through the entire building. Magazines and newspapers lay on tables and chairs. People were talking and laughing while a jukebox played the popular tunes of the day.

We flight-planned quickly and got burgers, fries and shakes.

Then we left the flashing neon hubbub and laughter, climbed up into our airplane for a nighttime ride to take us home. That was once upon a time, and it was a long, long time ago.

★ ★ ★

Tonight it is November 17, 1970. We land our KC-135 at Westover AFB, Massachusetts, en route from Minot to Torrejon AFB, near Madrid.

Base Operations has two empty newspaper racks in a hallway near an alcove with four dispensing machines that dispense a flickering fluorescent glare. There is a candy machine, a soda machine, a coffee machine and a machine with chips and desserts. A smell of burned and stale instant coffee permeates the place. Our footsteps echo through the empty hallway.

As we receive our weather briefing I can't help but think of my last trip here eleven years ago. I AM impressed at how much better the modern weather data has become, yet I feel we have lost something important since the old cafeteria that was so full of life is now just an empty hallway of our own echoes. I wonder if someday we might not receive our weather briefings from a dispensing machine in a darkened and echoing hallway. I can almost visualize the instructions above the coin slots: "Twenty five cents for local briefing, One dollar for entire east coast, Five dollars for transatlantic information".

While we are busy in base operations, civilian technicians are installing two black boxes in the back of our airplane. We meet with those technicians briefly and they enthusiastically explain how their work is part of a nearly completed testing program that will eventually provide all Air Force and commercial aircraft with navigational equipment that will track the flight of each aircraft. They point out that this equipment does not require any external information such as celestial or radio input.

We are told we must taxi to a spot near the middle of the airfield before we depart, into a large circle, which has been painted on the tarmac. While the pilots stop there, I am to open a cover on one of the black boxes and insert a set of coordinates they have given me for that spot. When we get to Spain, we are to taxi to another circle there, and I will copy the coordinates from the machine into a special logbook. One of the technicians tells me I can go back to the boxes and read my coordinates while we are in flight. "Any time you want to." He encourages me to do so, like it would be a real big deal.

"Sure." I say. "Thanks." It has already become apparent that the flight ahead is going to have its interesting points as we are forecast to encounter some heavy weather since we will make a frontal passage. I am going to have a busy night without the added problem of nursing along some new and wondrous toy.

We lift into the dark sky as a nearly full waning moon rises ahead of us. It is a bewitching sight, not only hanging out there in the vastness of space but also rippling in the waters so close below where it lies reflecting, full and moonlike in the sounds of Rhode Island and the sheltered bays of Massachusetts, then exploding into endless shimmering brilliance as we pass over wind-ruffled open water.

Later we coast out over Nantucket and the shimmering column of moonlight glitter leaps out to the ocean horizon, now on a level with our eyes. Later we enter light clouds and watch the lights of Boston fade and blink out.

John Womack navigating a KB-50

We fly on, south of Nova Scotia, leaving the entire world behind us. We sail on, far above the foggy sea below us, denizens of our own small world of subdued lights and humming power. Six silent people we are, separately engrossed in our own thoughts and work as we crawl across a small-scale map through a primitive fog, heading for Spain.

The ride tonight is a typical Atlantic winter trip, full of bounces and strange drifts. The ground speeds are far away from those forecast by the weather people.

When the clouds encapsulate us we rise, climbing higher into a shining night sky that is suddenly full of stars again and a bright pale, now high-riding moon. It is mid-November; some call this moon the Hunter's Moon and we are sailing under it hunting Spain at 600 MPH.

I remember again the ancient KB-50 flights across this same ocean, years ago. Those planes flew with props, not jets like the KC-135. The difference is much the same as swimming across the top of the water using a "crawl" stroke (the prop flight), and swimming underwater (the jet flight). Then it was at 7,000 or 8,000 feet instead of 35,000 as it is tonight. Then it was 180 MPH and the radio was a simple

HF with a range of less than 500 miles, not the 3000 to 4000 mile range of our new Single Sideband equipment. The improvements are astonishing and have increased our capabilities immensely. Of course they have also brought with them new restrictions and requirements. Back then, we just drew a line on our GNC (Global Navigation Chart) maps that covered the entire ocean. We drew one straight line that ran from coast-out point to entry point, and it was our great-circle pathway for that night. Now we fly on "highways" that reach invisibly through the sky and our new job is to stay "on course".

I run this crossing with night celestial, our only over water navigational equipment, since our Doppler is not working tonight.

Even at 35,000 feet, the celestial "seeing" is not good due to a developing high cirrus cloud layer and some altostratus. The wonderful selection of autumnal stars becomes more limited as the night progresses. The sky is clear to the north, but it closes under great clouds toward the south and east. I use Polaris for courseline and cross it with any bright star I can find ahead or behind us for a speedline. Sometimes I can see Betelgeuse or Rigel, or I look behind and find Deneb, or ahead and get Sirius. Here and there I can find a three star fix; it's a little like playing pick-up-sticks.

We fly on through a fast dawn and sunrise and into a quickly flowing morning. We land in Torrejon at noon local time and taxi into a circle on the ramp. I go to the back of the airplane to read the coordinates off the Wondrous Toy and am amazed to find they are in error by less than 1/4 mile – about 4 football fields. I think: *This could be a big, BIG deal!* We go through debriefing.

Other civilian tech representatives are there and review with us the amazing prowess of the black boxes.

I ask, "What *are* those things?"

One of the tech reps replies: "We call them IMUs – that's for Inertial Measurement Units – we know they work beautifully," he says, smiling. "We just need actual inflight data so we can prove it to other people."

"Well, I'm impressed!" I comment. "How can I get one?"

Turns out they cost about $400,000 each. But the second guy says "As soon as we can get them in mass production the price will drop like a rock!"

The first tech rep adds, "Five years from now every Air Force airplane will have one of them."

A third guy, quiet until now, speaks up "Well wait 'till the GSPSs get into action!"

"What's a 'GSPS'?" I ask

"Global Satellite Positioning System " he says carefully. "It will tell you where you are within 20 feet and you can carry it in your pocket!"

"Wow!" I raise my eyebrows at that, "Just like Dick Tracy and his wristwatch radio!"

"Yep – all you do is just press a button!"

We get to the BOQ in the very early afternoon. I grab a beer then go to bed for a quick nap, still engrossed by the wonders yet to come. I can't wait until I can get my hands on a – what was it – a GSPS? But then, I wonder, what if these new wondrous toys take the "life" out of navigation, like those "improvements" that made a lifeless shell out of the magic that once was Base Operations in Westover?

That's way too much to think about right now . . It's clearly time for a quick nap; a busy night is behind us, a busy day still awaits. I lie down on my bed, and drift off into a sleep filled with dreams of wondrous toys.

# 20
# Carpe Nocturne:
# The Lament of the Ancient Navigator

I've heard the GPS is here.
They say it's quick and ready to use,
it's easy to work
and calmly tells you where you are.
No muss or fuss,
no math to curse,
no lines to plot,
no watch to rate,
no sextant reading to collimate.
Just a button you learn to press!
No work of art, carefully made
with great prowess, and certainly not
an answered prayer.

But I remember a different time,
back in an ancient, golden age
when Navigators rode those winds
that soar above the earth
through dark night skies.
Creatures of heaven, more than earth,
Who winked at twinkles from the stars
and weaved strange angles 'cross their charts,
cobwebbery secrets from the skies,
while solving mystic cosmic clues
as they made magik out of stars!

★ ★ ★

Ah yes. Back in those old days we would mount up in our KC-135s and leap off from the North Dakota plains, and sometimes we headed northward. Two hours after launch we might rendezvous with a B-52, offload fuel and fly on through the arctic night sky to our next refueling.

We might fly east then, or west, or even farther north to finely hone those hard-earned skills of racing through the northern skies without a compass to show our way.
On top of the Earth the compass needle gets confused and

really wants to point straight down. But it can't point down, so it might point to the north for a while, then wander off to find a hill, or a western part of an ocean, or maybe a speck of tundra, then perhaps it would fondly point, hintingly perhaps, towards its home far away, way down south in North Dakota!

So instead of following the headings our compass showed us, up here we flew by gyro headings, plotting and rating on graphs and charts their slow precession.

During preflight planning, we navigators would plot the place where we might find the "Beginning of Morning Twilight", that special point at a special time when the very first lightning of the eastern sky would start to dim the faintest stars. We would also mark the "Beginning of Evening Twilight", that place and time when the boldest stars could first be found in a sky still bright with light.

We were not just observing diurnal passage across the globe but were marking out sectors of day and night that we could find and use for our own special needs. We found and caught and flew in those swiftly moving lanes of light and darkness, using them to find our way.

We explorers of our own dark world, delighting in this strange new sky for speedy jets where stars might move west OR east, and we might fly – in local time – from four o'clock to three o'clock and then onward back to two. Proud masters of the ancient world of time we were, with Greenwich still ticking on our wrists.

Rating and plotting gyro readings was not that hard — our challenge was the Twilight Zone. As long as we flew in the bright daylight, we could measure the height of the sun up in its sky through our sextant, or as we navigators used to say, we could "shoot" the sun.

If we were flying at night, we could "shoot" certain stars. One always knows the height of the sun or a star above any given place on earth. It only depends on the date and the time. So if we find our sun or star to be "out of place," then it's supposed discrepancy is really the distance **we** are away from where we had "assumed" we were.

If we measured three stars and marked each "error," either away or toward each star, we could plot on our chart a "three star fix", and know exactly where we were. But if we were flying in the twilight time, we needed a Jupiter or a Venus, or another planet bright and clear, or to compute and shoot the careless moon – the only thing up in the sky which runs on its own sweet time, and has its own galaxy of corrections to apply, to make some sense of what we found.

Sometimes though we had to fly - captured by chance - in the Twilight Zone. Then our choices were always poor, and our results often poor as well. If we flew west at 600 mph up near the top the globe, the twilight zone would lengthen out from 20 minutes to sometimes – half a day! In two and a half hours we could cross 1,500 to 1,800 miles, depending on our wind, while the sun would go 2,200 miles in that same length of time.

Combat aircraft of the Strategic Air Command did not carry the navigation gear that all other aircraft had. We flew only with that which would survive after nuclear weapons began their blasting. So we found our way very much as Prince Henry and Columbus had.

Yes, we had Tacan and radar, both of which were useless for navigation in high arctic regions or over water. Pressure Differential was usable way up there, but never reliable over land, especially if mountains or hills were down below. So we SAC navigators lived in a conflicted world of modern jet aircraft and ancient navigator tools.

The best aid to navigation in the northern twilight was a navigator who *loved* the sky. One who knew the stars by sight, and was familiar with the sun, who could seek and find the wandering moon, and knew the planets of the night. He could find and "shoot" both moon and Venus in a daylight sky, then cross them through with a parting shot from the setting sun and make of that a "three star fix"! One who equally was at home, high in a dark night sky, that abode of cold and windy clouds – that place where stars hang out. One whose mistress <u>was</u> the sky, who had tuned his senses to her soul, harmonizing with her pulse; rising, falling with her breath, swaying with her every mood, and quick to note her slightest shift in thought or glance, which told him of a weather change, or that the wind was new.

★ ★ ★

So now they say you press a button!
And you leave and go and then arrive;
no surprise, no cares, no wrinkled brow,
no breathless prayers; no one's *amazed*
you found your way!

But remember always, that you still fly
with cockpit ghosts who sail each dusk,
and soar and haunt the dark night sky
with gyros spinning on their desks.
Ghostly figures who sketch and plot
curious symbols, unknown today,
in sepiaceaiously ancient ink
on faded parchment charts.
Masters of forgotten arts
no longer practiced on the earth,
they still fly through skies they love,

silently blowing tiny bubbles
in polished D-1 sextant chambers,
computating and rechecking,
then cranking Greenwich hour angles and
declinating elevations, and
through sextant eyepiece quietly peeking,
with pursed lips, discretely seeking
secrets of the starry realm
where they have chosen to remain . . .
and never leave the sky again.

# 21
# Tosca Tales

I awaken about two in the afternoon from a dream-tossed nap. Reality brings me back into a world of navigation without benefit of black boxes or GSPSES or whatever.

I walk across Torrejon Air Base, just northeast of Madrid, through a slow rain to the "Steak Pit" for filet mignon and sangria, and then back through the rain to our Detachment Operations and flight plan three missions.

Later at the club I meet some old friends from KB-50 days and two more from missile crew duty, all of whom are also passing through, headed in opposite directions.

During the night I am awakened several times as gusty winds drive heavy rain against my BOQ window.

We're up at 0430. Our flight leads us from Madrid out over Balboa, then on to Nantes, France, and on to Jersey and into the UK.

We refuel fighters between Ibsley and Lands End, out over the coast of the Irish Sea. Below us great sweeping seas and towering, resolute cliffs of rock meet in surge after surge of crashing foam.

On we fly, over Brittany, a land that appears to be either rising from or sinking into the sea. From our altitude it glows greenly with darkly furrowed hedgerows and they and their rock fences form careless quilt-like patterns.

Here lies England, a land that's careful with its sunshine. And when the sun does come upon this countryside, its light slants in low and seems bleak, watery and pretentiously cheerful.

Next morning we climb on the crew bus at 0530. Then we take off, and fly over Lisbon, down to the point, around the Bay of Cadiz, through the Straits of Gibraltar and on over Majorca, Sardinia, Sicily and down to the toe of Italy.

We carry fighters on someplace east of there, and then pick up others headed westward and lead them back over Sardinia, to Barcelona and finally we land back at Torrejon.

**Outside of Botins**

Tonight our crew heads into Madrid. We're going tosca-hopping!

For dinner we go to "Antigva Casa Sobrino de Botin," well known throughout the United States Air Force simply as "Botins (bo-TEENS)."

Cigarette smoke is always heavy here but good wine flows freely and musicians play lively Spanish songs as they stroll through the seated crowd. Violin melodies and guitar rhythms resonate against the cellar walls of brick and stucco. Gypsy rhythms and flamenco tempos whirl wild energies that dance through the merry throng.

Waiters carry Castilian-roasted suckling pig complete with apple in its mouth, in great silver platters held in a single hand, high enough to pass safely through the throng, and high enough for all the world to see.

Heavily laden, steaming plates are placed before wide-eyed and openmouthed patrons, who sit with hands clasped in astonished delight, their eyebrows arched in wonder.

I order Andalusian cold soup (also called gazpacho) followed by roast pork with earthy-smelling vegetables accompanied by a deep red wine.

After eating, we climb back up to street level. It's 10:30 p.m., and Madrid is busy. People are everywhere, street cars are running on Calle de Toledo, shops are open, artists stand, engrossed as if in another world, braced in front of their easels painting city nightscapes from the sidewalk.

Next morning we rent a car and drive thirty or so miles into Toledo. The entire trip is through heavy fog and armed national policemen. "La Shareria", are standing every 300 feet along the way. We find out later that President Franco was coming back from a visit to Toledo.

After visiting the cathedral we prepare for lunch. I was tasked to buy the wine, and I find a small shop. The owner offers me his best "house" dinner wine. I buy it, thinking it thrifty at $2.50, in American money. He brings me back change: $2.25. I had lost a decimal point in the conversion process – the bottle cost 25¢ in American money!

We eat lunch in a park sitting on benches. Spanish salami and Spanish ham goes well with Spanish bread and Spanish cheese, and a few Spanish olives and some Spanish peanuts, and a bottle of good, really good, and cheap, really cheap, Spanish wine.

We buy souvenirs and presents as usual. I can't pass up a fantastic Martini Sword Set. Indeed, a tiny set of eight fine swords for impaling olives to place in one's martini! There is an épée, a foil, dagger, saber, rapier, cutlass, scimitar and stiletto, all of them three inches long, and all, of course, made out of the finest (they say) Toledo steel with hand-painted and user-friendly handles.

We tour the Alcazar, a gloomy and depressing place. I am afraid to tarry here lest I be nabbed by some ancient ghost and dragged below to a place where screams are never heard.

Then on to El Greco's house – very different – How could one live like that I wondered? To go to bed at night next to the fireplace with the wind blowing in through those nearby trees, and stars just outside the window, and to sleep above that clay-brick patio. Then to rise in the morning and walk to the balcony and there to gaze down upon the patio below or to look up into the clear blue Spanish sky . . . and then to paint. Wow.

The drab brown color of buildings seen throughout Madrid seems to pick up a teasing pinkish hue here in Toledo, especially when seen against a ringing blue sky.

View of Toledo, Spain

From across the Tagus River, Toledo looks like a miniature Grand Canyon, obviously accessible, yet as impenetrable as an ancient tomb; a place of revelation, mystery, wonder; full of light, but also full of darkness, especially the dread Alcazar.

As the fog creeps back under the sunlit skies of Toledo, we drive back north headed for Madrid.

Tomorrow we will fly into England.

# 22
# Big Ben

The Eiffel Tower rises out of a fog below us and later, German fields lie suddenly exposed. More refueling is done over Holland, then we go back across Norway over the North Sea for more refueling, and finally we drop down toward England.

The land here is astonishingly green, incredibly green. Moss seems to be everywhere, growing on all the trees, on the roof tops, on telephone poles, on the roofs of buses, on tennis courts and even on the road. No wonder the English talk so funny; they have to work hard just to move their lips, probably because of all the moss. At night the land turns black and quiet, and smoke sifts through the air, more reminiscent of coal than the wood smoke we remember from Spain.

After a couple of days flying missions out of Mindenhall RAFB, we have a day off and I head into London. I catch a train out of Shippea Hill, amazed to find there are tables between the seats! Why don't we Americans think of such things? I ride the Underground to Lancaster Gate, and on to the Columbia Club. Then I take a series of London Cabs to Westminister Abbey, past Big Ben, over the Thames, back to Victoria Circle via Whitehall & No

10 Downing Street, to Buckingham Palace and through Hyde Park, past Kensington Gardens back to the hotel.

Later I go pub-crawling and try to figure why the English drink this thing they call beer. And the English monetary system seems to be totally beyond comprehension. I quickly learn that when it is time to pay any reasonably small item such as a bus fare or to buy a drink, it is best to simply dig into my pockets and haul out all my pences, shillings, tupences, ha-pennys and quadrilles, dimes, nickels, quarters and whatevers, and hold them in my open palm. Then, the person collecting the money can pick quickly through the pile and take what they need, or want, and leave whatever is proper.

Next morning I go to Westminster Cathedral for morning prayer. A sense of deep beauty gives way to sacred awe as the organ music reaches down low and grabs and shakes the earth during the venite: "For the Lord is a gr-eat God (shake . . . rumble . . . tremble); and a great kiING above all gods (shudder . . . quake . . . quiver)! In his hands, are all the corners of - the - earth. . . (vibrato in excelsior!)."

During a quieter part of the music, Big Ben is heard, and it sounds again during the sermon.

I sit near the Poets Corner and for communion I move to the choir area. Throughout the services, tourists wander through the area with flashing cameras, snapping pictures of us and the sundry goings-on.

After the service is completed I have to race through London to make connections to get back to Mindenhall.

During the next two days we fly more refueling missions up over the Shetland Islands and Orkney. After those flights we will go back to Madrid for one more week; then we'll go home.

Finally our European trip is over. As we prepare to leave Madrid, headed back home, we already know that our crew is going home to go back on alert. That will be boring. After these wonderful days running cross-Europe in a KC-135 it will be hard to go sit in an alert pad where nothing ever happens.

As we rise into the air above the Spanish countryside, an old folk song that we used to sing at the bar comes back to my mind: "Goodbye to my Juan, farewell Rosearita."

Somehow that seems to fit the day.

# 23
# The Dark at the Top of the Stairs

This is the part of the Air Force that civilians don't know about, and never will.

There were periods when the long nights and short days of the North Country would get to people. Sometimes the winds way up there became personal; they would blow *your* car off the road, drift snow high against *your* door, seal *your* driveway with black ice, and moan and scream and cry through the wires above *your* house. It could seem that they weren't doing this to everybody; it was *you* they were after. Sometimes they would grab *your* house and shake it just to scare *you*.

The cold was personal too; there was no way to get warm sometimes. You would push the limits of flesh and time, knowing the flesh-freezing time was less than 60 seconds and you would work quickly, and fumble without gloves under the raised hood of your car trying to get it started. Some days there would be joy at finally getting above zero. Then it would drop to 35 below that night.

There was no smell of grass, or earth or water for five months. Sometime around the end of March, when the world finally went above freezing again, you still couldn't smell earth or water because all the animal excrement that had accumulated since November would thaw out – all in the same week, and that was all you could smell for that week.

The house was too dry in the winter even with two humidifiers working constantly. Your furniture split and cracked, and every member of your family always had a dry cough. Then both of your humidifiers would dry out and burn up.

The snow would cover the basement windows, then the ground floor windows, and then the upper windows. Sometimes it would drift up over the upper windows and reach the roof of your two-story house.

We all heard about people who had been stationed up here for six, seven or eight years. There were always rumors of suicides, and occasional reports of actual suicides.

Dogs, abandoned by former owners who had moved south during the preceding summer, would sometimes form packs in the winter and roam through the base. There were stories of packs of wild dogs attacking school children. One day each year, usually in the short autumn, there would be a notice in the base newspaper for all personnel to keep their dogs in the house (they were not supposed to run loose anyway). The next day Air Policemen would drive across the base with shotguns shooting every dog they could find.

We would go to work at 8:00 a.m., thirty minutes before sunrise and leave the building at 5:00 p.m. It was dark when we went to work, and it was dark when we came out again. Those who worked in staff jobs often worked inside buildings that had no windows. You could go crazy living like that; and some people did. Some of them could regain themselves, some couldn't. You could tell some of them had gone over. There were others who just left the base – quickly, quietly – they disappeared; nobody ever said what happened to them, but everybody knew.

People got crafty at getting their cars started. Three plugs hung brazenly out the front of the Minot cars; some nights they were all three plugged in. Sometimes the next morning, the car still wouldn't start. And when it did start, it might run five minutes and quit – or it would take your wife and kids to the BX and not start when they came out. In those days few families had more than one car. When you finally did get the stalled car started again after two days in the BX parking lot, the tires would be frozen to the asphalt and you still couldn't go anywhere. When you finally got the tires loose, a day or two after that and could drive again, you drove on tires that were frozen flat on one side and you would bounce every time they turned until they warmed up - for the first five or ten minutes you had to stay below about 10 MPH or you would shake all the fillings out of your teeth and all the bolts off of your car.

You would have slush flung up against your car doors and later at night, that slush would freeze solid and it would expand and crack your door open enough to turn your dome light on. That was the end of another battery. The second winter you would remove all interior light bulbs in November. Why does the far northern winter hate light so much? You would also get a new clock to stick on your dash because the one that came with your car had frozen and burned out the first winter. You had your automatic choke removed and a manual choke installed with a knob you could pull out to help you get the engine started and keep it running.

The far northern bases had magnificent snowplows. They were as good as money could buy. But if they were SAC bases, the first priority of the snowplows was to keep the runway open so the alert aircraft could take off if thermonuclear war came. Sometimes the rest of the base would be snow clogged. The base would be completely snowed in, all vehicle traffic ceased, wives and children were stuck in their houses, the schools were closed, Air Force training classes were canceled because of snow on the roads, even the runway would be officially closed and no aircraft allowed to takeoff or land and heavy snow would be falling and drifting, driven by strong winds. Yet even then, those great snowplows were out plowing and re-plowing again and again and yet again, the main runway. A runway that was officially closed because of the weather. But, then – if IT happened, even though the airfield was closed, the alert force would go.

One wife went shopping at the BX and then the commissary. That makes a long day when three children are with you every step of the way. Coming home, while she was skidding here and there on glare ice in the high winds, she was also trying to handle her kids who were fighting in the back seat. Then there was a flashing blue light in her mirror, and an Air Policeman appeared alongside and ticketed her for doing 27 mph in a 25 mph zone. Her husband, a sergeant who was midway through a seven-day alert tour, and confined for those seven days to the alert facility, was officially notified of the event the next day and reprimanded for not adequately supervising his wife.

An officer, who was flight planning for a TDY to Vietnam, was reprimanded because his porch light was still on in daylight hours. It was the second time he had been guilty of that this winter. He had left for work before daylight, so obviously it was his wife who had failed to turn the light off. "If you can't control your wife and kids, how in the hell are you going to be able to control men in combat?"

Navigators could never command a flying crew. Consequently, many navigators enjoyed working staff jobs, or serving in non-flying assignments. There they could develop and apply their skills as an officer and work their way up the chain of command to acquire experience denied them in their flying assignments. One navigator had spent years in a missile wing and had become a crew commander, been assigned to instructor status at the Alternate Command Post. He had been one of the senior men in the wing and was ripe for assignment to a high-level job in the wing. But he was reassigned to a flying organization because of the Vietnam personnel needs. Six months later he was flying on a crew and his commanding officer was a Captain. This senior Major was now working for a young man who had less time in grade as a Captain than he had as a Major. The work the Major had accomplished the past six years in missile duty was of no value to him at this point and his low flying hours during that period put him at a disadvantage working with other navigators who were younger than he. Officer Effectiveness Reports were no longer written by Lt. Colonels and endorsed by Colonels, but now were written by a Captain and endorsed by a Major, who although a field-grade pilot, was also junior in time of grade to the navigator.

There were accidents. People you knew well were killed. Your kids knew them too, in a way. They knew them as "Billy's Daddy" or something like that. Most funerals were back in somebody's hometown in another state. The families would leave the base and disappear, and you would lose contact with them too. When you tucked your kids in at night they might ask if Billy's daddy really was burned up like a cinder. "Where is Billy's daddy now? Could that happen to you? What about me? Where is Billy? Why did he leave? If you die will we get to go live with Billy?"

When people went overseas, especially to Vietnam, most of them received several letters each week from their loved ones back home. Some people didn't get any. Often the mailroom was not convenient to the workplace so you would go over in a government vehicle once a day with three or four other guys. There was always mail. Some people would go a day or two without mail, then get a package. For the ones who didn't get mail at all it was hard. At first the other guys would kid them: "Boy they don't care about you, do they – heh – heh. . . ." as they opened up their own letters and packages. Later they would pass their photographs around. After a week or so the kidding ceased. Sometimes these people who didn't get mail would not go to the mailroom for a day. Next day, though, when there was still no mail, that only made it seem worse. Then they might skip a couple of days, maybe a week, then – ahah! There would have to be mail! Then they would go there again, and there would only be an empty mailbox. Empty, empty, everything would seem empty, just empty and lost like their empty, aching heart.

"Have a cookie" Joe might say, opening up a large package.

"Hey, look at Angie, wow! That's her new tricycle!" Said someone named Bill, and he started passing a photograph around.

Tom, I think it was Tom, got a letter one day with a return address reading Hiram, Smith, Delet, and Johnson. It was his first notice from his wife's lawyers that she was suing him for divorce. He applied for emergency leave. Turned down. He had six months to go before his tour in Vietnam was up. He couldn't contact his wife. It turned out that she had run away with another guy, taken his kids with her and gone somewhere. You couldn't telephone the states from Vietnam. He didn't know any lawyers back there. What should he do?

Back in the states, the husbands and fathers were on alert, seven days straight. They would come home at noon, have the next day off, then fly three times the next week, then go back on alert for a week. When they got off of that alert tour, they would go TDY for three weeks. Then they would come home and go on alert again. The wives and mothers would have the whole bag: all the shopping, kids, paying the bills, fixing things that broke and so on. When some men finally did come home after seven days with other people in that fish bowl type of existence, people everywhere all the time, endless light and noise, all they really wanted to do was just go sit in a corner in the basement – all by themselves for an hour or so. That night after the kids were in bed they might go upstairs and find their wife sitting at the top of the stairs crying in the dark while the wind was moaning and screaming through the wires and the house was shivering and shaking in the cold icy wind.

There were Grass Police. Not looking for marijuana – this was back in the 1960's. The Grass Police would drive by your on-base quarters in the summer checking out the height of your grass. If it looked high, they would stop, get out and poke a ruler into the grass and measure it. If it was higher than two inches, you got a ticket. Some people pointed out to the Base Civil Engineering Section (BCE) that local farm extension people recommended that grass should never be cut *lower* than two inches. But that didn't fly.

One sergeant, at Little Rock AFB, came home from alert and found two 80-pound bags of fertilizer that the Base Civil Engineering section had dropped off in every yard on the base.

Sgt. Kelly was already mad because he had to cut his grass every week, sometimes every six days, and he was ready for revolt. This was *too* much!

He read the instructions about spreading the fertilizer on the lawn over a two-week program. You would have to put a small amount on the grass and water it thoroughly to get it into the ground. The instructions emphasized that too much fertilizer or not using a very large amount of water with a small amount of fertilizer would kill the grass.

*I'm not a professional gardener!* He reasoned. He spread both bags on his lawn in less than an hour. *That will kill all the damn grass, and it will be their fault!* He woke the next morning to rain. A tropical depression had come ashore and it died there as it stayed over the base. It rained just the right amount for four straight days.

Sgt. Kelly cut his grass every three days for the rest of the summer. He got a lot of compliments. It was acknowledged that he surely had a "green thumb." The base newspaper had a picture of him in his front yard shaking hands with the base commander. The commander pointed out that Sgt. Kelly had shown how people could take care of government property. He said the Air Force needed more men like Sgt. Kelly.

"Because base personnel apparently cannot discipline themselves in the use of Band-Aids, the BX will no longer carry these products. In the near future, we will stock adhesive tape and gauze which can easily be used in place of Band-Aids."

This notice was posted on an official bulletin board in the Minot AFB, BX back in 1968. A couple of weeks later there was a comment from the base commander in the base newspaper to the effect that the Band-Aid shortage was a good example of the type of problem that could be prevented if military personnel used proper management methods and exercised adequate supervision and leadership over their dependents who "had the privilege of living with them on the base".

The "Band-Aid Curtain" descended because of a series of chance occurrences. There had to have been a middle event, an enabling thing, but it was lost in the vast world of everyday rub-a-dub. Vaguely though, base personnel slowly became aware that they were low on Band-Aids. This was duly noted on various personal shopping lists, and on the next trip taken to the BX many of them bought Band-Aids, thus further depleting the overall base inventory. Eventually, there were only one or two boxes to be found. So some unnamed and unknown perpetrator precipitated this great tragedy when he (or she) bought both boxes! This created a run on Band-Aids.

A month later word would get around: "Hey - they got Band-Aids at the BX!"

"You're kidding! I gotta go!"

People began leaving work, without permission, to race to the BX for their Band-Aids. A shipment would come in, and be gone within hours when the word got around fast. People would drive to the BX just to get Band-Aids and find they had all been sold. The BX manager would catch hell.

Now this was up North – the weather was too bad to run into town to get Band-Aids, but when people did go into town they brought home Band-Aids. When they went to

Minneapolis they brought home Band-Aids. When they went to Winnipeg they brought home Band-Aids – wasn't there some law about smuggling contraband from a foreign country into a military installation in the U.S?

Your mother and father might call and tell you they were coming to visit.

"Great! " You say, "Can I ask a favor?"

"Of course, anything you want, what is it?"

"Bring a lot of Band-Aids, please."

"Band-Aids . . . what on earth happened to you?"

# 24
# Black Sky Morning - Teddy Bear's Warning

About nine o'clock in the morning the sky turned black. There may have been a sound but I didn't hear anything. I am scheduled to fly tonight and am home studying Air War College and baby-sitting my kids. My first thought is that somebody is burning trash over by the runway - although part of me already knows better than that. Snow is still on the North Dakota ground, and now black soot is falling upon it from the sky.

The Today Show is conducting an interview that suddenly stops. "We interrupt this program to bring you a special news bulletin! Word has reached us from the United States Air Force that a B-52 jet bomber has just crashed on the runway at Minot Air Force Base in North Dakota. There is no word about survivors or whether or not nuclear weapons were on board. More news will be coming as soon as we receive it. We repeat . . ."

There is not much for me to do. My kids are unaware of anything, my wife is shopping; there is nothing I can do. Including studying. Heavy, black, choking smoke now hugs the ground and slowly creeps between the homes on the base, finding everyone as if to ask: "Have you heard?"

The news is not good. There are no survivors. Eight crewmembers are dead. Twenty children on the base have just lost their fathers.

Bulletins continue to come in on TV throughout the day, all of them concerned with nuclear warheads. Finally comes the statement that no nuclear bombs were on board. That is the last bulletin, and then there are no more words.

The evening news does mention the event: "The Air Force reports that a giant B-52 bomber crashed today at Minot AFB, North Dakota, killing all eight crew members. No nuclear weapons were reported to be involved." The newsman turns to his left to look at another camera. "Meanwhile, the Labor Department reports unemployment continues to decrease slightly as housing starts continue . . . "

A roar from the runway announces the launch of a B-52 on a training mission.

Later, I finish placing my bags in my car, and prepare to head to the flight line for a long, all-night flight. I hug my wife and kids. Then I leave.

★ ★ ★

"I am . . . resurrection . . . life. . . though . . . were dead . . . yetshallhelive."

The wind slices through all of us, grabbing under our coats and shaking us. The familiar message of the priest is only half heard but then, we are really only half listening.

"Man that is bornaWO-man ..." the words are blasted and whipped away. "Shor'time t'live. . . isfulla...mis'ry!"

The canopy over the gravesite has been taken down lest it be blown away. The coffin sits above the grave shaking in the cold gusty wind as if it were shivering.

" . . . and . . . cuttdown . . . likeflower . . . fleeth . . . a'shadow .. weare . . . i'death . . . ."

The clouds are dark and brooding; low, ragged shapes that gallop swiftly through the sky, occasionally dipping down to slap the land.

"OLrdGd . . . most'Tholy . . . bitr pains of death . . . fall frm thee."

About thirty mourners are gathered at the gravesite, grimly rigid in the fifteen-degree late evening chill. Most are in military uniform, almost all have fur-fringed parkas pulled over their heads, and their hands are stuffed in pockets. The new widow is seated with her family around her. Her young son, Thomas, who is four years old, stands at the edge of the grave, looking stunned. He is sucking his thumb and hugging his teddy bear.

"My heartis glad. . . glory . . . rejoiceth!"

The coffin is lowered into the grave.

When Tom's widow shakes her head and draws back, a friend steps to the grave, picks up a handful of dirt and throws it upon the coffin.

"Unto Almi-ty God we commd . . . soul . . . our. . . brotherd'parted . . . commitearth . . . earth . . . ash . . . ash . . . dust t'dust."

Then the service is over and the family turns to leave as several of the group who remain shovel dirt into the grave.

Suddenly young Thomas pulls away from his mother. He runs back to the gravesite and calls out loudly: "Wait – *Daddy*! – Wait!!"

The little boy runs to the edge of the grave.

"Here's *Teddy*! He's going *with* you!"

Teddy Bear arcs through the air, climbing surprisingly high, then seemingly pauses for a moment before falling like a lost soul upon the coffin, already with dirt on it.

The world stops for a long, long time.

Then shovels of dirt commence falling again, falling on grave, falling on coffin; falling on Teddy Bear. Falling on all.

# 25
# Greenfish

Thirty seconds before takeoff. We taxi our KC-135 onto the active runway. Power comes up on all four engines. Final adjustments are made as I count down over the interphone ". . . five, four, three, two, one, hack."

The brakes are released and our aircraft surges forward on its takeoff roll. I start my stopwatch as I say the word "hack" and will use that timing to check our progress over the next thirty seconds.

The thirty-second check is good and we continue our acceleration to the rotation point where we will have enough speed to bring the aircraft into takeoff attitude.

"Rotate," the copilot calls as we accelerate past that pre-calculated speed, and the Aircraft Commander pulls the yoke back into his lap.

The nose gear lifts off the runway and the aircraft settles into its climb-out angle, gathering its last 20 knots of speed with only two main gear still on the ground. The ride has become rough with increasing bounces as the distance between runway lines and cracks are compressed by our 120-knot speed into a constant jiggle. The end of the runway races toward us like a car that was pulling off the highway in front of you but suddenly stopped and didn't clear the road. We are committed to flight but still seven knots too slow to fly. The aircraft becomes more difficult to handle, everything in the aircraft is pounding up and down.

Suddenly we slip into the air, the vibrations cease and we slide out over the end of the runway. Airborne.

"Gear up," calls the pilot

"Gear coming up." The copilot responds.

A grinding noise from the bottom of the aircraft announces that the gear is rising.

There is a "thump, thump-thump" as the gear locks into place and cover panels close over them, and we glide more easily.

"Flaps up, five-ten-ten" calls the pilot.

"Flaps coming up, five-ten-ten" responds the copilot and immediately a whirrrr sound is heard from below as the flaps begin their rise, pausing for a moment after a five degree rise, and then resuming as the aircraft increases speed. The flaps, which had traded lift for drag, now slide back into our clean wing.

"Pilot, nav, come right zero-eight-seven." I call over the interphone.

"Roger, coming right zero-eight-seven." The pilot sets the bezel on his compass to 087, and the aircraft banks to the right.

Three hours from now we will rendezvous with a B-52 bomber to transfer fuel from our tanks to his. His call sign is "Greenfish two-one".

★ ★ ★

"Hello Greenfish 2-1, this is Maple 3-2, how do you read?"

"Greenfish here, read you loud and clear Maple, how copy?"

"Greenfish, you're loud and clear. We have a paint, say your squawk."

"Greenfish squawking 1-3."

"Roger Greenfish, have a 1-3, strangle your parrot."

"Parrot's dead, Greenfish." The B-52 pilot turns his radar beacon off.

"Copy Greenfish, come 3-2."

The B-52 pilot turns his radar beacon back on and sets it to frequency 3-2. "Greenfish 3-2 – now."

"Maple has positive ID, Greenfish you are one-two-six nautical miles, zero-seven-two degrees, we are inbound your position, say airspeed."

"Greenfish five-eight-zero."

“Maple copies five-eight-zero, we will turn to refueling track when you reach four-seven nautical miles range from us – should be about three minutes and . . . thirty . . . six seconds. Say heading Greenfish, Maple over.”

“Greenfish copies . . . heading two-six-zero.”

“Greenfish, your heading is good, refueling heading will be two-four-niner degrees.”

“Greenfish copies two-four-niner refueling.”

Then on the intercom, “Pilot-nav, come left please, two degrees zero-six-three degrees.”

“Roger nav, coming left two degrees, zero-six-three.”

I check the heading, then call: “Greenfish come left seven degrees two-five-three.”

“Greenfish steady two-five-three.”

* * *

“Pilot-nav, standby turn to refueling – thirty seconds.”

“Roger Pilot.”

“Roger nav, rollout heading two-four-niner degrees.”

“Pilot copies rollout two-four-niner.”

“Roger nav, begin your turn in ten seconds . . . five, four, three, two, one, hack. Rollout heading is two-four-niner degrees.”

“Roger. Now turning, rollout two-four-niner.”

“Greenfish, Maple turning to refueling track, roll out two-four-niner degrees, request Greenfish come left two-four-niner degrees. We are now four-three nautical miles from you, ten o’clock your position, level, moving across in front of you, do you have joy, over?”

“Greenfish copies, no joy; Greenfish holding two-four-niner degrees.”

“Maple, Greenfish tallyho! Coming six-two-zero knots to join up.”

The copilot responds, “Hello Greenfish, we’re prepared to transfer five-zero thousand pounds of fuel, and looking forward to about a six-minute ride with you. Are you ready for hook-up?"

"Greenfish ready for pre-contact checklist."

"Roger, Maple - pre-contact checklist."

"Roger Greenfish copies, coming in – Do you read me, Boomer?"

"Hello Greenfish, this is your friendly Boom Operator, all systems are "go," you're looking good and cleared to pre-contact position."

"Greenfish coming in to pre-contact."

Boom operator again: "Looking good . . . good . . . good . . . hold it there – that's good . . . hold it . . . I'm extending . . . Contact!"

"Copy contact – Greenfish shows contact also."

"Roger Greenfish we have good contact, are you ready to receive fuel?"

"Roger Greenfish is ready, fill'er up."

"Roger Greenfish – transfer underway . . . need your windshield cleaned?"

"Yeah, and check my oil and tires too . . . got a restroom handy?"

"Roger that, we got one, it's back in our bowling alley."

"You bastards, I bet you do, too."

"Yeah . . . 'cross from the swimming pool . . . twenty-five thousand, looking good . . . how're you hanging?"

"We're hanging-in . . . I'm boosting power for the weight."

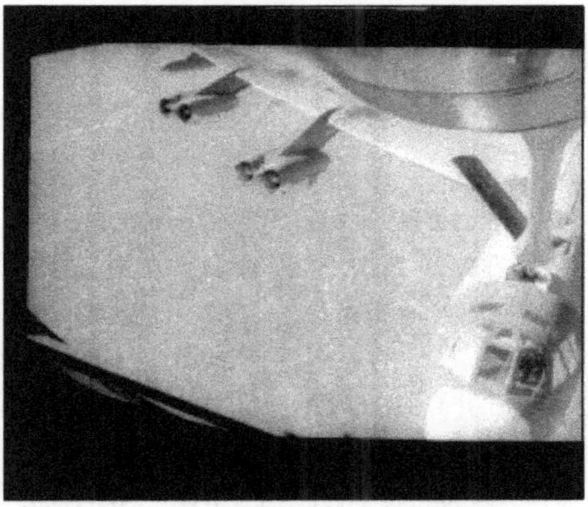

We feel our aircraft accelerate as Greenfish adds power.

"Thirty-eight thousand now, how you doing?"

"We're wallowing a little, can you pop it up to about four-niner-zero?"

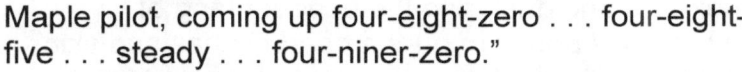

"Roger, this is Maple pilot, coming up four-eight-zero . . . four-eight-five . . . steady . . . four-niner-zero."

"Forty-eight thousand, coming up forty-nine."

"Roger, Greenfish is ready to prepare for disconnect."

"Roger, copy, five-one thousand, two hundred pounds transferred, are you ready for disconnect?"

"Greenfish ready . . . coming disconnect . . . Greenfish clear."

"Roger copy, disconnect here . . . you're looking good, Greenfish . . . all panels closed . . . your ship looks clean, sir."

"Greenfish departing."

"Copy Greenfish, catch you later, sir."

"Greenfish out."

"Have a good ride, Maple out."

# 26
# Hoodoo

The sign reads "Theodore Roosevelt National Park," but there is nothing else that could possibly prove it to be true. There are no buildings or people in sight. Our family appears to have landed on an isolated planet and we cautiously step out of our station wagon and rally beside the trailer that it pulls.

A slow swell of late August breeze brings the smell of summer heat and dust, and the pungent tang of sagebrush quickly bonds to our hair and clothes and skin. Great swirls of brilliant white cirrus have been recklessly spun into the deep blue northern sky. Pine and piñon needles hum sweetly in the soft dry air.

Another sign proclaims: "Honor System – Two Dollars per Vehicle Please." I deposit two one-dollar bills in the small receptacle, wondering if they will ever be found. Archeologists someday I think, will theorize over this money if it is ever seen again.

I start up the station wagon and we wind our way around curves and over small hills. We pass large boulders and thread through a couple of ridges and drive down into a tree-covered valley through which flows the Little Missouri River and enter the best campsite we have ever seen.

Large oak trees grow on a gentle hill that rises behind the area and cottonwoods wave in the dry breezes down along the creek. Tall rocky spires, locally called "hoodoos," rise above the trees.

Twenty campsites are here, all are pull-through and they are all vacant. We have our own private national park! After disconnecting the trailer and setting up camp, we drive around the area.

Interpretive signs in front of amazing rock formations explain how different layers were stratified over unfathomable periods of time, diagrams show how they slid - in an instant - downhill and now continue that previous process of stratification, but from a new level.

Pines grow on the upland areas, piñon trees stand lookout on bluffs, and cottonwoods dance in the breezes down by the creek. We see bison and antelope slowly grazing, completely at home among the hoodoos. A climb up a "mountain" (perhaps eighty feet high) reveals cactus scattered through the sagebrush.

Great numbers of round rocks that resemble cannonballs litter the landscape. Large, metallic-like pieces of shattered rock jut out of the shale and limestone and they look like broken pieces of cast iron. One can imagine a story about an ancient cannon-ball-firing space ship that crashed here eons ago, and has not yet been discovered.

**Theodore Roosevelt National Park**

We return to camp and walk down to the river, which is really a small creek that winds through the area. We listen to its singing and gurgling as it travels over its stream bed while light flashes from bright rocks as the water runs along its stony waterway. Birds hop across the rocks that fill the creek bed, and raccoons and foxes walk beside and wade into it, keeping an eye on us. A couple of friendly looking coyotes watch from a small rise. Everybody here is looking at us; *we're* the strange ones. We can get the feeling that they have come down to the campsite exclusively to see us. A magpie plays the role of docent, clearly pointing to us, while making interpretive comments to explain our presence. *Wonder if she has an honor system? "Deposit two pine nuts, please!"*

Later, we cook and eat sumptuous steaks and potatoes grilled slowly over a campfire built in a brick fireplace under the great oaks.

Evening brings blue shadows that reach as far into our souls as they lean across the land. The wind, always present in the northern Dakotas, now slows as if to linger here to see the sun set in this special place and watch with us as it falls behind a rocky cliff. Gold and crimson clouds seem to touch the high bronze canyon rocks.

Far below, out across the desert floor, bent sagebrush glows with purple luminosity, each wiry plant seeming to scatter dusk out of its labyrinthine maze. A puff of contented breeze brings the scent of dust to my nostrils. *The earth smells good.*

Stars seem to perch on our shoulders and surround our heads throughout the bright night. Owls fly in and out of the overhead trees and watch our campfire in amazement; small rocks tumble as tiny creatures peek or run in alarm. The night wind brings again the smell of sage, christening us one more time with its scent and anointing us as one of its own.

The next morning is cool, down into the forties; but that's just summer in the high plains. I pull on my hooded sweat jacket. Its color is dark blue. *Just like the sky*, I think. I look up as I wrap the jacket about me.

The cobalt brilliance above is so deep and powerful that it seems to stream straight through my eyes, headlong into my brain, staggering the unprepared mind and stealing my breath with awe. There is something about that view of the Dakota morning sky that seems to be an open window into "Somewhere Else", and you can't ever see *that* morning sky and be the same person you were before. Somehow I sense that I should stay here forever and never go anywhere else. There is a magic “something” here that I sense as being my own true self, and I feel I am finally “here” in my own real home.

I awaken the family by gently thumping on the trailer wall as if it were a drum. I play a semi-native rhythm I had never heard before, at least not in my present form.

Sausages and eggs cooked on a cedarwood fire fill our souls with the best food of our entire life.

Then we go for another short hike.

Finally it is time to return to the base; tomorrow is a workday and I need to prepare for the week which will follow.

Thursday, I leave for Vietnam.

# 27
# Gone

Today is the last day I will be at home for a long time.

I try to pack the things I think I'll need, and with a heavy heart prepare to leave. I had wanted to savor this special day but it flies past with breakneck speed and is gone before I even know that it has passed away.

What an ache – every pore of my body and every facet of my soul explore this pending separation as a tongue becomes fascinated by a cavity in a tooth.

I have become obsessed by a figure. It is the number 62. That is the number of days this Temporary Tour of Duty (TDY) will last, and the obsession began several weeks ago as a small 62, but the size of that number has grown in my mind day by day and now it pounds and pulses and doubles by the hour until I almost yearn to *leave,* to just *GO*, so I can see that hideous figure become a 61. Then I can begin to count it down, backwards to 60, and push it into the fifties and then I will have something to look forward to again. I feel helpless, a victim of fate, and while I realize the length of the forthcoming TDY is minor in comparison with that experienced by so many others today, and also by myself in the past, yet even that awareness is no consolation. This trip to Southeast Asia ("SEA" as it is called by the Defense Department) to participate in the Vietnam War will not count even as part of a tour over there. I fear this may be only the beginning of a very long trip down a steeply falling river that plunges into that great SEA.

Now it is night. My last night at home. I put my kids to bed late and my oldest daughter, who is eight years old and has some small concept of what is happening, looks deeply into my eyes as I prepare to leave her room, slowly shaking her head and telling me "Daddy, I will remember you all the rest of my life". I can't think about this now, it is too much for me to handle. And there is much that I still have to do before I leave. I kiss her forehead, and then I smile at her from the door as I close it.

Next morning I depart the house at 5:00 a.m., after getting to sleep at 1:00. I kiss my sleeping children, and go to base operations. Weather briefings for the trip and other preparations all seem so normal that it is hard to comprehend the significance of the changes which have already begun. We go through these familiar processes mechanically and halfheartedly, because while our minds are fully engaged, each of our hearts still linger in a warm house that is not so very far from here. We load our equipment on our aircraft and await the arrival of passengers. Finally we start engines and takeoff at 7:00 a.m. As we rise into the air, I bid farewell to my home, to my family and my kids, and also to my soul, which remains behind, unable to tear itself away.

We fly westward, coincidentally following a trail I traveled in the past with my young family in a travel-trailer. The towns and places we pass quickly over are filled with nostalgia for me and now they assume the aura of holy shrines. We race westward as part of my life seems to pass before me. Abilene, Buffalo Gap State Park, El Paso, Demming, Lordsburg, Tucson, Gila Bend, Thermal, Banning Pass and on to Castle AFB.

There are no rooms on the base so the Air Force has secured lodging for us in a Big 6 Motel. Tomorrow we will turn our attention to the Pacific Ocean. Our crew will fly the aircraft to Hawaii, then augmented by another crew whom we will pick-up tomorrow, we'll sleep in the back of the airplane as they fly through to Guam, and then to Okinawa. Later, the other crew will sleep as we fly on into Taiwan.

I put off calling home as long as I can because I know that when I hang up this time it will be a final act of severance. Someday, telephones will reach across the great Pacific, but not now. Finally, I do call home and talk with and hear those wonderful familiar voices, already insouciant and occupied with other important affairs of life like dolls and baseballs. I even hear our dog bark. Then I hang up, and as I sit on the edge of the motel bed I can feel myself disappearing.

Finally, it is over.

I am gone.

# 28
# Crossing

We take off late the next day, at 3:40 p.m., in a cool, dark, California rain. Our last look at mainland U.S. is of Monterey Bay to our southeast and San Francisco to our northeast.

It is an easy ride, the last two hours of which take place after the sun has set and before the first stars become visible. I use speedlines from Venus, low in the sky ahead of us, and a rough courseline from a half-full moon to penetrate the Hawaiian ADIZ (Air Defense Identification Zone) and my first radar fix is only four miles away from my dead reckoning position!

We descend through small fluffy clouds and watch Honolulu glisten in the early night. Tropical clouds rise off on our left, like the mountains of Bali and they tower above Oahu, and the forests below lie dark under heavy shadows. Ahead, Waikiki Beach and Pearl Harbor shine clearly and brilliantly in the moonlight.

We land and head to the MAC terminal to prepare for takeoff again. There we find the next part of the mission has been canceled because of rough weather at Guam. We'll spend the night in Hawaii and depart the next afternoon.

Next morning I am amazed all over again at the beauty on this island. I stare at the palm trees, some of which stand tall and skinny and others are short and dark. Some carry bananas, some have coconuts, others wave fans or fronds; and there are banyan trees and strange, tall, leaning hemlocks. Yellow and red leaves flutter in the breezes. Orchids peer out through great vines below the palms. Beyond this stand the mountains, and then dark clouds rise above them into the blue tropical sky.

The warm green sea carries the pulse of the pounding trade winds that wash the earth and sea and sky with a faint smell of grass and sun and salt. Many of the people here are of Asian descent and much of the music on the radio also reflects that culture. There is a real feeling of having gone somewhere else.

I try to call home again, but the lines are "down." We hear that they usually work about two or three days a week now, and may be up again soon. Tomorrow will be day 60! I send postcards home and wonder what is going on back there. They are already five hours behind us. Here at 3:00 p.m., it's warm and sunny; at home it's 7:00 p.m., and it's dark and cold.

We takeoff at 4:40 p.m. heavy with cargo and fifty-eight passengers headed for Guam, and then Okinawa. Far out over the Pacific Ocean while flying into the setting sun we pass through the International Dateline and into the Eastern Hemisphere. The great sea far below seems a dark blue corduroy mantle stretching out before us with its lines of warp running north and south. On either side of us tall, skinny clouds rise like sentinel-snakes, appearing to turn and watch our passage. Long cloud shadows cast by the setting sun fall east and west, interlacing with the corduroy pattern of the ocean, forming a pink and blue weave that seems to reach out across all eternity. Darkness rises up out of the ocean to engulf us, and later Wake Island moves below us as a small semicircle of lights, then there is total darkness for four more hours. It's already day 59! Our relief crew is asleep in the back.

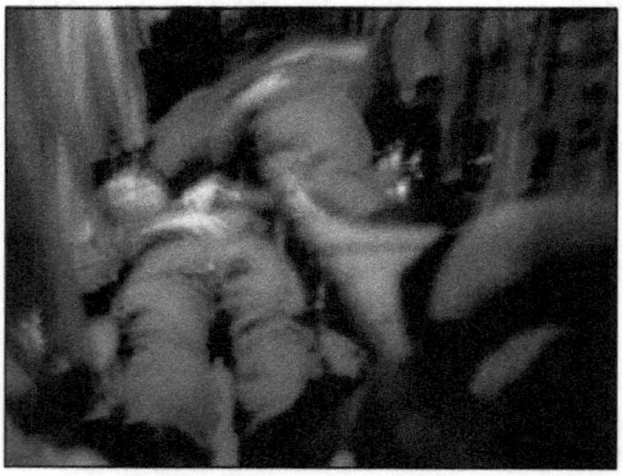

A nine-hour flight brings us to Guam. We land there at one o'clock in their morning. We have a short stop in this busy place that is washed with balmy breezes and the warm scent of unfamiliar flowers. The flight line and ramps are filled with B-52s and KC-135s, and after a quick snack and another weather briefing we're off again, now with the other crew at the controls. For four hours we fly over the dark sea, finally landing on Okinawa. Meanwhile, I have headed to the back of the airplane about 5 a.m. and turned this last leg of the trip into a four-hour nap.

Our first day on Okinawa is filled with briefings about our work in SEA. Later, our crew travels into the city of Naha for our first shopping trip of the tour. I discover that you have to buy what you might want when you see it – you can't come back later because you don't know where you are – the street signs are in Japanese so you can't even write down the names and if you "drew" them like an artist, you couldn't "read" them again later. Naha's streets appear wide enough for only one car to crawl along, yet the Toyotas and Datsuns go both ways, and move along right smartly.

The Naha Trading Center is an area about two blocks wide and perhaps eight or ten blocks long and is served by only five or six of these small streets or alleys, so it is virtually one solid shop, honeycombed with walkways that enter and exit upon alleys. No single store appears to be bigger than about fifteen by twenty feet or so. The owners all work here on the ground floor with their wives and children working with them, and they live and sleep above their shop on a second floor. This seems poignant to us new travelers as we remember our own families, now – already – so far away from us both in time and distance. These people however, live in the shop where they work, and that part of town is their whole life. All their markets are right here and the entire area is constantly filled with the smell of frying onion and garlic, along with cumin and chili and cabbage and also that of cooking fish and chicken.

The sewers are generally open little trenches about one and a half feet deep, and of the same width, and covered here and there with concrete slates. Later in the evening as the smell from the trenches begins to become more noticeable, a new one emerges, that of burning incense that is both effective and welcome. As the day wears on and the evening blossoms, the air becomes filled with the smell of flowers, frying onions, herbs, sandalwood and that other thing.

After supper, we return to the BOQ to pack and prepare for bed. We will fly our first combat mission tomorrow and we all are quiet and write long letters that will be mailed home from here after we leave in the morning. Off and on all night long, I keep waking up as strong winds and heavy rains pound and shake our quarters.

# 29
# Ground Spares and Rice Paddies

After breakfast at 4:00 a.m., we proceed to detachment operations for our briefing and to find out which aircraft we will fly. The airplane we brought in from our home station – "our" airplane – is gone, already flown out by another crew and now entered into the great pool of "theater aircraft". We will not see it or its crew chiefs again, except by coincidence, until we get back to Hawaii in almost two months.

At the briefing we find we are also scheduled to preflight the Ground Spare aircraft, an aircraft that is to be prepared for immediate flight in case any of the scheduled aircraft cannot make their takeoff. Apparently the crew previously scheduled to preflight the Ground Spare aircraft is already flying.

We are briefed on the weather, pick up our lunches and head off to preflight the Ground Spare. But the aircraft is not parked at its proper ramp location and we can't find it.

After conferring with the Command Post several times, and driving around the ramp checking out several parking spots they give us, the Command Post discovers it is already flying. *Welcome to the world of combat operations!*

We are given another aircraft that will be the new Ground Spare, and we finally find and preflight it. Then we then race to the aircraft we are scheduled to fly today and can't find it! All this in the dark, with a native driver who *can* speak English but doesn't really understand it, who is not at all interested in either his work or our problems, a radio that cuts in and out and is filled with static, while torrential rain bounces like bullets off our bus.

Finally we find our airplane, get our bags on board, quickly preflight it, and start engines twelve minutes before scheduled takeoff instead of the normal thirty minutes.

We race down the taxiways, roll on to the active runway five minutes late, get clearance and go. We are three knots low on rotation timing and the aircraft won't accelerate after we rotate – so we race into the black rain, finally bouncing up into the air with about 100 feet left on the runway. A great explosion shakes the aircraft as we raise the gear but we never found out what that was.

Now we are headed for the Gulf of Tonkin to set up an orbit and refuel aircraft. I have no Doppler, the computer is dead, the radar altimeter is inoperable, and the radar does not show returns that are farther away than about 70 miles, so I make my first penetration into a combat area using only celestial observations from the sun.

A speedline from Saturn, which glows faintly yellowish and is hard to find in the daylight sky, provides important help. About three hours into the flight, Hainan Island just off the Red China coast and a part of Red China, becomes visible on my radar at a distance of 60 miles. We are only three miles from where my navigational position indicated we were!

Red China claims a 50-mile territorial limit so this is about as close to them as we want to get. If you go down over Hainan you will never get out of there again. We have all heard the story about how the Air Force abandoned one crewmember who went down there.

Vietnam looks lonely from the air. It reminds me of both Arkansas and West Virginia except no towns or roads are visible, only mountains and jungle. The sea races in to wash up on apparently deserted beaches. Many of the valleys disappear under light clouds that fill in to them looking like a great lake with many arms.

We seem to be the first aircraft over the Gulf today but the radios tell a different story. We share this air with both MiG's and enemy Surface-to-Air Missiles (SAM's).

Finally, after orbiting for more than five hours, we leave the area and head back over the South China Sea. A United airliner passes under us, bound for Hong Kong perhaps.

Later we penetrate and land at Ching Chuan Kang Air Base, better known as CCK, in Taiwan. As we approach the base, even from above, we sense that the land is cold and to us it seems lonely. We glide on, sailing above a landscape covered with empty rice paddies and dirt-streeted villages.

We check into the base and eat supper at the Officer's Club and are glad to get to bed. Just ten hours from now we will fly a twelve and one-half hour flight back into the Gulf of Tonkin.

As I drift off to sleep I wonder about my family on the other side of the planet. I can't imagine what is going on back there now, they're in bed too I guess, then I remember it's 7:00 a.m. back there, the day is just underway. *Oh well* . . . I think, *it's day . . . what? . . . 57? . . . let me think about that a moment* . . . .

# 30
# Klongs and Gardens

it's 5:00 a.m., and we are on the runway, rolling with a heavyweight takeoff and find that number one engine won't take water. We abort the takeoff roll, taxi back to find the Second Ground Spare aircraft while we send our box lunches, in a maintenance truck, to the Primary Ground Spare crew. I have already eaten the hard-boiled egg; *hope nobody minds!*

They get on the runway but at 114 knots, abort due to low speed. That's the predicament we all fear, being in a heavyweight aircraft going full power but still too slow to fly and too fast to stop. They are barely able to stay on the far end of the runway with brakes steaming and smoking.

We have already boarded the Second Ground Spare aircraft, and now it's our turn again. The other crew sends the lunches back to us, and I notice that somebody has eaten the fried chicken! This adds new meaning to the concept of a "movable feast."

We blast off for eleven hours up into the Gulf of Tonkin and finally complete the mission, arriving back at our BOQ about 8:00 p.m. Tomorrow, we brief at 5:00 a.m.

The day after that we spend eight hours over Laos refueling RC-135s. The land below is very smoky and seems quiet, glittering in the glare of the afternoon sun. Only the tops of hills can be seen for a long time. Then, I catch a glimpse of the setting sun reflecting off of a bluff above a river far below me and it seems for a moment as if I am down there, and I am shaken by how familiar that place and its river looks. I've been down there before . . . somehow, I know that beyond any question.

What has happened to my own real home? Suddenly my kids and wife seem as if they had been blown into an ancient part of someone else's past. I shake my head and try to find "Reality," but another trick of the war has already taken place: This is now my new reality, these machines of noise and rattles and bounces and power. My world has become just a map, and it lies before me on my desk. I watch it under a dim cone of light in a darkened cockpit filled with red-lighted gauges. My galaxy has become an empty space of endless static and radio bearings that constantly conflict with each other, and my universe is now a spiteful realm of constantly malfunctioning equipment, and decisions that struggle under mounds of misinformation sucked out by the forces of collapsing time. Yes, this is now my "Reality," and those little girls and boys, playing happily somewhere else, far, far away – do they really exist anymore? My family now is only my crew: a pilot, a copilot a boom operator . . . and me. We live together, eat together, and place our lives in one another's hands. Suddenly I don't know what is real – I don't have time to think about it. I look out again and glance below as if called by that river.

The Mekong appears from this altitude (about 6,000 feet) as a narrow waterway winding through an enormous flat jungle. After the sun sets, a thousand campfires burn below in the jungle. Whose fires? Good question. Whose jungle? Some base camps below clearly belong to us. They are easily identified by the rings of fire that surround them. Most of those people down there have families who are far away, too; but they also now have a new family of buddies. What is their "Reality?" Some of the rings lie beneath brilliant yellow flares that float slowly down over them; flares dropped by unseen aircraft flying far below us. The flares drift down in pairs and as they burn out, two more appear with explosions that briefly light up a charred and blackened fragment of forest that is filled with distorted black things that once were trees, perhaps just this morning. Large areas of the jungle are on fire. It's good to get back over the South China Sea. Tonight Taiwan looks like home.

Next day, we go into Taichung. Walking along the sidewalks of the Air Force Base is very much like taking a walk along streets like those in Orlando or Columbus or Sacramento. Then you walk off base and pass immediately into a world of dirt roads, oxen, and wooden carts.

**Taichung, Taiwan, 1970**

With great rattles and bangings, small "trucks" that look more like With gr rototillers than anything else slowly grind down the road carrying unbelievably large amounts of stuff. "Station wagons" that have been assembled out of wrecked and discarded parts of motorcycles, cars and bicycles clatter along. All of the vehicles emit a foul-smelling blue exhaust that coats your skin and lips with a thin film of oil, and all the drivers seem to be honking horns or ringing bells or slapping pieces of wood against each other as they move along among the oxen-pulled wooden carts. The streets are wide dirt boulevards lined with rubble and broken stones. Several open sewers run through the town, tiny rivers that indifferently carry rotting garbage and human waste, slowly drifting along, winding from house to house, making a thorough tour through the town. Someone mentions that any disease carried by the refuse in the sewers would be carefully paraded from house to house. Next to the open sewers (which are called "klongs") are houses, and people live in balconies that hang out over the klongs. We all make pictures and buy some trinkets for our kids.

The following week we head into Taipei. We leave Ching Chuan Kang in 60° sunshine, pass over great river washes filled with large boulders, past large sand mountains and up into foothills through vineyards and tea fields. Tiny children hang like ticks onto motorcycles that are loaded with three, four, five people. Other children casually use the sewers for potties, but so do grown men, some of whom, every now and then, stand with one hand on a hip, urinating into a sewer, regarding us on the bus with curiosity as we slowly pass by them. We continue up the mountains climbing through Hsinchu where the wind and the fog form together into a wicked swirling tapestry out of which dragons or witches are expected to appear momentarily. But we pass safely by and descend into Taipei.

Klong, Taiwan. 1970

We search first for a room and find some for $2.36, but there will be inscrutable roommates, there is no toilet or drinking water, and all the rooms seem to be heated to about 110°. Our pilot insists we go over to Peitou, also known as the "Sin City of the East," and as we check out more of the few rooms that remain available, sin starts to look better. We cross into Peitou and find rooms at a resort hotel. I get a palatial cottage inside the wall of the hotel grounds for $7.50, and as we sign in, a group of nine very nice looking young Taiwanese ladies all dressed in western clothing are bought out and assembled for us to review, to select one for "companionship" for the night. We are told they will be glad to disrobe if we wish to "check them out." They grin and giggle and twist and turn. One begins to undo her blouse. We thank them politely and tell them no. We enjoy our stay at the hotel and most of the other occupants we see appear to be families with small children. Later, there are knocks on my door several times during the early night by an older lady (forty years old?) asking if I would like water, or beer or "a girl." I order a couple of beers, and am brought two one-liter bottles of Japanese beer!

Next morning I wake about 7:00 a.m. and go outside in the cool dark gardens for a long walk and to make some pictures. Again, the grounds and restaurants are filled with very happy-looking families and their young children. Part of me cries out at the sight of these people and I can't help but wonder why am I not with my own children, and something seems very wrong about that.

The garden is part of a park and they set together on a hill with the top portion beginning in the steam clouds of a hot springs waterfall. The stream then flows through the length of the little park, passing at first through a dark wooded ravine and then out across a landscaped garden where it flows under a small, arched, oriental bridge and widens into a little river that passes from here into the vibrant city. The park is well forested, some of the trees still have leaves on them and some are even bearing flowers. The borders of this park grow wild, becoming more landscaped as one approaches the boulevard that serves the hotel and its cottages. Flowers and palm trees grow in great abundance. Somehow, all this has taken on an intimate sense of familiarity. What I can remember of my own home with my children seems like something I read about in a book somewhere. We've been gone a week. There are fifty-five days to go. Tomorrow we fly again, briefing at 2:00 a.m., so it's already time to go back to the base. Next week we will fly back to Okinawa for two days, then after a couple of missions from there, on into Vietnam.

We leave Taipei, and from a turn in the road, see it one last time; now from a distance. It is a beautiful city, gleaming in the rain with wide curving, graceful, tree-lined boulevards bordered by wide sidewalks. I remember the cloistered walkways that open into shops, bookstores, jewelry and art stores, hotels, and restaurants. Everywhere there is the smell of flowers, incense and good food. Above this lovely memory rise the mountains and then there is the bridge at the end of town, and the river runs under it. I watch helplessly as it falls into the great sea.

# 31
# The Yellow Umbrella

The sky today is a low, dark stratus that covers the city and a quiet rain slowly falls.

Streets are wet and on the hills water slowly descends. It's a rainy day in Okinawa, the one day we are not flying on this first part of our deployment and my pilot, co-pilot and I are going into the city of Naha.

Being good Air Force officers, we don't take any umbrellas. We don't have any. In the 1960's, as during the preceding 200 years, umbrellas have been considered taboo for military officers, whether they are in uniform or not.

As the afternoon turns to evening we walk through a city filled with smiles. The rain, the people and the peaceful city all seem to belong to each another. Somehow this all seems to be so right. How could anything ever be different from this?

Naha, Okinawa, 1970

Everyone in town seems to have an umbrella. Everyone but us. We don't notice because we are busy shopping for families back in the states. We're looking for gifts for our wives and our children, parents too and other members of our clan. And we have come to the perfect place to shop.

Clocks, woodcarvings, boxes and filigree, and paintings fill every store. There are watches, of course, and pencils and pens; carved coffee tables and fancy clothes, chess sets, bracelets, rings and more, and it's all on sale today! That's what they say. But we are seasoned veterans, lavishly decorated – not in ribbons, but in presents we have bought, and we know exactly what to buy: Jewelry!

Jewelry will hold its value well and probably appreciate over the years. One can carry a lot of jewelry home in a briefcase. Not so with coffee tables or suits of armor. Jewelry doesn't get wet and run, or turn magically from "leather" to wet cardboard. One doesn't really "buy" jewelry for that matter, one just exchanges dollars for something of more lasting value and beauty.

We tarry a while in a store filled with sandalwood carvings, pieces of jade and brilliant fire-opal broaches. Smells of incense are part of the decorations, but there's a greater smell that comes from the back: fried pork and onion, cayenne and curry.

The owner's children work and play in the store, dusting and arranging merchandise, and the oldest, a boy about seven years old, is already helping customers. We asked the owner about his son's help, and he said that his grandfather had inherited the store, then his father had run it, and now it is his. Then he smiles at his son, and says, to us "It's been a good store, and we've met a lot of nice people."

We are halfway around the world from our own families.

"Makes you wonder if it is all worth it." Muses Ben, the pilot. "Here we see a man who really is at home with his family, his wife, his store, and everything he owns." He continues, "We roll the dice every time we race down the runway and pull that heavy load off into the turbulence and rain – and then we head for enemy territory."

Every store seemed to be filled with wonderful things and happy people, and they all had umbrellas, and everything was always on sale!

"You like-a parasol?" We are asked, in Pidgin English. (And I'm not making fun of them because I can't speak pidgin anything!)

"No Way!" We reply, also in pidgin English. "We Air Force officers, no can carry umbrella!"

"Oh, you no fly in rain?"

"Not today!" With a grin. "You gottum opal ring I mebbe catch, huh ?"

"Ahhhh, yessss. . ." with a smile and a bow. "We gottum lots'a opals, lots'a ring!" And with a swirl and a dramatic gesture, "You folla me!"

There are sandalwood boxes built to hold jewelry, mahogany tables with Asian scenes carved deeply into their tops, and then covered with glass. They would sell in the States for two thousand dollars, and you can buy them today for one hundred bucks!

Incense always floats in the air and umbrellas are everywhere, and everything's on sale, but only today!

Finally, in one store we shop for a long time. We buy rather extravagantly of princes rings, while the rain outside increases. A lovely young lady tries to give us umbrellas as souvenirs.

The pilot says "Oh, no, we no usem umbrella, not happy thing to do!"

The young lady says "Oh, so wet outside, you needum parasol!" She reaches into a bin and produces a blue parasol and gives it to him. "Here! – It belong to you, now you gotta use it!" And she reaches up and kisses him.

"OK" Ben says, as he opens up his new umbrella. "Now me understan!"

The copilot and I pucker up too, but all we get are umbrellas; his is red, mine is yellow.

Now we're back on the street again. After a brief clash of umbrellas, we learn how to keep a certain vital distance from each other. But it is raining harder now so we learn very quickly and are grateful for our gifts, it's like flying formation – well, in a way. And we are amazed at the difference they make!

Darkness falls, enhancing the glow of the colored lights, and the city becomes a great neon jewel through which we wander in a form of rapture.

Savory fragrances float through the air. Sizzling soy sauce, ah . . . exhale, inhale . . . ah, frying pork! Exhale, inhale . . . ah, roast beef! Exhale, inhale . . . ah, shrimp? Yes, *barbecued* shrimp! Exhale, inhale . . . ah, potatoes and beans and peas; and noodles and rice! Exhale, inhale . . . ah, chili peppers, cumin, curry, and basil!

Wood smoke drifts along the sidewalks and sounds of food preparation sizzles from every door in town.

We close our umbrellas as we climb steep stairs that rise under a bright red neon sign into the "Kobe Steak House."

The smells intensify as we enter into a bright red room where a "geisha" meets us. She bows deeply, and then leads us to an unusual table. We three all sit on the same side of this table and on the other side is a griddle, already hot.

Another waitress, also dressed like a geisha, brings us water and a menu. Then, tall glasses of Japanese beer appear. Later, she comes back to take our order. We all want the special: the Kobe Beef.

Now, we have a few brief moments to review our prizes. Nice opal rings and princess rings and children's rings, "worry rings," and puzzle rings.

"Chop-chop!" We look up to see a small white cloud hovering above the griddle. It takes an instant to realize we are looking at the top of a chef's hat, which slowly lifts and turns into a broadly smiling Japanese face as our chef raises his head from his greeting bow. He bows again, and smacks his large cleaver against the griddle again. "Chop-chop!"

"Gleetings!" He shouts. "I am Toby!" He smiles broadly. "I will COOK for you!"

With the gesture of a magician, he pours sesame seed oil onto the griddle, and spreads it across with his cleaver. A great cloud of steam and smoke arise as he pours into the foaming bubbles a substantial amount of soy sauce. To his left a flame suddenly appears under a grill and three enormous, extremely marbled, steaks are placed on top of the grill. Sliced onions are swept into the sauce on the griddle, and liberal amounts of Sake wine and a little bit of vinegar follow along with minced garlic and mushrooms. The steaks are turned with much sizzle and pop, and flames lick above them and smoke fills the air. Thin strips of green pepper are added into the sauce, back on the griddle. Butter then falls on top of the beans, and a light pink powder also.

Then they all are spun together and the steaks are turned again and, now nicely browned, are added to the griddle. All this with various "Chop-chop's" from Toby's deft cleaver, and great, magnificent smiles from his expressive face.

With deep sighs of satisfaction, he lifts his nose into the air after smelling our cooking food. Finally, a special sauce is placed over the steaks, and as they are turned again, another sauce is added to the beans. Baked potatoes roll out onto the griddle, cleft by Toby's cleaver, they are turned and mashed, then over again and another sauce falls upon them. Now they are turned over, and pressed down, then swept onto plates and placed, still steaming and bubbling, right in front of each of us. All this with just a cleaver!

Toby beams and bows at us. Then reaching with the cleaver again, he pushes a small plastic glass into our midst, with the word "Tipp! Thanks You" on its side and five or six quarters already inside. Toby bows again and smiles broadly and says: "I hope your lick you sticks!"

We have knives, but don't use them. Cutting the Kobe beef is like cutting butter, except that thick, dark, rich juices run from every slice.

Now it's bus time. Out, into the pouring rain we go again, safely protected by our wonderful umbrellas and we catch the last bus back to base. We bounce along, pockets filled with family treasures, bellies full of bliss; but the greatest treasures we carry with us are the memories of a wonderful day.

Since they really *are* taboo, the last bus from the base carries away with it our beautiful umbrellas. The yellow umbrella I leave on the bus was the first one I ever had.

We've been on Okinawa for three weeks, and we've flown every day; this is the first day we've had off. Tomorrow, we leave for Taiwan, beginning a series of sixteen-hour flights into the Gulf of Tonkin up next to Hainan Island. Up into MiG country. It will be a different day.

# 32
# Bandit

It's midnight. Low clouds race over the island scattering rain onto the flight line and filling the night air with the smell of wet grass.

We're flying out of Ching Chuan Kang (CCK) Air Base in Taiwan tonight and it will be a long ride, fourteen or fifteen hours, maybe sixteen. We will orbit over the Gulf of Tonkin while specialists in the back of our airplane monitor electronic data and messages sent by Chinese and North Vietnamese forces. We will also help relay messages to and from "Crown," our Airborne Battlefield Commander.

A blue bus pulls up to our EC-135 as we complete our pre-flight checks. Twelve men get off, each with a briefcase and some carry two. Both officers and enlisted, they seem to be quiet people and are called "spooks" by the rest of the Air Force. Such a name seems appropriate for those who fine-tune black boxes and catch and study electronic energies which float otherwise unseen across the world.

The crew chief and his assistant are exhausted from working on the plane all night and will collapse in bed as soon as we get airborne. Our departure is scheduled for 3:00 a.m.

Faraway screams rend the night air like banshee shrieks as Chinese steam engines race through nearby foothills and begin their charge at the mountains. Their cries seem to echo our mission tonight since our call sign will be "Specter."

The take-off is rough. We bounce into the night with our sky left wing low, then rise as we catch a little air that helps us clear the foothills. We bounce up and down, shake and fishtail a little, and climb in moderate turbulence through pitch-black clouds. Twenty minutes later, we break out into a smooth, serene and silent sky filled with stars.

I run a night-celestial navigation leg, westward almost eight hundred miles out over the South China Sea then turn the aircraft northwest as we pass above the Paracel Islands. Below us lie atolls, fabulously rich we have heard, incredibly endowed with priceless oil fields not far below the surface of the sea. Later I turn northeast and we fly deeply into the Gulf of Tonkin.

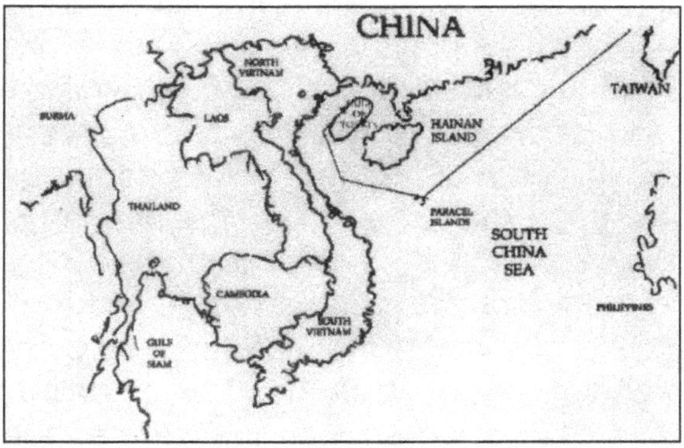


North Vietnam is visible on our left, and on our right we can see Hainan Island, a well-fortified part of Red China that now lies below an inland fog.

I drive the aircraft right up to the edge of Red China's boundary then turn right to set up our orbit. We have already been airborne for three hours, and it will take three more to get home; but we will remain here for eight hours while our "spooks" in the back do their silent work.

We are scheduled for an eight-hour orbit. North Vietnam will be on our west, mainland China to our north, and Hainan Island on our east. We plan four-minute long, aproximately180° turns to the right at the top of the orbit, then to fly southwest for about a twenty minute leg, make another four-minute turn to the right and run back northeast for about twenty minutes. The wind is 120 knots out of the west. Later, it increases to 190 knots and swings more out of the northwest. We set up our orbit about 6:00 a.m., and will remain here until 2:00 p.m. Then we can begin our three-hour flight home. We might get in just before dark.

We complete our first full orbit, and then start back southwest as the eastern sky begins lightening. When we come back up, a brilliant sun is rising out of China slightly off to the right of our nose. I remember an old song about a road to Mandalay, where the sun "comes up like thunder" out of China and where flying fishes play. I wonder if there are any fishes playing in the Gulf of Tonkin six and a half miles beneath us. I look out my window and see a quiet stretch of water with plumes of smoke drifting uncertainly out over the gulf. Several white "toothpicks," each with a black head, can be seen on the ocean far beneath us. The Navy! How tiny their ships look. We know from the briefing that there is an aircraft carrier down there. Its call sign today is "Martha" – must be the long black head. The white "toothpick" is the wake they leave behind them. They are in a different world from us. They are supposed to be our "air cover" in case we run into any "Bandits," or enemy fighters. If that happens "Martha" will launch some of her fighter aircraft. Today their call sign is "Skullcap." Doesn't look encouraging. Co-pilot thinks it would take about 10 minutes for them to get airborne and up here. We seem to be pretty much on our own.

Sunrise is always a difficult time on flights that run from the night before into the following afternoon. Energy departs us. I begin to feel like a huge Hershey "Kiss" sitting in my chair, as if all of me had settled into the bottom of my rear end. I notice the co-pilot is nodding; the pilot sits like a statute without moving. Is he asleep? Is he breathing? It is time to turn back right again.

"Pilot, nav."

"Go ahead nav."

"Come right 261 degrees"

"Coming right, 261."

We head back southwest again. We will run about twelve orbits on this flight; we have now done one and a half.

I think of my family on the other side of the world – my boy and my little girl. I can't help but feel that I should be back there with them, helping them grow up. It's 7 a.m. here, back there it's 7 p.m. They're getting ready for bed, but they will have no stories from Daddy tonight.

Radios crackle continuously. Most of it is jargon that borders on gibberish, carrying snippets and pieces of interrupted conversation, much of it monotonously banal yet some is uttered almost hysterically. Helicopter pilots are always recognizable because they sound like someone talking while sliding down a long flight of stairs on a piece of cardboard. Someone else screams out, in a high-pitched voice in apparent terror: "Two Pop is *airborne*! All systems *normal*! . . . lookin' *good*!!!" Artillery coordinates are passed on. Weather comments are debated. Questions are asked without response. Radio checks are conducted: "This is Flatfish on 432.8 - anybody read? Over?" Some of the conversation is passed over "Guard Channel" in violation of international flight rules. Guard channel is always reserved for emergency use; all aircraft are required to monitor that frequency and forbidden to use it except to make initial distress calls. The Air Force and civilian aircraft generally respect that requirement but the Navy has been accused (by the Air Force) of using it routinely to establish casual contact with other Navy aircraft. Sometimes we sarcastically call it "Navy Common."

Another hour drags by. The drone of the air passing by becomes hypnotic. Sun glare glances off of every bright piece of metal in the cockpit. The air in the cabin takes on a bluish cast. We seem to be passing through some kind of a thin place that separates "reality" from "somewhere else." I try to concentrate on my work but begin to feel like a man in a dream who can't wake up.

"WHEEP! WHEEP! WHEEP!" A SAM up-link call is broadcast over guard channel. It warns of a surface-to-air missile launched by the North Vietnamese at one of our aircraft, but it is for a location inland near the Laos-Vietnam border and doesn't concern us.

We reach the top of the orbit again and now the sun is well up in the sky and its glare is blinding. Another hour has passed away.

The box lunch is a mess. The ham in the sandwich is mainly gristle and fat and the cheese has mold on it in places. The lettuce has wilted far beyond even being able to pull it out of the bread. I fish my hard-boiled egg out of the box, crack it against my navigation desk, and after picking the shards of shell off the egg I take a big bite.

"*BANDIT! BANDIT! BANDIT!* This is Crown on Guard with a Bandit call! Two Bandits in the Gulf, Hainan, 243° range, 120 nautical miles, heading 360° at 800 knots . . . these are MiG- 21's . . . heading for Specter . . . Specter stand by to begin evasive action. Martha this is Crown on Guard, scramble Skullcap now."

"Martha, aye aye, Skullcap is airborne."

I have pieces of egg in both hands and my mouth is filled with an old hard-boiled egg that feels like a dry feather ball, and we've got MiG 21s! Coming for us!

"Heeee, he!" comes a wild scream over the radios . . . "Heeeehehehe HAW HA!" Nothing else can be heard on the radios because of the screaming that is suddenly coming over Guard channel.

"Nav-pilot, what's our heading?"

"Hahaha ha HA!"

("Gasp")

"Ah ho HO! Hohoho-HO!"

Where the hell are the bandits? "Chuckle, chuckle, ha ha - ahhhhhhah (drawing a great breath of air) Yaaaaha ha Ha ha, HA HA HA HA!!"

It's a laughing box!

"He, HEHEHE - **HE**!"

What idiot is playing that damn thing?

"Pilot-nav; We (gulp) gotta' come (swallow) left, North Vietnam is (glomp) better than (cough) Hainan!"

"This is Crown on Guard . . . New Bandit Report: Bandits now over Hainan, heading zero four seven, speed 1200 knots, area safe, Skullcap say position."

"Roger Skullcap, we're holdin' hands with Specter."

Unbelievingly, I look out my window and there is a Navy fighter setting inside our left wing. The aircraft is slowly rising and falling beside us. I think of a man on a galloping horse. The pilot sees me - he salutes, then lifts his visor & winks at me.

"Hello Specter, heard yu got some MiGs, where yu keepin' em?

Silence.

"Golly, Bill . . . " one Navy pilot says to the other.

" . . . ah think these here Air Force guys have died a' fright."

"Naw, they're probably still asleep. It's early for them."

"Hello Specter, how copy Skullcap?"

"Ah, roger Skullcap, gosh you guys look good!" How'd you get up here so quick?"

"Well, you said you had something important you wanted to show us."

"What I want to know," asked the co-pilot, "how did you get up here so damn fast? We're at 34,000 feet and you were at sea level . . . how long does it take you to get airborne and up here?"

" About half-a-minute."

"MiG's are gone?"

"Yeah dammit, we launched too quick."

"Were you guys playing that laughing box?"

"I didn't hear anything."

Our escort remains with us for about 20 minutes, then they "peel-off" and depart with afterburners popping in and out, along with wing rolls and other ado. They seem to be trying to enjoy the last few moments of their short flight. But we drone on. Five more hours before we can leave. The hours did not pass quickly to begin with, now they slow down as if they are the final moments of eternity.

Part of my attempts to adjust to the culture of Asia has been to study a little about Buddhism. One of the things I recall about that was their attitude toward Time and Eternity. Eternity, they say, is not just a "long time" but it is the "total absence of time." They even refer to what they call the "Eternal Now," a moment in which time does not even exist. That had puzzled me. Now I see. They must have flown missions like this too, perhaps centuries ago.

Even the minutes drag by more and more slowly. Then the seconds quit. I check my watch again and am amazed to see that it actually *has* stopped - the second hand is not moving. *My watch has died,* I think. I wonder what time it really is. Then I see the second hand jerk over a bit and then it stops again. It appears to be running very, very slowly. What is wrong? I check my master watch and it has the same problem. Time *has* slowed down. *What is going on?* I dial in WWV, the worldwide shortwave radio time hack station, but can't pick it up on any of its frequencies – that is not unusual though in this part of the world.

Another hour goes by and I feel numb. I eat the cold chicken in my in-flight lunch box. Incredibly, it tastes good. Well, it's something to do. Another hour goes by and my left leg starts to jerk. I clench my toes and tense my calf. Finally, I get up and walk about and do some deep knee bends. Another hour goes by - only one more to go. Thank God!

"Hello Specter, this is Crown, how copy?"

"Roger Crown, this is Specter, (sigh) loud and clear."

"Roger Specter, your replacement will be about an hour late - can you extend your orbit for one more hour?"

Silence.

"Hello Specter, this is Crown, do you copy?"

"Roger Crown, this is Specter . . . standby . . ."

Fuel consumption computation begins to take place in our cockpit, punctuated by occasional coarse language, then, "Crown, Specter."

"Go ahead Specter, this is Crown."

"Affirmative, Specter can extend for almost fifty minutes."

"Good boy, Specter. Let us know when you leave; Crown out."

"Specter out."

Another hour goes by – only one more to go - again.

Finally we call: "Hello Crown, this is Specter."

"Go ahead Specter, Crown here."

"Specter is preparing to depart station in two-zero minutes, Crown copy?"

"Crown copies, out."

"Specter out."

We finish the last run on the southern part of the orbit and head back down to the Paracel Islands. Later, we head north-east out over the South China Sea. The remainder of the flight works us into increasingly rough weather. The last hour finds us bouncing in and out of moderate turbulence. Finally we begin our descent through heavy clouds and strong crosswinds. Eventually we break out of the overcast and the ground looks dark and cold. It's going to be a rough night for a hard landing.

Now we're on final approach, descending quickly through heavy dark scud, bouncing hard up and down, crabbed 12° to the left for the wind, fighting to keep the left wing down. My navigation kit lifts up and then is slammed to the floor of the aircraft. We have power on, engines pulling hard, yet everything we can find is also out for drag. Our wheels are down, flaps are down, we're bouncing, tilting, hard up and suddenly down - back up again. Finally, we're on the runway. It is a hard landing, and it has taken the last speck of energy we had on this sixteen-hour and twelve-minute flight.

At debriefing we are all pulsating from fatigue. Wired. Our next flight will be a repeat of this one. Briefing will be in ten hours. My body throbs, and my left leg has started jerking again.

Finally we are back at the BOQ. I go outside in the pitch-black night and sit down at a picnic bench next to our room with a frothy Japanese beer. Taiwan is dark as the bottom of a deep pit but there is a breeze that smells of grass and rain. The wind is gusty and cool.

Faraway, out there somewhere, a train screams its shrill cry as it runs toward the mountains and it reminds me of a Bandit call sailing out over the Gulf.

# 33
# NKP

After a week of flying electronic reconnaissance missions out of Taiwan, we returned to U-Tapao and finally flew a mission that went exactly as planned. We went to the scheduled orbit, refueled the scheduled bombers, and then came home as planned. Amazing. We didn't know such a thing was possible over here.

Then we found that U-Tapao was closed due to an accident and we would have to land our KC-135 at Nakhon Phanom (NKP), a fighter base in northeastern Thailand.

One thing led to another, and we wound up having to spend the night there. Even worse, at the Officer's Club we found a great sign over the swinging doors that were the entrance to the bar: "Only Fighter Pilots Allowed in This Bar!" So we sat at a table in the dining room and ordered a drink. We were complaining about our luck, being stuck in here for the night, when our table exploded.

An open palm had slammed against it. The hand was still on the table and it led our eyes up a fighter pilot's arm, then on to his rank: a full colonel! His face sported a wild, bushy mustache and his bloodshot eyes burned like fire pits. He resembled David Niven gone stark, raving mad. His name tag read "Wolf." We had all heard of him; he was one of the legends of Vietnam.

"What's yer *problem* boys?" He asked, glaring at me, his eyes three inches from mine, our noses almost touching.

"Uh . . ." I said.

"Why don't ye come in th'*bar,* boys?" Now he stares, Dracula-like at our pilot.

"Oh, ah . . ." ventures our pilot " . . . we're ah, not fighter. . . ah, you know, pilots."

"See the sign . . . sir?" Adds our copilot.

The colonel looks astonished and turns to the copilot

as if he hadn't noticed he was there. "Hello, boy . . ." the colonel said jovially, then more softly, "Well you fly *some*thing don't you?" He picked at the copilot's flight suit, and then suddenly in a very loud voice asked him "Do you remember what it was you flew in here *on*, boy?"

"Tankers!" Our pilot whispered out loudly.

"Tankers?" Col. Wolf exclaimed and beamed, "Ahhhhhhhhhh! Yes, I *saw* a 135 on the ramp – is that yours?"

"Yessir." said the pilot sadly, perhaps like it might be an admission of guilt about something worthy of shame.

"Come'*ERE!*" The colonel commanded, pulling us up out of our chairs, leading us to the bar and shoving us through the swinging doors into the forbidden area!

"MEN" he shouted in a stentorian voice. "We got *Tanker* Troops here!"

"*Tankers?*" Somebody yelled.

"Dong! Dong! Dong! Dong!" The bell that always hangs over every Air Force stag bar started ringing as a lieutenant pulled on its rope. Of course we all knew that anytime a bell is rung in an Air Force Officer's Club stag bar, that means there are free drinks for everybody. Normally the person ringing the bell has to buy those drinks unless someone else had walked in with his hat on, or had gotten a phone call from his wife while he was at the bar, then the hat-wearer, or the husband had to buy the drinks. And every base also had local "ground rules." I wondered how much all this was going to cost us.

But it seemed that every fighter pilot there had a story to tell us about how a tanker had "saved his life" at least once, and they all bought drinks for *us*.

"Where's yer boomer?" Someone suddenly asked.

"Probably at the NCO Club." Replied our pilot.

"*Get* him!" Ordered Col. Wolf, and pointing with his right hand in a Thor-like gesture, "Smith – Jones – go *get* him!" Then half-turning like a ballerina, with his left hand pointing to our pilot. "What's his name, boy?"

"Clark, sir! " said our pilot, "Tech sergeant."

Ten minutes later, an MA-151 Jeep without a top, drove up the stairs and through the swinging doors into the bar, two lieutenants in the front and a bewildered, confused and flustered boom operator sitting high in the back. The fighter pilots broke into cheers when they saw him and started chanting "Boomer! Boomer!" Col. Wolf dragged him out of the jeep and shoved a drink in his hand "Have a *drink*, boy!"

So that was the beginning of a long night, but it all ended well.

# 34
# City of Angels

We've been back in Thailand flying out of the base at U-Tapao for several days. Now we have a "day off" and my pilot, co-pilot and I are headed in to Bangkok.

Even out here in the farmland the road is busy. We pass Thai soldiers with guns; Buddhist monks with beggar bowls, and people with tote poles springing across their shoulders. We meet oxen pulling wooden carts, rickshaws filled with riders, archaic "trucks" that surely must date from the twelfth century, and buses painted fantastic colors and decorated with religious effigies, animal horns and great splobs of wild and clashing paint. Coconut palms rise on either side of the road.

Our bus drives on, past Pattaya Beach and its famous Nipa Lodge, then the road angles away from the sea, through jungles of twisting vines and dark, secret-looking trees. Later we enter open country and cross a flat delta with rice paddies and water buffalo. The sky takes on a high blue-gray look that tells of rain to come. Later in the morning we arrive in the great city. The Thais call it "Krung Thep" which means "City of Angels." We find rooms in the Chao Phraya (CHOP'-e-ah) Hotel for $1.50 a night, and head off for shopping.

There are westerners here, as well as Chinese and Koreans, and Thai and Vietnamese of course, along with Laotians and Cambodians, but the most remarkable visages we see belong to Indians, huge men with enormously large faces, big mustaches and bushy beards. They also wear colorful turbans and great cummerbunds – I can't help but look for jeweled daggers around their waists - perhaps they are hidden.

A large open field is swarming with kids flying kites. I buy several kites for my own kids, also a couple of paper parasols. We stop at Wat Arun, which is the Temple of the Dawn. Sunlight and color flash from its outer walls that are a mosaic made from pieces of porcelain plates, cups and saucers.

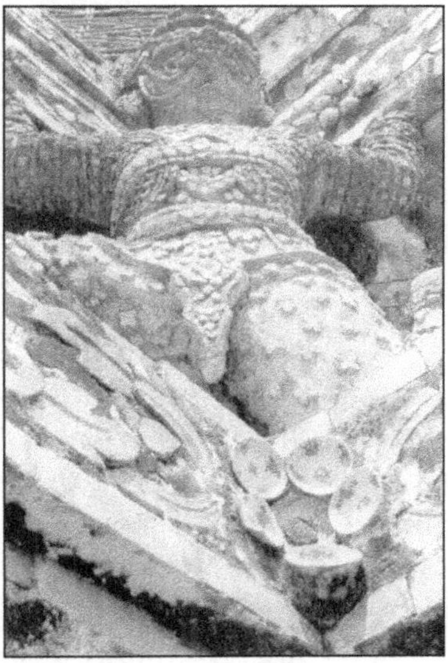

We take in the nightlife and enjoy some of the many bars and fine restaurants. We see amazing and astonishing dancing which I won't even attempt to describe here.

We had several restaurants recommended to us before we left U-Tapao. We eat in one of them and find it a very different experience from what we have been used to. I have a marvelous fried beef and rice, the rice being mounded in a small saucer and the beef floating in gravy the color of soy sauce after having been slowly cooked with garlic and ginger and other things I was not familiar with. The rice and meat are combined in the plate and garnished with side dishes of sautéed onion, green peppers and awesome Thai bird peppers. Wow. Kirin beer helps control the internal temperatures.

While eating at the restaurant we see one of our tech-reps and he has some recommendations for places that are not as touristy as those we had been to earlier. We enjoy a couple of these more traditional Bangkok bars and nightclubs and count ourselves lucky.

Next day a riverboat tour on the Chao Phraya River takes us through canals leading to the Old Market area. Here policemen stand on boat roofs, whistle in mouth, directing the river traffic with cool white gloves.

A young elephant about six-feet tall is available for petting. Tourists gather around it along with an array of young Thai boys. A beautiful young woman, blonde and blue-eyed, probably about twenty-five or thirty years old approaches the elephant as its trainer motions her to do so. She reaches to pet it and the elephant grabs her skirt with its trunk and lifts it far above her head, revealing bright red panties and resulting in screaming and stamping of feet and nervous laughter. The boys laugh and giggle, clapping their hands, and the lady backs away, smoothing her skirt over her thighs, blushing and smiling embarrassedly, speaking rapidly in German. The elephant's trainer, an older man with a large beard and a large belly and wearing a large blue turban, also appears embarrassed and apologizes profusely, bowing toward her and speaking sorrowfully in Thai, shaking his head in regret. I notice the elephant's trunk briefly nestled into its trainer's hand then carried something back and places it into its mouth.

Probably happens several times every day.

Thais who live on the river seem to have no fear of the water. Young kids swim naked in the polluted mess from about the age of three (and probably earlier). Mothers bathe tiny children in it. Clothes are washed in it. Dishes are washed in it, teeth are brushed there and the people apparently drink from the river too. To them it is a constant source of life.

Tiring of Bangkok and its tourists, I leave my pilot and copilot at noon for a bus back to Pattaya Beach, catching a cool nap on the trip. I get a room at the Nippa Lodge and get to the beach to watch an orange sunset spread through the sky and cover the earth.

Later at the lodge I eat outside in a dining room on a deck, up above the jungle, with a nice view of the beach and the Gulf of Thailand. A delicious tomato-wine-mushroom-marinade-smothered-fillet with melodious dark red wine helps the evening turn into night under an unreal sky of slowly changing colors bright with orange, purple, shades of red reflecting from towering thunderstorms which have now begun to anvil out on top, and with a lonesome blue sky way up above it all. Cool breezes from the bay fan the torches on the deck and ruffle palm fronds by the porch, bringing with them the salty scent of the sea.

Next morning I walk the beach at dawn, barefoot and shirtless, wading and swimming in water so clear that only the sky and the bottom can be seen, each alternating with the other as the morning light dances upon it. Smells of water, salt, fish and ancient heat caress my skin. The ocean spins varying crests and troughs that swirl together and then part, and

while rising and falling they fill the morning with endless flashes of light.

I walk the length of the beach and watch the dhows slowly glide by, powered by their single small sail. Other boats ply these shores with engines that fire like a slow-hitting hammer firing only once each second. I eat lunch at the lodge, then board a bus and return to U-Tapao where I find that the schedule still shows that we will "rotate" (leave here and go home) in just nine more days!

# 35
# Jiggity-Jig

The day after returning from Bangkok I pull all day duty as “Ramp Tramp.” In other words, I drive a pickup truck down the runway after each wave of B-52 takeoffs and landings looking for pieces of aircraft that might have fallen off, crew members who might have tried to escape, or other whatnots.

We fly three more flights, all of which proceed without a single hitch; they are the first ones so far on the entire trip! Now we’re wearing our Sa-Wa-Dee Caps and ready to go home.

Suddenly, it is over. Our last mission has been flown and we are feverishly shopping for last-minute things. Then comes time for my last trip to U-Tapao beach, and a long walk down it alone. The beauty of this beach though, has now lost its charm and like the land-pools and sky-pools of Pattaya Beach we too, now ebb away from the war to flow back to our homes and reunite again with our families.

Next morning we’re airborne. We fly over northeast Thailand for the last time this trip. Then east over Laos, and finally over South Vietnam.

We coast out over the South China Sea, flying south of the Gulf of Tonkin with its EC-135’s and carrier escorts, and we land later in the Philippines. A quick turnaround has us airborne again for a fast run down to Okinawa where we find the weather is cold on a mid-March day.

Beautiful high cliffs jut upward, out of the Philippine Sea, and are mostly covered with rich-looking jungle but we don't have time to enjoy the spectacular view, we are busy! We are off for Guam, then Hawaii.

The trip to Hawaii is a long ride. It is a navigational challenge because all of our navigation gear was stripped from the plane in Thailand for other aircraft still flying combat missions. Our Doppler doesn't work, and the radar altimeter was removed from the airplane! We are leading three F-4s back across, and I contact each pilot and find they have no navigational gear at all, their "flight plan" is just to keep *us* in sight! I find myself crossing the Pacific with only a sextant – just like Magellan!

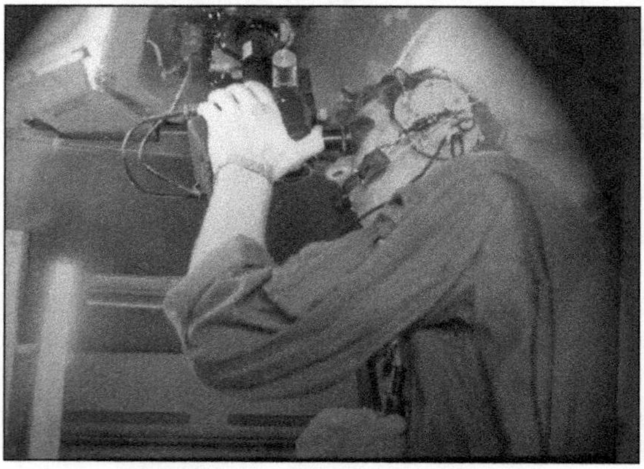

I fly a long day-celestial leg, with sunlines running quickly from speedline to half-cut to courseline and on. Jupiter becomes barely visible through the sextant to the south and gives a nice speedline for several shots. Then the full moon rises with the sunset and I finally cross it with Jupiter and Venus about thirty minutes before ADIZ penetration, and plot my first "fix" of the trip. It is six miles from my MPP (Most Probable Position). Forty minutes later we get our first TACAN fix and that also is six miles off. I'll take that any day.

After we land I try to call home but the telephone connections are still not up to the task. The word is that sometimes you can get through to the mainland, and sometimes the connection is pretty good; often though, it doesn't work at all. So I spend a quiet Saturday night at the Hickam AFB Officers' Club.

Now we have two days to wait for our aircraft to arrive. The first night I go back to the only place on Oahu that I feel at home. For some inexplicable reason that's the Moana Hotel. Probably that's because everything else has changed since my first visit here back in 1957, but now I can still see the moon through the Banyan tree as it rises over Diamond Head reflecting down off the waters of Waikiki. I can't help but remember having listened to a radio program, "Hawaii Calls" that broadcast from this very spot, many years ago, and I used to listen to it every Sunday evening when I was a kid.

Next day I rent a car and drive up to Diamond Head and on around to the Pali Lookout, up through the rain forest and to the place of the cool fog and fierce winds to see again that fantastic view. Here the sides of the mountains fall into an ascending mist and from there one can look back up and around to the left and gaze at the mountains that stand side-by-side all the way to the end of the island.

I drive on, first to warm and brilliant Kaneohe Bay, then around the northern end of the island, with the ocean on the right, mountains on the left, great ranches nestled within little twisting roads. Down past Sunset Beach where five to eight foot waves come rolling in, often running crossways at one another and whipping up a boiling, seething and grinding surf. Finally, I come back across the pineapple fields to Honolulu, and drive past the vast Schofield Barracks, which look grim and smoky.

I unwind on Waikiki, surfing! With toes clenched into the surfboard, knees bent, arms flapping in the air, I probably resemble a gigantic carnivorous bird trying to lift its flat prey out of the ocean.

The breezes at U-Tapao had been salty with a fishy tang to them, a steady eight to ten knot wind. Palms were bent easily with the fringe of the fronds always flapping gently. Here in Hawaii, the wind is stronger and much gustier. It runs the palm fronds ragged and it blows toward California, ready to take us home.

Next morning we're up at 5:45 for a quick breakfast. We hurry to flight planning and buying orchids, then we are airborne again – it's our old airplane that we haven't seen for two months, naturally without navigational gear, of course – but we're headed home. I know I can find that!

We land back home again at ten minutes after midnight on Easter morning. Gifts are distributed and I finally get to bed at 4 a.m. Back up at 6 a.m. to greet my youngest child, a two-year old who is amazed.

Later in the day I call the Scheduling Office and find that I will begin a seven-day alert tour three days from today. Tomorrow I will file for per diem pay so my family can finally become financially solvent again in about three weeks. Tuesday I will get re-certified in SAC's Emergency War Order Operations. Back home –trying to fall into the old routine again.

Then the phone rings and I find out that I have received PCS (Permanent Change of Station) orders reassigning me to a staff position at another base. Later, I go by Central Base Personnel Office to pick up the orders and get more information about the assignment.

It will be to a small Air Force Station whose mission is to score B-52 bomb runs. The good news is that half the time I will have an ordinary staff position there, the bad news is that the other half of the time I will be completing a one year tour-of-duty in Vietnam, broken into two six-month segments. That way I will not get any "credit" for a tour in SEA, and will still be eligible for a one-year assignment to SEA when this new tour is completed.

# 36
# Death Ray

My new assignment was to an Air Force Station in a small southern town called College Heights. At the end of the town was a small commercial airport that supported Cessna and Beechcraft aircraft and not much more. We were located in the corner of the airport and had three or four small buildings and a couple of radar antennas we used in our mission. Our total personnel consisted of about 300 enlisted and NCOs and about 10 officers, approximately half of which were always overseas in Thailand or Vietnam. I was to work while in the states as Operations Officer, or second in command, of this detachment.

The stateside mission was to score the accuracy of B-52 practice runs in the local area. We would track the "bomb runs" and when the aircraft "dropped" its "electronic bomb" we scored where it would have hit if it had been a real bomb. This was useful in training the aircrews.

When B-52's began bombing in Vietnam, they encountered problems finding suitable radar returns since the jungle looked somewhat like a plate of scrambled eggs on the radarscope. The solution was to have some of SAC's bomb scoring sites moved to SEA where they could direct the B-52 bomb runs by giving the crews headings to fly, and telling them when to drop their bombs.

This procedure was designated "Operation Skyspot". The crews rotate to SEA for a six-month tour, come back home for six months, then they return to SEA. After the second tour most of the officers returned to flying on an aircrew, while the enlisted men remained in their career field. There were a total of eleven Skyspot sites in operation although not all eleven were operational at the same time.

SAC required that the person who directed the B-52's flight path and who told them when to drop their bombs must be an officer (called the Mission Director) who was currently rated as a pilot or navigator. Each B-52 mission also required a supervisor to be present and responsible for the mission, and he (the Senior Mission Director) was required to be a field-grade pilot or navigator. I was one of the Senior Mission Directors for Operation Skyspot.

When stateside, the Senior Mission Directors functioned basically as Squadron Operations Officers, where the work was pretty routine and basically boring, including a lot of paper work and responding to telephone calls from higher headquarters. Like this one.

"Now Major, I'm not going to suggest that this matter actually *is* classified but I am asking you to consider treating it as if it were, shall we say, 'Top Secret?' . . . you know what I mean?"

"Well, Mr. Blue," I reply to the voice on the other end of the telephone, who had been identified by his secretary as being THE Assistant Executive Director of the FBI, "if what you have just told me is as you have said it *might* be, then it would *have* to be classified '*Top* Secret.' Then, both you and I would have to submit a violation report on each other since we have just discussed the matter on an unsecured telephone line. However, I think I know what you mean, and you can rest assured that we will handle the matter with discretion. We will not pass it to the press or otherwise disseminate information about it."

"Thank you Major, we're counting on you – goodbye."

"Wait a minute! What about a report?"

"Oh yes, of course, thank you; just write it up and submit it."

"What kind of format?"

"Well we really don't have a format for anything like this; just write it up and send it in. Goodbye."

"By courier?"

"Oh no, just put a stamp on it and drop it in the mail. Thanks, Major."

"OK, do you have an address?"

"Here's Buzzy, she will give that to you. Goodbye."

As I write down the address, Sgt. Swen walks by my open door. Sgt. Swen is our medical corpsman. He wears a white uniform that sets him apart from our other personnel, and he provides medical services here at our tiny Air Force Station. He helps take care of the officers and men who are assigned here, and schedules their medical appointments at the nearest Air Force Base, 120 miles away.

"Sgt. Swen!"

"Yes sir!" He spins around and comes in.

"What do you know about Death Rays?" I ask him as I hang up the telephone.

"Well, we used to use them in the Pentagon, going around and zapping people down the hallways. Sometimes they work, sometimes they don't; you know, they're so-so."

"No, no . . . " I reach for the telephone again. "I mean really?"

I buzz Sgt. Roloc, our First Sergeant.

"Yesssir?"

"Can you come into my office, please?"

"Be right there, sir."

I ask my secretary to hold all calls until further notice, and when Sgt Roloc comes in I ask him to shut the door and have a seat.

"Well, here's a different problem," I begin, looking at two brightly expectant faces. "I just got a telephone call from Headquarters SAC asking me to contact some guy who claims to be a high muck-a-muck in the FBI; seems like there may be a Death Ray machine roaming around our peaceful town of College Heights." I pause a moment to look at the faces, still bright and expectant, smiles beginning to form at the corners of their lips. "Have either of you heard anything about this?"

Swen shakes his head, Roloc grins: "No major, how does it go?"

"All right, here's what I know: I just talked on the telephone to a Mr. Joseph Cabot Blue, from Washington, who is allegedly THE Assistant Director of the FBI. He tells me that a professor at the university here in College Heights had contacted Pentagon Intelligence to say that several years ago he had been working on a 'Death Ray' for the United States Government, and that another professor, also here in College Heights, has stolen some of his concepts and has constructed a 'Death Ray' machine in his own home and is aiming it at the first professor's house and 'beaming rays' at it day and night."

The two sergeants look as if they really would like to leave now.

I continue. "The first professor says he can't call the police or sheriff because the thing is classified Top Secret."

The two sergeants look at each other. "Can't call the police?" Sgt. Roloc asks.

"Well, because he says it's classified. At any rate, he contacted the Pentagon, the Pentagon contacted the FBI and they say they're trying to get a Federal Marshall out here to investigate but don't have any marshals available around here right now . . . "

Sergeant Roloc interrupts: "Yeah, I bet they've heard about this one and cleared out of the whole area."

"So, at any rate," I say sternly, "then they started looking for a military installation and found us – since we're in the town of College Heights. I'm going to call the first professor and set up an appointment if I can, and then this afternoon we will go out there. Roloc, I want you to secure a station wagon for this afternoon, probably about 2 p.m. I'll keep you posted."

Roloc nods his head.

"And, by the way, let's not talk about this 'till we know what is really going on, OK?"

"Yes sir," says Swen

"Oh, I don't want anybody to know about this one," Roloc says, shaking his head, as he ambles off for lunch.

I get a cup of coffee and dial the number of Professor Number One, a Dr. J. William Capp. Busy. I keep dialing while reviewing the bombing run charts from last night. Finally, the telephone rings. On the eighth ring it is picked up. I hear heavy breathing coming over the phone along with a lot of static and faint noise that sounds a little bit like some strange music.

"Hello," I say. "Hello?"

"Yes!" A voice responds sharply.

"Is this Dr. Capp?" I ask.

"Who are *you*?" The question is threatening and the voice now intimidating.

I introduce myself.

"Thank GOD!" I can hear a deep breath. "Mildred, we're *saved*!" Then I can hear him speak as he apparently turns his head, "The Air Force is *here*!"

The phone connection is not good, and he is very hard to understand but we finally set up an appointment at his place at 2:30 today. He says the force from the death ray is usually very strong at that time of day.

★ ★ ★

When we arrive at the Capp residence, I knock on the door several times before I hear a key inserted into the slot and after a moment I hear it turn. Then another key is inserted and turned. Then another, and another. I hear chains being unlatched and the door slowly opens to reveal a small elderly woman. She introduces herself as Mrs. Capp. She tells us that Dr. Capp will be home momentarily and invites us into a house that seems very dark even though every light in the place appears to be on. A haunting cacophony of noise comes from every part of the place and a sinister aura seems to permeate everything. Swen and Roloc exchange wide-eyed glances and pause for a moment before entering. As I step through the door I feel vulnerable to danger. I unconsciously think: *Watch out now*!

Mrs. Capp leads us into the living room that has been wallpapered in aluminum foil. Even the windows are covered with foil, and the strange background noise that fills the house appears to periodically break into a cadence of rhythmic patterns faintly reminiscent of speech. A premonition of doom envelops me.

"Can you feel the ray now?" I ask Mrs. Capp.

"Oh yes, it was very strong just a minute ago." She seems coordinated and responsive, coherent, lucid. "While you were out on the porch, I could feel the 'force' very strongly." She smiles a sad smile. "But it has weakened quite a bit now."

"Do you associate this force, or ray, with any particular location?" asks Sgt. Swen.

"It's worst of all right here!" She says, walking into the kitchen and pointing to the sink. I notice the telephone is off its hook and lying next to a radio that is playing music very softly.

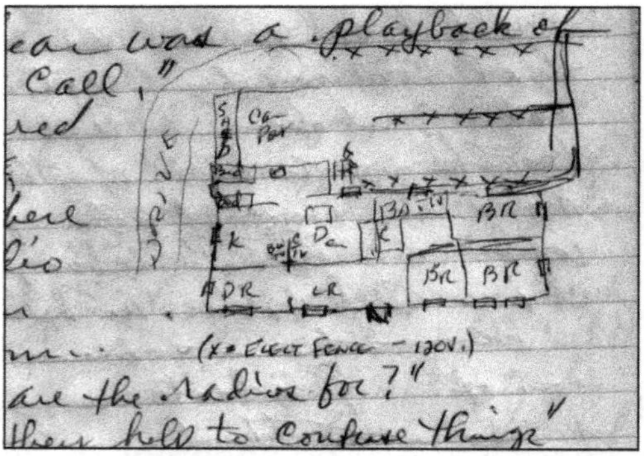


I walk over by the sink and stand there for a moment. I feel nothing except the perception of dread which does seem to be getting a bit weaker, perhaps fading slowly away. *It's a smell!* I think, and then am not sure about that – maybe more like a bad dream. I want to get out of this house as fast as I can!

I open my notebook and make some comments and sketch the layout of the house.

"The force amplifies noise, too," she adds. Indeed the radio is louder here, but not supernaturally so, since it is in a corner.

Sgt. Swen asks, "What makes you believe that a force is present? Can you describe its effects?"

Mrs. Capp looked wistful. "Oh, it comes in through the mouth or the nose, you can just feel it pouring in - sometimes it comes in through the ears and sometimes it comes in through the eyes. It's just like being hit in the face . . ." She pauses and almost winces, as she glances down toward the floor and her words become more melancholy. "It fills your stomach and swells it till it hurts. Or it gives you headaches or makes you dizzy. Sometimes it makes your vision burr so you can't see anything."

"Why is your telephone off the hook? " I interrupt her.

But she goes on, now intensely. "Sometimes it gets on your skin and then it snaps and crackles like electricity and it just waits to get you whenever you open your mouth to speak or listen to something or try to look somewhere!"

"Why is your telephone off the hook?" I ask again.

She turns to look at the telephone lying on the counter like it might be a dead pet. "It doesn't work. Nobody can fix it." She shakes her head. "They've been out here several times."

"The telephone company can't fix the telephone?" Asks Sgt. Roloc.

She tosses her head and looks at Roloc. "Oh, it's all right when *they* are here."

He nods his head as if his understanding has suddenly deepened.

Suddenly she grabs his arm, startling him, and she continues in a husky voice. "Listen, last week I tried to call one of my daughters, long distance, and it was awful – I couldn't understand her but she could hear me. Then I called my other daughter and all I could hear was a playback of the first call . . . " She looks at Roloc with intense and worried eyes.

I see hairs rise on the back of Roloc's neck, and he pulls his arm free of her grasp.

Mrs. Capp leads us on a tour of the house and I note there is a radio playing very quietly in every room – that is the strange noise I had noticed when we first came in. Most of the radios seem to be tuned to the same station, but a few are tuned to different stations. Every blind and shade in the house is pulled down. There seems to be a faint trace of a smell permeating the house but I can't identify it, and am not even sure that it is really there.

"What are the radios for?" Sgt. Swen asks.

Mrs. Capp replies in a rather businesslike manner "Well, they help to confuse things."

Swen says "Umm."

"So where are these rays coming from?" I ask.

Mrs. Capp pulls back a piece of tinfoil, parts the curtains and lifts the blinds a little. "They come from the brick house - that one, over there." She points to a large house on the other side of the street and about two houses down. I ask the sergeants to take a look around the yard and to see what the brick house looks like. They walk out the front door in welcome relief.

A shed has been added and attached to the back of the Capp's house. I ask if I can look inside. The shed door is locked with three padlocks, but she gets them all open and we look inside at a collection of garden items. As I step inside the shed I feel as if I have been trapped – the horrible presence I had sensed when I first came in the house is *here!* Evil, Itself, is here in these dark shadows! I stop and spread my legs to steady myself. I mentally ask myself, *What are the facts*? There is a smell. It is that same smell that faintly permeates the entire house. Here though, it is heavy and dense and seems full of death. There is a radio playing but only static is heard, it had drifted off its frequency. Mrs. Capp shakes her head. "Just an hour ago it was very loud!" Then I boldly step to the back of the shed and pick up a container that is sitting on a dark shelf. There is a faded label that I turn to the light.

"Strychnine." I put it back and pick up the one next to it. "Lead Arsenic." There is also Diazinon, Chlordane, Malathion and Dursban.

"What do you use these for?" I ask.

She smiles a beautiful smile. "Oh, we grow roses!"

We go back inside the house as the sergeants return. Roloc raises his eyebrows and rolls his eyes, and Sven shrugs his shoulders.

Dr. Capp drives up in a big Chrysler sedan. He is a plump, heavy man, about five feet five inches tall, a person of obvious dignity who has the look of one who has been deeply hurt. He seems so deeply preoccupied that he gives the impression of being a man without eyes. He moves slowly and thoughtfully, and speaks in a deeply resonate monotone voice that constantly makes sound and creates a noise which is unbroken except for his labored breathing, and out of this endless sound he carefully fashions words as he slowly thinks. Meanwhile, he constantly searches with his hidden eyes, looking under chairs and tables and occasionally tilting his head so he can see more clearly into dark corners.

"He ahhhhhhas ahhhhh someuhhhhhhsome sortof of ofalistening ahhhh deavice I. I know that we ahad them back inahthe 19aahhh50's he. He hecan <u>tellllll</u> when I aaam inahthehouse and thennnn he directs his ahMASER atme." He whispers his words while shifting his gaze from under the dining room table to below the couch on which his wife is sitting.

"Yes," she says, nodding her head. "You can just smell the *ozone*!"

"Who is 'He'?" I ask, opening up my notebook again.

"Oh he's uhhh that he he's athat ahhhh rascal acrosstheahstreet." Dr. Capp lifts a tablecloth to peer beneath the table, then under the cloth. "He's uhhhh been divorced two two . . . two ahhhhtimes and has he's had had two otherawives ahhhhdie from bone boneacancer where he uhhhhhkicks them on the alegs, oh he's ahhhno good. " Dr. Capp separates each fold of the tablecloth, then releases it, and looks at me. "He's no good at ALL, not at all, not at all!"

Mrs. Capp adds, "He killed our roses!"

"Yes anduhhh yeswe took him to uhhhhcourt, we took him toacourt over over over ahhthat and he's uhhhhstill he's still mad . . . " Dr. Capp trails off, his interest now focused on a shadow under the easy chair across the room. "Yes, . . . he's uhhhhhstill mad over . . . overuthat."

Roloc takes his glasses off to rub his face and his glasses pick up light from the chandelier and send reflections gliding across the floor, then up the wall. Dr. Capp watches these reflections seriously.

"He's no good . . . " Mrs. Capp adds, " . . . he doesn't even *work*!"

Roloc puts his glasses back on and the reflections cease. Dr. Capp pauses as if on the verge of making an important discovery. Carefully he opens his mouth to speak. "No, he runs ahhhhdrugs from the border on up. . . up to aSeattle . . . all the way. They've got those MASERS for ahhhhhsale now. I saw uhhhh one in the magazine the other . . . the other day. They wanted $3900 for it. He's got one. They'll stop at nothing, you know. They won't let anything get in their . . . ah in their ahway." Now he is bending down looking under their buffet.

I look up from my notebook. "What do the letters in 'MASER' stand for?"

"Oh don'tuhknow . . . I don'tahhhthink . . . It'sato uh toahdo uhh with uhh microwaveah–amplificationah but I uhhhdon't . . . uhhh . . . I'm uhhhnot really ahsure." He straightens back up and scans the tops of the open doors.

I write that down. "And where do you work?"

"Oh, I work atathe. . . at the uhcollege . . . I'm athe ahhhchairman . . . the chairman of the ahphysics departuhment." Now he's staring intently into my eyes as if looking for something that bothers him.

"You *were* the chairman, Honey," his wife says sadly.

"I *am* the chairman." Dr. Capp's voice now has a ring of victory.

"You've had some experience in hypnosis, haven't you?" I asked suddenly, partly because of his monotone answers.

"Oh no . . . no . . . no . . . no . . . no . . . uhno . . . no."

"Have you done any work in matters pertaining to the occult?"

"No . . . no. I need you to uhh get me some ahhhsomthing thatawill ahhdetect . . . uhdetect MASER rays." He is glancing behind their sofa which sets a foot out from the wall.

I tell them that I will check into the matter and that while I have no way of giving the Capps official advice that unofficially, until the report is finished, I suggest they have a medical checkup, and have their gas furnace inspected for leaks. I emphasize the importance of removing the garden chemicals from such a close proximity to the house.

Later, back at the Air Force station, after reviewing the afternoon bomb run scores, I go into my secretary's office. Shelia has gone for the day, but no matter. I sit down at her desk and put a piece of paper in her typewriter and begin typing a letter.

Dear Mr. Blue:

I have completed my investigation about the Capp matter and have come to the following conclusions:

1) There is, in fact, credible evidence of a death ray being used in the streets of College Heights.
2) I have reliable eyewitness reports of a similar weapon being routinely used in the Pentagon.
3) If you need more information about this matter, or have any questions, please feel free to contact me at the above address.

I review my report.

I like it.

Seems to be the most sensible thing I have seen all day.

I take the letter out of the typewriter, fold it carefully and put it in my briefcase. Then I turn the lights off and go home.

Tomorrow I will write the real letter.

# 37
# Alfalfa

My secretary brings a large envelope into my office. I open it and find orders assigning me to a court-martial! Wow! Members of missile and flying crews are exempt from jury duty, both military and civilian, but now, reasonably late in my Air Force career, I am in a staff position and for the first time available for such tasks.

I report to the Staff Judge Advocate building at 0900 hours on the scheduled day and am directed to a small classroom. Other members of the court-martial pool file in. There are two Lt. Colonels, one major (me), a second lieutenant, and the others are enlisted men.

About 9:15 a young airman comes in and begins a quick briefing.

"OK gentlemen, there is only one trial today. It concerns an airman, Smith, who has been charged with the possession of marijuana." He refers to a black briefing book. "Judge Bob Jones will be presiding." Then he looks up. "Everybody here been on a court-martial before, right?"

I hold up my hand.

"Major?" He looks puzzled. "This is your *first* court-martial?"

"First time." I respond.

"We'll take care of him," one of the Lt. Colonels says with a smile, pointing to the other Lt. Colonel who nods his head and grins.

"Major, I'll get you a handout." The Airman looks at his watch. "Any questions?" He glances around the room. "OK, follow me."

He leads us down a hallway into a courtroom. We sit in seats that will be used later by the audience.

A voice from the back of the room calls out "All rise."

We stand up as a black-robbed judge comes through a door and sits at a large desk up front.

"Be seated." Someone says.

We sit down.

Two first lieutenants come through the back door and approach the judge. They are the prosecutor and defense attorneys and both look like they could be 18 or 19 years old. They speak quietly with the judge at his table for a few moments, and then sit at separate tables facing the judge but in front of us.

The judge says something that I don't understand and one of the lieutenants quickly checks in a notebook and says "Lt. Colonel Hebrim."

The judge looks our way and says "Colonel Hebrim?"

One of the lieutenant colonels stands up.

The other lawyer speaks: "Colonel Barnes."

The other lieutenant colonel stands up.

"The judge looks our way again and says "Thank you gentlemen, you are dismissed."

The Lieutenant Colonels get their hats and leave.

Now the bailiff comes to the judge, turns and looks at us and calls my name. I feel very relieved and rise, fingering my cap, ready to leave. The second lieutenant's name is called and he also rises. Then ten sergeants and airmen names are called and they rise. The judge addresses us: "Gentlemen, please be seated at the table to my right."

The judge rises and looks at me "Major?"

"Yes?" I reply.

"You are the senior officer of the board and will be in charge of the court." He turns and walks out of the room, followed by the lawyer lieutenants.

I think, *I gotta get my handout.* I look around for the airman who had given us our first briefing but he is not in the room. I start to go out and find him but the bailiff tells us to sit down at our new table near the front of the room, and as we do, the door opens and a middle-aged woman, obviously dressed in her finest Sunday clothes walks in. She has been crying. A middle-aged man walking heavy-footed like a farmer might walk through plowed land is right behind her. He is dressed in a blue jacket, black shiny trousers, and is wearing brown shoes and a light green tie, and he carries a gray hat in his hand. He looks like he has just received very bad news. A young woman, perhaps nineteen or twenty years old follows him. She is wearing a print dress and her hair is almost well done; she wobbles as she walks, apparently she is not used to high heel shoes. Bright lipstick clashes with her clothes. She has been crying. An older man wearing a blue pinstripe suit, with a large stomach and great bushy eyebrows walks in right behind them. He has a fiery look in his eyes as if he had just seen God, and is carrying a badly worn Bible in his left hand. A young man with a large belly and small glasses is next. He is wearing a light gray suit and a very thin, bright blue tie. A lieutenant and a sergeant, both wearing Dress Blue uniforms come in. All these people sit down where we had been sitting just a few moments before. A young airman with two stripes and a press camera slips in and sits down. Then an Air Policeman dressed in a khaki short-sleeved shirt with a black "AP" armband comes in and sits down. He is wearing a .38 caliber pistol and his hat remains on.

A woman in civilian clothes brings in a court recorder and places it on a small table and sits down behind it. The two lieutenant lawyers come in again. One of them has a very young airman walking beside him. The airman has one stripe on his uniform. They all stand at the two tables in front of the room. The bailiff now walks to the front of the judge's desk and calls out "All rise!" We all stand up as the judge enters and sits down at his desk.

"Please be seated." The judge reads a bill of particulars from a sheet of paper on his desk and then the discussion rested largely between him and the two attorneys.

It is not much of a case. Airman Smith has been charged with use and possession of marijuana. A package, about a quarter the size of a football, is introduced as 'Exhibit A'. It appears to be some dark green substance wrapped in clear plastic with a large 'A' marked in red ink on its side, giving it an oddly Christmas motif. It was allegedly found in Smith's locker and is the entirety of the case.

The sergeant wearing dress blues is called forward and testifies that he had noticed Airman Smith had been acting peculiarly in his work area, and that the smell of marijuana was often around wherever Airman Smith was working. The sergeant tells of questioning Airman Smith who denied having ever used marijuana. The sergeant explains that he then notified his superior, Lt. Hash.

Lt. Hash is now called forward and testifies that he had questioned Airman Smith and asked him to open his locker but that Smith said he had lost his key. Hash then called the Air Police.

The Air Policeman is summoned and sworn in. He testifies how he had cut the lock off Airman Smith's locker and found the material that is now contained in and presented as Exhibit A. He states when asked, that it is his opinion that the contents might be an illegal substance, and when asked to explain, states that he thinks it might be marijuana. He is dismissed from the witness chair, walks back to his seat and sits down.

The young man in the gray coat with the large belly and small glasses is summoned and he comes to the chair by the judge's desk and is sworn in. He is motioned to sit down.

The prosecuting attorney approaches the witness.

"State your name, please."

"Bill Budd."

"Mr. Budd, where are you employed?"

"I work for the State of Ohio."

"And in what capacity?"

"I am a Chemist III."

"Have you ever testified in any court before?"

"Yes, this is the 38th case I have testified in."

"Have you ever been certified as an Expert Witness?"

"Yes, I have been certified and have testified as an Expert Witness in my last 18 court testimonies."

"Have you had the opportunity to examine the contents of the package marked Exhibit A?"

"Both my staff and I have examined the contents of Exhibit A."

"Have you reached a conclusion about the contents of Exhibit A?"

"In my professional opinion, the contents of Exhibit A are *Cannabis sativa*."

"Also sometimes known as . . .?"

"Marijuana."

"The prosecution rests its case."

The lieutenant turns around and walks back to his table and sits down.

The other lieutenant rises and approaches the man in the gray suit. It appears from the demeanor of the two men that they know each other well, but are not friendly.

"What college did you attend, sir?"

"The Ohio State University."

"Ohio State, eh?"

"It's located here in Columbus, Ohio, Lieutenant, about six miles north of here."

"What did you major in, sir?"

"Organic chemistry."

"And is that where you received your Ph.D., Dr. Budd?"

"I do not have a Ph.D., we talked about that the last time I was questioned by you."

"I'm sorry, Mr. Budd, I meant, you got . . . then . . . ah . . . what . . . a Master's degree in Science . . . ?"

"I have a BS in Organic Chemistry."

"Oh – only a BS? Well . . . ah . . . perhaps you would like to explain to the court, Mr. Budd, why did you not even attempt to upgrade your education?"

The other lieutenant rises: "Objection, your honor."

"Objection sustained . . . please confine your questions to the issues of the case."

"Mr. Budd, what position did you occupy in the academic order of your class?"

"I don't understand the question."

"Oh, yes . . . I see . . . maybe you can understand if I ask it like this: did you graduate number one in your class, sir, number two, three . . . any idea . . . sir?

The other lieutenant rises: "Objection, your honor, these questions are irrelevant. The witness has already testified that he has earned and was awarded a degree in organic chemistry from the Ohio State University, he is currently employed by the State of Ohio as a Chemist III, and has been certified by the Fourth Judicial Circuit as an Expert Witness in the field of organic chemistry."

"Sustained; Lt. Jones, you may proceed with your questions – please confine them to the facts of the case."

"Mr. Budd, how did you determine the nature of the contents of the exhibit? Was that from your college experiences or what?"

"Lt. Jones, qualified and certified personnel in my office proceeded with the Standard Substance Determination Worksheet in accordance with Ohio State Statute, 421.45, parentheses 3, sub-paragraphs 14 through 26, as outlined in our report already submitted. If you wish, I will be glad to read the procedures in detail and explain the results to you again at length."

"That will not be necessary Mr. Budd. Thank you, I have no further questions."

The man in the gray suit with the thin blue tie pushes his glasses back to the top of his nose with his middle finger while frowning intently at the lieutenant, then he turns and glances at the judge.

The judge looks over the top of his glasses and said "Thank you Mr. Budd. If there are no further questions, you are excused and we thank you for your attendance and testimony."

Mr. Budd gets up and walks out of the courtroom.

The judge now directs the bailiff to come to the front of his desk.

"Sergeant Doe, hand Exhibit A to the Officer of the Court."

The bailiff picks up the exhibit and brings it over and hands it to me.

I gingerly accept the package and lay it on the table in front of me.

"Major, " the judge continues, "can you confirm the nature of the contents of Exhibit A?"

I look at the package.

"Well . . ." I begin.

"Yes . . .?" says the judge, as he glances at his watch, "What is your opinion of the contents?"

"Hmmm. . ." I ponder "Well, I'm not sure . . . ah, exactly . . . what it is." If it really is marijuana, it is the first marijuana I have ever seen in my life.

"Yes, Major, what do you think it looks like?"

"Ahem . . . "I look hard at the package, staring at the close cropped dark stuff which really looks like the clippings I got out of the bag on the back of my lawnmower. I clear my throat, "Well, it looks like . . . ah . . . *grass*?" I say, not really sure.

A snicker runs through the courtroom. I am surprised and look up.

The judge looks straight at me. "What *kind* of 'grass', Major?"

I don't know, so I will be honest. "Lawn clippings."

There are chuckles and one person laughs out loud.

"*Silence*!" The judge says. He seems angry. The Lieutenant lawyer for the prosecution looks at me like I might have just said something that really required clarification; the recorder is looking at me with cocked head, raised eyebrows and puckered lips, her fingers poised above the keyboard; the sergeant next to me chuckles and is looking downward at the edge of his desk and shaking his head with a smile. I glance over toward the judge who is now staring at me with raised eyebrows too.

"Open the package Major," he says in a commanding tone.

"Open . . . ? the package . . . ?" I ask.

"Open - the - package - Major."

I reach for the exhibit and find a taped edge and peel it back. The flaps of the package unfold.

I look back at the judge.

"Now, what does Exhibit A look like, Major?"

I am wishing that I was somewhere else, almost anywhere else. I am not going to say 'grass' again, but that is what it looks like.

I stare into the open container, speechless.

"Smell it Major."

"*Smell* it?"

"Smell Exhibit A, major!"

I hold it to my nose and sniff. It smells good. It takes me back to my high school days, back when I worked on a farm and we used to harvest hay. I smell it again. *it's alfalfa! That's what it is! It's really good alfalfa*. Somehow I can almost remember the warm sun and the breezes that carried the smell of earth and water. I smell it again and seem to hear once more the call of the plovers and killdeer that used to race across the fields . . . I remember the cooling afternoon breezes and the evening dusk . . . .

"What does it *smell* like, Major?"

"Oh! . . . uh, I don't know . . . exactly. . ."

"Well, what does it *remind* you of, Major, speak up?"

"Well . . . ah . . . really, it reminds me of . . . " Now I am starting to get mad. "Alfalfa, it reminds me of *alfalfa*!" I say decisively.

The judge gestures in an irritated manner. "Pass it to the next man!" The recorder is typing rapidly on her keyboard.

I hand it to the sergeant who passes it under his nose and hands it straight to the lieutenant next to him. "Marijuana," he says matter of factly.

The lieutenant passes it to the airman next to him, commenting "Marijuana."

"Marijuana."

"Marijuana."

"Marijuana."

The bailiff retrieves the exhibit and securely tapes it back together again while staring at me and places it on the table in front of the judge.

The judge stares at me for a moment, then he turns to the young airman. "Do you wish to enter a plea?"

The airman mutters something.

"Stand and face the court!" the judge orders.

The young man stands up and faces the judge.

"Now how do you plead – guilty or not!"

"Guilty, your honor."

There are faint signs of sobbing from the audience.

"Your honor," The lieutenant lawyer representing the young man stands up. "We would like to introduce character witnesses for the accused."

The judge looks down on his table at a list. "Hmmm, let's see, we have his mother, father, girl friend, and preacher, is that it?"

"Yes, your honor."

"I believe we can dispense with that." He turns to me. "Major, does the jury have any questions before you begin deliberations?"

I look at the others sitting at my table. They are all looking down at the table in front of them.

"All rise!"

We stand up as the judge leaves. Then the bailiff leads us out to another room.

The deliberation is pretty brief, there's not much to say. We summon the bailiff who leads us back to the courtroom.

The judge enters and sits down. He looks at me.

"Have you reached a verdict?"

"Yes we have," I respond.

"Will you stand and face the defendant?" the judge asks.

I stand, holding a piece of paper.

"Stand and face the Officer of the Court," the judge commands the young airman.

The airman stands and faces me.

"What is your verdict?" the judge asks.

"We, the jury, find you guilty as charged." I say. Then the young airman and I both sit down.

The judge speaks to the airman: "You are sentenced to ten years at hard labor, and a dishonorable discharge from the United States Air Force." A flashbulb goes off. The judge motions to the bailiff. "Take him away."

"All rise!"

★ ★ ★

I go home to find orders. They always come in when you least expect them. It's kind of like you let your guard down and then they sneak in and get you. I will be leaving for my first tour in Vietnam and Thailand to direct B-52 bombing attacks. I will leave the day before Christmas.

A couple of days later, over at the Officer's Club, I see the lieutenant lawyer who had prosecuted the young airman. I go over to him.

"Hi, major, " he smiles " You're the 'alfalfa guy'!"

"I am amazed at that sentence – ten years!" I say, "That was awful!"

"Oh, no big deal . . ." the lieutenant sips his drink. "It will be appealed – has to be, since it's military – and the sentence will be overturned and converted to a special discharge and he'll be out of the service in two months."

"Well, what was the ten years at hard labor and dishonorable discharge about?"

"That was for the base newspaper - to scare the other kids. So, you're an old farm boy eh?"

# 38
# Over Easy

My orders were delayed 48 hours so I will leave for Vietnam on December 26, and I get to spend Christmas at home. It's a strange Christmas though, nothing seems to work quite right and we're not sure what is wrong. Long pauses appear in our sentences and my eyes seem to be focused both near at hand, at the faces of my kids, and at the same time far away on the other side of the world. I see their bright smiles and also dark shadows of approaching events.

We toss a small rubber football about, watch specials on TV and pretend it's all OK. I fix some presents that break early enough, and about mid-afternoon get a stepladder and begin taking down the lights, then the tree. I pack the pretty decorations into old cardboard boxes, and can't help but wonder if I will be the one who opens them up next year. Last minute work is spent on income tax forms so they can be completed when the other forms come in so they can be filed on time. War being not an acceptable excuse for a late return.

I tuck my kids in bed for the last time this year. The next time I hear their prayers they will have grown a good bit. Important days of their lives will take place and I won't be with them to take part in those things. I will have to find a way to make that up. It will have to wait though until I get back. I just can't think about that right now.

This trip to Vietnam I will not be flying as a crewmember but will travel almost like a civilian tourist. On the first leg I will even wear civilian clothes and fly on a Delta airliner. This is really going "Over Easy." What could possibly go wrong?

At the airport though, I find there is a problem with my orders. They looked normal to me, and my administrative section back in the squadron saw nothing wrong with them. The reservations have been made all the way through, and there is even a boarding pass ready for me, but they won't let me have it. The Air Force has not yet paid for the ticket. I can't find a telephone to use, there is only one at the counter and it has a line of about six people waiting to use it. So, I pull out my personal charge card and pay my own way to Vietnam – the first leg, at least. I assume the Air Force will eventually reimburse me but that will probably be at least ninety days from now. Then, when my baggage is searched, my Swiss Army knife fails to pass, and it is confiscated.

"Why do you want a knife on this flight?" I am asked.

"Because I'm going to war, and may need it to fight with when I get there." I reply, trying not to appear too edgy-looking. Finally I get the knife back and put it into my checked baggage.

Eventually, I am off from New York en route to San Francisco, Travis, and Vietnam. First part of the trip will be in a 707, and we'll chase the sun to California. I settle back to read a magazine although really I just hold it and look at it from time to time. Occasionally I turn a page or two. Emotionally, I feel totally uninvolved in anything. I am quiet and complacent. My nerves are well shielded. I have not yet been stung by those great feelings of loss, which I know are coming. I have not yet thought of what I will do when I get back home tonight, or what I will do with the kids this weekend. It is normal working hours right now; I would be at work at this time of day anyway, and all still seems well. I feel calm and can actually enjoy the refreshing change from the frantic days of racing breathlessly through my life, chasing after fleeting time. Right now I have all the time in the world. A contrail appears beside us, far off our left wing, it is wispy and curly, like ocean waves sketched through the thin blue air. Below lie dark foothills, and ahead great shining mountains rise out of the snow. A martini and shish kebab dinner make the trip more pleasant.

The airport in San Francisco seems neglected, and shows signs of wear and tear; *probably all the war traffic,* I think. The bus ride to Travis is surprisingly quick and it is over before I am ready for it to end. The base is a sprawling and messy dirty place filled with sullen people. The Military Airlift Command Terminal is choked with cigarette smoke and everything stinks. I buy postcards and mail them home, and then I quickly call and talk to my family. My youngest even leaves Popeye on TV to come talk with me – how deep is her love!

We're airborne with the sunset, rising out of the smog. Five and a half hours later we pass over Anchorage. With no other lights around, it looks like an open cluster of stars – one might try to remember its Messier number. Now we have seven and a half hours left. Hours later, through cupped hands I watch stars rise and set in the December Siberian night over our right wing. It is a thirteen-hour ride with 225 people in an aircraft filled with cigarette smoke so thick that it has become a pallid, foul and greasy stench that burns our eyes and noses and throats. From somewhere comes a new smell - a cigar has been lighted by a lt. colonel. He is asked to put it out and he refuses, and points out all the cigarette smoke. "Make them put theirs out." Finally the pilot comes out to ask him to extinguish his cigar and the lt. colonel - who is a command pilot himself, tells the pilot to get back to his job and get to work. When he is threatened with being "reported", he waves his cigar in the air and says, "What the hell *can* happen? I'm on my way to Vietnam! What can be worse than *that*?" Then he points to the cockpit and tells the pilot (who is civilian) to get back to his job and pretend he knows how to do it.

Tokyo appears as a spreading cluster of large towns that look like they have been woven together into a lace-work of lights. When we land at Yokoto AB, I buy more cards, write messages to my kids and drop them in the mail.

An hour and ten minutes later we are airborne again, en route to Kadena Air Base on Okinawa and another one-hour layover. Finally, we are airborne again, this time heading for Clark Field in the Philippines and a BOQ room. I walked out of my home 33 hours ago, and it has been dark for the last consecutive 25 of them. This much darkness seems unreal, and encountering it reminds me of stories I have heard about alien abductions. When I walk off the airplane I find I wobble. Tomorrow morning I will go in-country.

Vietnam is visible in the early morning light from quite a distance out, but we land at Saigon in dense brown smog. Tan-Son-Nhut is awesomely crowded. Airplanes seem to have been shoved together like part of a great traffic jam. Revetments are everywhere and tails of many more planes stick out above them.

I am driven over to "Camp Alpha," where I fill out endless forms and trade in my US dollars for "script." I have $22 dollars left out of the $50 I had taken with me from home.

Next, I go to the detachment where I meet my commander and the men of the organization. Two large notebooks are handed to me. I must study them later today and take a test on them tomorrow. One is titled "OI," or "Operating Instructions", and the other is "ROE," or "Rules of Engagement".

The world seems a bit too bright and it appears to slow its spin a little from time-to-time. I have a hoarse, racking cough and a sore throat from breathing the cigarette smoke of the long flight; otherwise, I am in good shape for having just come from the other side of the earth in one day, or was it two? (One day for us on the plane, two for the rest of the world.) The sky clears up & reminds me of days I've seen in southern Louisiana, down in the delta, or maybe on the Texas gulf coast. It is blue, pale blue, but there are shadows in the sky too, and its light lies on leaves and the ground in a manner that speaks of rain to come later in the day.

I am scheduled to return home on June 23 – 179 days from the day I left. If you are gone for over 181 days, you get credit for half a tour in SEA, if less than 181 days you get no credit. Like great numbers of SAC personnel fighting this war, I will get no credit for this tour to Southeast Asia. After I return home, I am scheduled to come back over here for another 179-day tour, again earning no credit. When I return after that second tour, I will be reassigned to another base. It will almost certainly be a year in Southeast Asia, because "officially" I will have never been over here.

I left home in a December snowfall; but that was yesterday, and a long, long time ago; today it's midsummer. Christmas never happened, it was just a strange dream. My kids seem like a memory from my own childhood. I try to think of what they are doing right now. But I'm eating lunch at noon; and it's midnight back there, and they are all asleep.

I have already met a few friends I knew in KB-50s, and KC-135s and one from the Titan II program. There are also a lot of new friends to make. Probably the best thing about coming to Southeast Asia is that you are warmly welcomed into your new, temporary Air Force family, and you never know whom you are going to see again for the first time in a long time.

# 39
# Effingies

When it is nine o'clock in New York it is also nine o'clock in Saigon, but one of them is a.m. and the other is p.m. That's just one of a number of adjustments awaiting new arrivals in Southeast Asia.

The weather is also different, and can be quite a change, especially for those arriving fresh from a Montana or New York winter. Most new arrivals are also in a small degree of shock having just gone through rather traumatic good-byes to family and friends, and some are almost unable to function for the first day or two. Generally, the most strongly affected are those who left very young children behind, or pregnant wives, or those who had recently married.

One thing that helps these New Guys is that everybody else over here has already been through the same thing, and they know how these new arrivals feel. So, the New Guys are welcomed and absorbed into a rather large family all of which have at least three things in common. One is that they are all in a war zone; second, that they have all left family behind; and the third is that each New Guy who arrives brings everybody else closer to the arrival of their own replacement and the day when they can go back home themselves.

The New Guys gradually become aware of a strange term they constantly hear, usually directed at them: "FNG."

As I recall, FNG is an acronym for something like "Friendly New Guy," or "Funny New Guy," or "Fresh New Guy", or something like that. Actually, I've kind of forgotten now, but I know the "New Guy" part is right. The first word probably is "Friendly," but then again, it could have been something else. At any rate, the term "F-N-G," is generally shortened to "FNG," or a phrase that sounds a lot like "Effingy." So, about the time you notice that you are being called an Effingy, you have already been over here for a few days, and people now newer than you are already arriving, and you find yourself automatically referring to them as Effingies.

You hear yourself asking "Who's the Effingy over there?" nodding your head in the general direction of a group of people.

The person you are with might glance in that direction, where perhaps fifty people are standing, and immediately respond, "Oh, he's from the 5th Bomb Wing back in Travis. He's been in a staff position so long, they had to send his desk and chair over with him."

Maybe someone will nudge you and ask you who the Effingy is as he points vaguely at another group. You will look for a moment, and then say "I know him, but I can't remember exactly where we met, maybe Offutt, once."

Now how does that happen? What do Effingies have in common?

An Effingy always has his fatigue shirtsleeves cut short. New fatigues are not a giveaway because the garments wear out and are replaced from time to time. But since they have heard that it is so hot over in SEA, Effingies want to have short sleeves so they can feel cooler. The older heads know it sometimes gets cold enough at night that rolled down sleeves can feel good. Also the sleeves provide some protection from mosquitoes, including the malaria carriers, and they provide a respite from the intense tropical sun. Many Air Force personnel work in vans and trailers with radar and computers where temperatures are often kept down to around 62° to 64°. While that would sound great to a grunt out in the steamy muck, the people who work in those temperatures for 10 to 14 hours each day get a bit chilly. So one way you could spot an Effingy was by his short sleeves.

Another sure give-away of the Effingies is when the topless dancers take the stage at the club. An Effingy is the guy who stares at them. There is usually a new girl who will replace one of the older dancers every month and when she comes out on the stage for the first time, completely dressed of course, she gets everybody's attention. Cries of "New Girl!" can be heard all over the bar, usually someone adds, "She's an Effingy!" ("Friendly" New Girl) "We got an Effingy on the stage!" As she dances, she will take her shirt off, then remove an undershirt, and then another undershirt, and continue to shed various layers of clothing accompanied by hoots and claps, as she goes through one or two short dance routines, finally becoming completely bare-breasted, and then everyone will turn back to their previous topic of conversation until next month. All, that is, except for one or two people in the audience who will sit and stare at the girls and their bare breasts. Other people might notice one of them and ask someone, "Who's the Effingy over there?"

Effingies try to pick the roach pieces out of their bread. Now some people who have been to Florida, for example, may be under the impression that they have seen roaches before; but if they have never been to Vietnam, they just don't understand. They may have seen some "roach impersonators," but those are not the Real Deal. Most of the Florida roaches are timid and run from man but over here they know this land is their land, and they are mastering it by eating it. So everything, including bread flour is full of roaches, and when the flour is kneaded by machine, the roaches that are in there, or that crawl in, still eating, are squashed and killed and torn apart, and then all the parts are mixed in together. The bread is baked at 450° and all is sterilized and sanitized. The final product is perfectly healthy (according to the veterinarians, who are responsible for inspecting the military food) and even tastes OK, except for two minor details. One is that it looks like

the bread has been sprinkled with pepper and slivered almonds, and the other is that it has a slightly almond-bacon taste to it. If some of these brownish specks are picked at, they may reveal various things like an occasional roach leg, or wing parts. Really brand new Effingies don't know about this and eat their bread like seasoned troopers. But after they have been over here for about three or four days, they ask questions and they find out. Then they don't eat any bread at all for a week or two, and when they do resume, for the next month or so they pick out all the pieces they can find. Often, when a guy is seen picking out part of a leg, with an expression on his face that looks like he is going to throw up, someone across the mess hall will ask the person sitting next to him, "Where is that Effingy assigned?" The other person will glance across the mess hall, surveying perhaps 50 or 60 people. "Oh, he's the new Morale Officer. He came here from MacDill."

If a person thinks the war is for a good cause, or we might yet win in the end, or that it is to make the

Vietnamese free, these are also sure signs that he is an Effingy. Anyone who thinks they will be personally enriched from their service over here is probably so new that they haven't really got here yet.

Effingies still think they might find a dark and quiet place in which to sleep. Constant light and endlessly pulsating boom boxes dominate the sweltering nights, at least on base.

Aircraft, including heavily loaded fighter bombers take off around the clock, shaking the ground and vibrating the buildings as they go. Effingies are easily spotted by their obvious signs of fatigue and by dozing at their desks during daylight hours. Sometimes they forget to take their earplugs out until they get to breakfast. Effingies are not yet so tired that they can go to sleep whenever they have even a poor excuse.

Effingies' rooms are filled with briefcases, shoes, belts and other beautiful items that are made out of the very finest leather-looking cardboard. For $40 you can buy a mahogany coffee table that would cost $2,000 back in the States. There are a lot of these tables in the barracks and billets because there is no way to take them home, and shipping heavy wood back to the States will cost about five dollars a mile. So when you finally do leave, unless you are a general or VIP (who do take these items back by the plane load), you will be allocated two bags and thirty-four pounds of baggage for all of your belongings.

Somewhere during the tour, usually long after they have officially ceased being a technical Effingy, most people make the complete break. Often that is signified by something like selling the $2000 coffee table that they bought for $40 to someone else for $50, and then investing the proceeds in jewelry or photo equipment. Who could you possibly sell a coffee table to if they could not take it back home?

Well, new Effingies arrive every day.

# 40
# Skyline Ridge

Two weeks ago, I sat on a couch with my dad in his old Kentucky home watching a news conference on TV. Members of the press constantly asked President Nixon questions. They kept hitting him about reports that American B-52s were bombing in Laos, a country that was officially neutral. Nixon kept insisting that we were NOT bombing there, that would be against international law and we would never even consider doing that. He got so mad that when he shook his head his jowls wobbled.

My dad was furious. “Why don’t they leave him alone? He’s not bombing there! They ask him if is he and he says ‘No!’ and they keep trying to trick him! He’s our president! They act like they think he is lying!”

I knew at the time several things: One was that we WERE bombing in Laos, two was that the missions were classified Top Secret, third that Nixon WAS lying, and fourth, that I could not say a word about any of this even to my father. He, in the view of the Defense Department, did not *need* to know and he did not *have a right* to that information. He was only an American citizen.

Now, two weeks later, in the northern jungles of Thailand on a base outside of Udon-Thani, we are running B-52 missions around the clock. We are striking the very targets those reporters had been seeking answers to and the president had been denying existed at that press conference.

These missions were supposedly classified “Top Secret”. I asked who had authorized such a classification when I got on base. The site commander told me “The Office of the President.” Furthermore, those same orders directed that all records pertaining to these strikes be destroyed by burning twenty-four hours after they were complete, again on orders from the Office of the President. I was perplexed. These were almost all the missions we were now working. What were we sending back to SAC headquarters? It must have looked like we were on vacation and not doing any thing at all.

This seemed even stranger when reports of the B-52 strikes were carried in local Thai papers from time to time, and Gen. Vang Pao, the commander of the Lao forces there, kept giving press conferences of his own, usually with European or Asian reporters about how "his" B-52s would destroy his enemies and how he called them in to strike in Laos again and again. There was even an occasional story or two about these missions that even showed up in the *Pacific Stars and Stripes*.

This was amazingly strange. It seemed that everybody on the base knew "we" (meaning we the United States) were bombing the hell out of Laos, especially that we had hit the almost mythical Skyline Ridge just under the Long Cheng area very hard on numerous occasions. Our organization seemed to be the only ones who knew the work was Top Secret and since it "officially" was, we had to act like we didn't know anything about it, so we appeared to be the only people on the base who didn't even know it was being done, or who might be doing it.

Then again, that was also true of many things over here including CIA, Air America, opium, gold, and endless other things - were they all true? Were any of them true? No - here in Vietnam, nothing is ever true. Here, there is no such thing as truth. Everything is an illusion. We are always being fooled. And to a fool, truth is just a word you say about something to make it feel good to other people. And then, who is the real fool?

All this is taking place as the Thais begin burning off their rice fields. They have probably done this for thousands of years but it is suffocating. At first it seemed good because it supplanted the normal smell of Thailand, which to me always had seemed like the smell of a wet shoe or sock. But now the smoke gives the impression that we are in a murky fish bowl. You can look steadily at the sun in the afternoon - a dull reddish blob. Black "snow" drifts lazily down and covers everything on the face of the earth. I wonder if that happens up in Laos. Probably not. Their main crops, we have heard, are poppies and 500 pound bombs.

# 41
# Fingers and Fists

Every American military installation has a chapel, and almost anywhere in Vietnam or Thailand during the war in Southeast Asia, when protestant fundamentalists gathered for a service, a remarkable sight could often be seen. Some of the guys would shake hands with each other, and then swivel their hands and fingers so that their index fingers were pointing upwards, and shout "Jesus! - The One!" Then they would break the handshake and hold their index finger pointing straight into the air, and say simultaneously, "Praise the Lord!" After that they would laugh and pat each other on the back, or maybe, after they have pointed their fingers skyward and said "Praise the Lord!" they would spin around in a 360° circle, bend over, slap their knees, swoop to an erect position, point straight skyward again and say "And brother, you *better* believe it!"

Usually this only took place at or around the chapel, and if it were seen elsewhere on the base it would be regarded as strange. However, when two people who attended the same protestant church service would meet on the base they often exchanged the sign of the raised index finger, signifying "Jesus the One." It was a kind of a salute.

Many African-American servicemen were often seen engaged in a practice they called the "Dap." The "Dap" is a ritual that could be carried out by two people on opposite sides of a road, with just one very subtle and virtually unnoticeable hand/arm gesture toward each other. But it can also be an elaborately complex and intricate ritual that might involve several people and block entire sidewalks, and go on for five minutes or longer. The participants might shuffle a "dance", touch hands, arms, backs, and bump fists, arms and maybe even rumps. It sometimes ended with all the "Dappers" holding their fists high in the air as in a salute, with their knuckles facing backward like the "salute" that John Carlos used to scandalize the 1968 Olympics. It has been called the Black Power salute, and the Air Force didn't like it but couldn't figure out what to do about it. Trying to ban it would have lead to a mutiny or worse – cries of racism. So it was rather commonplace, officially ignored and apparently a matter of great satisfaction to the participants.

The "Jesus the One" and the "Dap Salute" were only two of the gestures commonly seen by military personnel in Southeast Asia. Another symbol, well known in most parts of the world, the civilized world that is, is the fist pointed toward some antagonist with the middle finger pointed skyward, the well known, "screw you" gesture. This symbol is not unknown in the combat area either, although never to my knowledge directed at an authentic Rules of Engagement enemy; more often reserved for Rules of Engagement friendlies, usually those of superior rank who were not currently present.

And then, there is the good old "V For Victory" sign, made famous by FDR, and its Churchillian Corollary which is the same as FDR's except that the fist is aimed at the receptor, and not the grantee. All of these last three symbols are bone-fide military salutes and are related to each other; descendants, reputedly, from the Battle of Agincourt, back in 1415, wherein the English archers proudly and defiantly showed the French infantry (who would amputate the middle finger, or first two, of captured archers) that they still possessed the fingers that provided the power to pull the longbow, and thus could still shoot an arrow (called a "bird" because of its feathers) at them.

Most souvenir and jewelry stores in Thailand and Vietnam had Buddha's, unicorns, incense burners, dancing girls, minatours, and what nots for sale one after another. They caught on to what the GIs were doing and began making and stocking life-size statues of these fists and fingers for sale to their American customers. Some had them lined up row after row, rank and file. They were usually grouped in common collections with perhaps twenty "Jesus the One" fists right next to twenty "Screw You" fists, and then twenty more "Black Power" fists, and so on. Some of the fingers/ fists were hand carved out of mahogany, but most were made from monkey pod wood, and there were a large number that had been forged out of brass, left over from our spent artillery shells.

Many of the American service personnel who were working desk jobs had at least one of the fist/finger symbols. They were used as paperweights or simply desk decoration. You could often tell what kind of a person you were approaching by glancing at the fist/finger on his/her desk. Index finger skyward usually meant fundamentalist Christian; a fist with no fingers probably belonged to an African-American "brother"/"sister." The "V-for-Victory" sign probably indicated someone who had just arrived into Southeast Asia on his/her first tour, or perhaps the owner's supervisor was a high-ranking officer who was currently in the immediate vicinity. The "Churchillian Corollary" had to belong to either a history major or someone else who was equally mixed up. And the middle finger pointed skyward indicated someone who had an important story to tell about what had just happened to him/her. Often this symbol meant its owner was within 30 days of completing his/her tour of duty in Vietnam and returning to the States.

Some people had the entire collection and would move them on and off their desks from day to day or even as momentary moods possessed them, or as various people came and went.

Several of the bases had taken the jeeps assigned to the base chapel and had a GI drill a small hole in the front top of the hood and affix a "Jesus the One" brass index finger pointing skyward like a hood ornament. The fundamentalist chaplains apparently enjoyed riding around the base behind this magnificent ornament, so the Catholic chaplains often retaliated by having a brass "Jesus on the Cross" mounted on the dashboard. Crosses are OK with most protestants, but not crucifixes, so that was a subtle measure of vengeance of which the Lord would perhaps have been proud, or maybe not. No one ever seemed to have checked with the Jewish chaplains, but then there weren't many of them. I guess they rode around with a "Dashboard Jesus" and a "Jesus the One" brass hood ornament, as just a couple more justifications for the validity of the faith of their own fathers.

On at least one of these bases the chaplains were astonished to find that their brass "Jesus the One" hood ornament had been replaced with a brass "Screw You" hood ornament, and all the chaplains had been riding around in their "God Squad" jeeps, behind that salute to the base for several days before they discovered it. The culprit was never caught, but everybody on the base, except the chaplains, had known about it. One of the chaplains commented later, "I wondered why everybody was smiling and waving at us!"

One of the mysteries of the war has become what happened to all the fingers and fists? They were all over the war zone, so common that I never even thought about photographing one, but I have never seen one since I left.

# 42
# Calling Home

I arrived at the radar site at 1730. We conducted several B-52 bomb runs, and then ran TAC fighter-bombers from 0200 to 0400. Beginning at 0500, we had two more B-52 compression bomb runs. Later, four more runs finished the day for me.

I was relieved as Senior Mission Director at 0700 and went back down the hill. Ate breakfast, then to bed about 0815. Up again at 1430.

Then to the weight room, trying to start working out again.

Later to the library where I checked out some books on the stock market and read the Wall Street Journal, already a week old. I will start investing again when I get back home four months from now. I am too far out of the loop to try any of that now.

At the barbershop I looked through a pile of magazines on a table. As I picked up the third one, about 15 roaches ran out from under it. I decided to think instead of read. The Vietnamese barber grinned at me and kept repeating the Vietnamese word for roach. “Gong ka chep! Gong ka chep!” He tapped on a wall near his certificate that hung in a picture frame, and three roaches crawled out from behind it. He smiled. I didn’t.

Back to the site again for another night of bombing. A fine drippy mess of rain fell from the sky all night long.

Next morning I returned to my trailer, still in a fine mist which fell through a great fog. To bed at 0815, up at 1430. When I opened my door to throw my used tea leaves out, I stared at a world afloat in a shallow sea. An endless rain was falling. Everything was soaked and dripping. Water stood an inch deep everywhere.

I walked to the BX for shaving cream. They had none. Today starts their second week without any cream. And of course, beards are not permitted by Air Force regulations.

The chow hall had rubber shrimp, green liver and burned onions. I got a rancid cheeseburger served up on a brown paper towel since they were out of plates.

Back to work again later. Lost one run due to radar and had another that was a "withhold"; not sure why, will have to read the report tomorrow.

Walked around the site. Saw a beautiful back bird with brown wings, the size of a big crow. He looked at me and hissed. Then he hopped over to me and flapped his wings at me and hissed again. I waved my arms and hissed at him and he flew away.

To bed at 0815 and up at 1430. Again to the weight room. It is a dull, lifeless day with rain endlessly falling. Back to the trailer to play out a game of chess from the Fisher/Spasky match book. Later read the *Bridge Over San Louis Rey.*

The chow hall had a good evening meal and the sun came out. The world was beautiful and fresh. Birdsong was everywhere, and the smell of flowers and earth seemed good.

I rode up the hill to the site with a young sergeant, a happy guy. I realize he is the first happy person I have talked with in five days. The night was busy. Twelve bomb runs kept us hopping.

To bed about 0815, up about 1400. Paddle ball at the "gym" by myself, hitting the ball up against the wall since no body else was around.

Waited for a bus for 45 minutes. It never came.

Walked back to base supply, finally got a light bulb for my room. The BX also got a few, must have been a flight came through.

Capt Gone left today, and I got his refrigerator! Yea! Now I'm cooking! Hand-carried it all the way back to my trailer. Heavy!

Rearranged my room. The refrigerator makes it crowded in here now. Wow.

Ran two miles today.

The Thais were burning off the rice fields and the smoke was extremely dense. Couldn't see 100 feet. Couldn't breathe either.

Played tennis this afternoon. Then had dinner in an off-base restaurant where I ate wonderful food that smelled like the earth itself.

Outdoor movie. We sat there in front of the screen on benches. It was fine for the first hour. Then the rain started. We all left when it started coming down hard. The movie just stopped.

Up late, at 1000. Had a long breakfast, then to church. No protestant preachers showed up. Went to the Catholic services instead, and then lay in the sun for 45 minutes. After that ran three miles on a 105° day. Later had a good meal at an off-base restaurant.

Spent one and a half hours in the MARS (Military Affiliate Radio Service) station tonight trying to call home. The telephones don't reach back to the states and the only way you can "call home" is through MARS, which is an amateur radio service using radio broadcasts, meaning you have an operator listening in so you can tell him when to switch over, by saying "over". So it goes a little like this: "Hello honey, how are you - over" "Hi Sweetheart, we're fine, how are you - over" "I love you - over" "I love you too - over". Some people can't hack that kind of thing. The MARS people advise you to write home and tell them when you plan to call before you try, so there will be sure to be someone home. Since I hadn't gotten a letter from anybody back in the States for almost two months now, I had written three letters home last week saying I would try to call tonight. There were six people ahead of me. They all went within 30 minutes. Good connections with the states tonight! Finally my name was called and I went into the booth. The phone at my home rang several times and my heart sank with each ring after the third one.

"There's no answer Charlie", the guy on the other end, back in Arizona said.

"That's the first one out of 27 tonight." the guy on this end said.

"That's not bad – not bad at all."

"OK thanks" said the guy on my end.

"Sorry sir, there's no answer at your place, you might write them and let them know when you plan to call."

"When will you guys be up again?" I asked.

"Probably we'll try to get up next Thursday."

Back to the club, walking in the rain again. A couple of beers, then to bed. I wonder what is happening to my family. The war is slowly becoming more than we seem to be able to handle. I wish I could be there. But I can't. I can't call home, my letters don't seem to get through. I've got three more months. Now what?

# 43
# Genesis Loophole

Little Billy Jones was hurting bad. The news from home got worse everyday. Nobody knew what his problem was, the doctors weren't sure and Billy's mother was sick with grief. Billy and his mom were in Tennessee, and Billy's daddy was in Thailand. He worked in my detachment, and I was his Operations Officer. I talked to the commander and we agreed to meet with the chaplain's office to see if they could help us get Billy's daddy back home. I made an appointment and headed for the chapel.

The chaplain was in conference when I got there so I told the receptionist I would wait. She led me to a spacious covered patio with several tables.

She was a beautiful young Thai, one of those people who are probably descended from inhabitants of the islands south of Thailand. I wondered if she was still a teen-ager, and guessed she is probably about sixteen or seventeen years old.

"Thank you very much!" I said as she pulled out a chair for me and I sat down.

She placed her hands palm to palm with fingertips pointing upward near her heart and said, "Ef you need soam ething, jus scallmee!" and bowed slightly.

"OK, I will." I thought for a moment. "What is your name?"

She smiled and bowed again. "My nome ih s'Thuck Lieh."

Her eyes sparkled with the brilliance of Christian love, and her graceful gestures reminded me of peacefully flowing water. "OK, Thuck Lieh," I said, " thank you very much."

"Woo dyou car efo rteee?" she asked.

"Thank you," I said opening up my notebook. "That would be nice."

She bowed again and left. I briefly reflected on how fortunate she was to have escaped the ravages of war. If she had not found a job working at the base chapel she would probably be living with an airman as his girlfriend for a year, or working as a prostitute.

While I made some changes to a report I brought with me, a young airman sat down at the next table.

"Hello, Major," he said as I glanced at him.

"Hi," I answered. I had attended some of the Protestant services and remembered that this young man had been working as usher or assistant to the chaplain, and I had seen him doing some janitorial and administrative work here. "Are you assigned to the chapel?" I asked.

He grinned. "I get asked that a lot," as he shook his head. "I work at Base Supply, building T-780, but I guess I do spend a lot of time here too."

We talked for a few minutes before Thuck Lieh returned with two glasses of tea.

She placed one of the glasses on my table and bowed again, "Than kyoo for try ingsome of ourteee."

"Oh, thank *you*, Thuck Lieh," I responded.

She turned to the airman. "Woo dyou lyketeee, Broth therTomus?"

He gratefully reaches out for the glass.

*Nice seeing young people who treat each other so well*, I thought as Thuck Lieh left the patio. Well, they both spend a lot of time at the chapel!

"Isn't she wonderful?" the airman asked.

"Indeed." I responded. "Has she worked here very long?"

"I'm not sure, but she was working here when I arrived, about ten months ago."

"Then you're thinking about going home soon?"

He turned his eyes upward as if in a mock prayer, "Oh yes – can't wait!"

"Are you staying in the Air Force?"

"No, I've enjoyed it but I want to go to college." He looked thoughtful. "Maybe study theology. I'm not sure yet."

We talked a few minutes more and then he mentioned he was getting married as soon as he returned. He talked longingly of the lovely lady who was soon to be his bride. Her name was Vicky, and she was the daughter of a preacher in Bloomington, Indiana. She was very active in her father's church, she played the organ and did a lot of charity work. A photo from his wallet proved she was beautiful, complete with blue eyes and blonde hair. He seemed lost in another world as he talked of her on this warm and breezy summer evening on the patio of the base chapel in northern Thailand. He was probably no more than 20 years old and it was very refreshing to find someone of his generation who had put his life together so well.

Then he stood up, tossed down the last of his iced tea and announced he was off for the evening.

"So what do you do on these lonely days?" I asked him. "Where does a young man go for relaxation?"

"Well," he said, "I'm heading to my girl friend's place for the weekend."

"Girl friend? I thought she was in Indiana."

"Oh, that's Vickie – this is Thuck Lieh."

"What?" How could this guy lie so brazenly?

"Wait a minute!" I said as I stood up.

"You said you're in love with Vickie, and you know she is being true to you, and you are both Christians! So how can you spend the night with Thuck Lieh?"

"Oh, Vickie knows about it," he said as he pulled on his cap.

"We talked it over, and I explained about how much I miss her and how worked up I get just thinking about her. And then we talked about Onan and how he was cursed of God because he spilled his seed on the ground, you know, Genesis 38:9. Vickie doesn't want me to get into that kind of trouble with God, and so Thuck Lieh is just helping out Vickie and me."

He picked up his brief case and walked out. "See you Sunday, Sir!"

Suddenly the chaplain was standing beside me. He had a very concerned look in his eyes, and as he held out his hand he said, "What's on your mind, sir?"

# 44
# Songkran

Friday the Thirteenth fell on the first day of the Thai Water Festival in April of 1973. How fitting!

In the western world, Fridays and the number thirteen have been associated with events ranging from just unlucky to downright evil.

The Thai's call their festival "Songkran" (SON'kra) and it is an ancient custom commerating both the ending of the old year and the beginning of the new one. It always takes place in mid-April just before the beginning of the monsoon season. The festival is a four-day long Buddhist celebration in which people help celebrate it by sprinkling a few drops of water on each other and exchanging blessings.

That these two events should coincide seemed to bode something important for the American war in Southeast Asia. We were soon to find out.

I walk out of my hooch that morning in Udorn, Thailand, at about 6:20 a.m. and meet Sanji Puri, one of the maids who help keep our area and clothes clean and in order. She is a quiet, very proper young woman who is perhaps 25 years old, and today she has small brass bowl in her hands. With a bright and beaming face, she dips the fingertips of her right hand into water in the bowl and gently flicks a few drops my way, then she bows, saying something rapidly in Thai, and smiles at me. I am deeply moved and feel strangely cleansed by the beautiful and sacramental Buddhist blessing I have just received. I placed my palms together near my heart and bowed to her, "Thank you Sanji, God bless you." Then I headed over to the Air Force mess hall.

I spend the rest of the day inside my detachment's radar van which is basically a large, humming box filled with wires, computers and vacuum tubes. The so called "van" is actually a series of trailers bolted together with narrow walkways winding through a snakey maze of cables, fans and high voltage warning signs. Air conditioners keep the temperature at a constant 64°. Humidity is virtually zero and no liquid is ever allowed in that area.

One of the compartments of this collection of trailers is the bombing control center. It is a brilliantly lighted room filed with acrid electric smells, radio static and the whine of generators. Here we use ground-to-air radar and computers to direct B-52 bombers of the Strategic Air Command to their target. From here we give them headings and speeds to fly and tell them when to drop their bombs. I am Senior Mission Director, commander of eight to ten junior officer and enlisted crewmembers. We work twelve-hour shifts and usually direct from eight to twenty B-52 runs on each shift. Each bomb run includes three aircraft and each carries 108 five hundred pound bombs. The accuracy of those bomb runs is our responsibility. We also help Tactical Air Command fighter-bombers with their targets whenever they request assistance, which largely depends on visual contact with the ground – and that visibility is often poor. We stay very busy, twenty-four hours every day. Today, we are carrying out combat operations against a large North Vietnamese division that is about 45 miles from our location.

I left the van at about six o'clock in the afternoon, and saw one of our sergeants fling a cup of water at an airman who immediately responded with a cup of his own thrown at the sergeant. Then they both saw me, and mumble something that they hope would be taken as an excuse. I gave them a short look of surprise and walked past them toward my jeep, returning their hasty salute and leaving them in a sort of a bird-like semi-attention pose.

On the way to the mess hall, I noticed that the streets were wet. That seems strange because the monsoons are not due for another week and it hasn't rained in months. A Thai girl comes down the road on a bicycle and a GI raced out and flung a bucket-full of water at her. She lost her balance but didn't fall; he slid into the street, ramming his foot into a gutter rail. I heard the loud snap of his ankle breaking. A couple of his friends ran up to him as he buried his head in his arms shaking in pain; a third GI came up and drenched him with a bucket of water.

Cars and trucks driving across the base were saturated with water from buckets being thrown by GIs, and the streets were covered with water.

In the mess hall some people were dripping water from their soaked clothing, and a cup or two was thrown on people in the line. Then someone flung a bucket of water soaking a whole table of people, many of whom rose up with coffee and milk in their hands to retaliate against the perpetrator who has been caught by others. Suddenly an enormous sergeant with a foghorn voice appeared. He stomped across the mess hall using amazing and fantastic curse words, some of which I have never even heard before. He led the villain off to the sound of cheers and applause, and order returned again to the mess hall.

The great festival had gotten off to a slow start, but by evening it was beginning to build, seeking some kind of a crescendo. I went to the Officers' Club for a couple of beers, and noticed the floors were wet and there were no tablecloths on the tables. A captain, who is a pilot, came racing down the hallway at full blast, and ran into me. "Sorry Major!" he stared at me unsure of what to do next. Then another captain came skidding around a corner with a fire extinguisher in his hand. The first captain raced away but was caught by a dazzle of foam that sent him sliding into a table full of other officers who had been trying to eat a meal. The table, along with food, drink and candle, collapsed into a soggy sputtering mess filled with shouts, curses and orders.

I sneaked away to the outdoor movie – it 's a lot like the old drive-in movies, except that there are benches here instead of places where one might otherwise park a car. Charlton Heston was giving a macho interpretation of his impression of how a Southern Californian would look trying to deliver ten commandments to a batch of movie extras, most of whom do an excellent job of appearing to have never heard any of them before. A small group of Buddhist monks, in their scarlet and yellow robes, sat on the front row as if students completing an assignment. At some parts of the movie which were obviously intended to be dramatic, when Heston finished delivering a monologue in a thunderous voice to the semi-heathens, and then turned (on the screen) and looks up into the heavens as if seeking God's approval, a huge gecko would always rise up on a limb which reached out over the screen and scream: "Phuk KYOUUUU!" The audience roars every time this happens and the monks can be seen whispering among themselves. Finally one of them figured out the reason for the laughter, and then after more excited whispers, they laughed together during one of the quieter parts of the movie. Unexpectedly, someone hurled a bucketful of water on them, they gasped and leapt up; pulling their wet robes about themselves, then giggling, they placed their hands together near their hearts and turning in the general direction of the attack, bowed and said "Sank you, sank you." At least it is warm; when I left the theater at 11:00 p.m., it was 96°.

Saturday the 14th of April.

As I walk out of the hooch, Sanji is waiting for me. She is drenched to the skin and has a bucket of water in her hands and an evil grin on her face. While I am transfixed at the sight of her breasts which show plainly through her wet T-shirt, the thought of spending the next twelve hours in a radar van which has a constant and breezy temperature of 64° – in wet clothing – sends shivers up my spine. I have a cup of steaming coffee in my hand.

"You bastard . . . "I say as I impulsively draw my hand back to throw my coffee at her. I look her in the eye, realizing that the hot coffee could disfigure her, and we both freeze. She drops the bucket to her side and lowers her gaze.

"So solly," she says.

I walk over to the mess hall.

The streets are still wet, but there is no water being thrown. The mess hall is dry and quiet; no water is being thrown in here, either.

I find out there are fourteen personnel in the base hospital as a result of the first day of Songkran. There are large signs all throughout the mess hall stating that the base commander has canceled the remaining three days of the old Thai religious water festival. Anyone found throwing water now faces a court-martial for disobeying a direct order. Of course the Thais are not bound by his edict, but then they don't throw the water in bucketsful either.

At least they didn't used to.

# 45
# Pleiku

Today I fly into our detachment at Pleiku, which carries the call sign "Bongo". I will inspect its files, records, procedures, etc. I will also monitor a bomb run or two to verify that the crews are using basic standardized procedures required on all "Skyspot" operations, and look for any potential problem areas.

Prior to departure at the Tan son Nhut base terminal, I wandered into base operations and ran into a guy dressed in civvies - blue jeans, jungle hat, long-sleeved shirt and tennis shoes. I knew him from somewhere, but couldn't place him. He stared at me, too.

"Charlie," I say, "Charlie Underwood," as his name came back to me, "how are you doing?"

He grins, grabs my hand and says, "Bob – right? Bob Smith? How's it go'in' man?"

"No," I correct my name - he had me confused with someone else - "we spent a night at the BOQ in the Philippines, two months ago"

He stares at me

"You're the guy with the silverware!" I said.

"Oh yeah, Hey man, I gotta go."

He turned and left.

Of course I remembered him. We had met in Clark AB in the Philippines. We were assigned the same room in the BOQ. He had two enormous bags, a B-4 and an A-3, both bulging and both obviously way over the weight limits. I had asked him if he was carrying bombs to Vietnam, and he smiled and "No. It's silverware." And I did see silverware in one of the bags.

"Why you are bringing silverware into Vietnam?"

"Getting rid of stuff my wife doesn't like" he said with a quiet smile.

He was wearing a captain's uniform then, but the next morning he got up early and left before first light, and he also left his uniform hanging in the closet, minus the captain's bars and the name tag. I had always wondered what happened to him. Now I knew even less.

I saw him again later when our aircraft taxied out for take-off . He was standing in front of a C-130 with other guys dressed like he was. The airplane had no tail-number and it also did not have the USAF markings. In fact it had no markings at all. I mentioned that to my seatmate.

"Oh, that's Air America," He said.

"Air America? I've heard of them, but what do they really do?"

"We call it Air Opium," he said "They run drugs and gold out of the country and money into it."

"Well, yeah I've heard that too, but that's just a rumor." I said.

"And they've got secret prisons in Laos and Cambodia"

"How could they get away with all that?" I asked, "Don't they fly food and medicine to the native people?"

My seatmate turned and grinned at me as he rubbed his forefinger and thumb together, "Money?"

The flight was Ok. We landed at Pleiku and I got a ride into the detachment. Met with the site commander, Lt. Col. Jim Smith, We had met briefly before at Vandenberg.

AFB, in California. He had impressed me as being a fine officer well on his way to distinction. Today he looked tired and seemed confused. Turns out he will be rotating home in three weeks and retiring from the service.

I ate at the Officers' Club and had a fancy Mongolian Bar-be-que. By the time it finally got cooked, it had a bit of everything on the buffet line. While in the line, I ran into Jack Jones from the KB-50 days. We ate together. He is on his last tour. He too will retire three months after he returns stateside from this tour.

Next morning I begin my work in the detachment office. First, I check their files. I am surprised to find they are generally sloppy, poorly organized and the documents have inconsistent notations on their margins. My notepad begins filling up. Then I found a document marked "Secret" in the general file. More notes: Why is this document here? Why has it not been missed in the Classified File?

In the afternoon I monitor six bomb runs. I notice a very strange relationship between one of the crew chiefs and his crew.

The crew chief is a Staff Sergeant by the name of Clark. He's a burley guy, mean looking, a real rough-tough guy. He stared his men down and they seemed afraid of him - he pushed them out of his way when he walked around.

I noticed most of his guys had bruises on arms or faces. Later, I found Col. Smith and asked him about this and he said he had not heard anything or noticed any problems.

During a break in the day's bomb runs I borrowed Smith's office and called in each member of Clark's crew

I got strange answers - eye contact was hard to get and hard to keep. I asked questions but got no straight answers. Finally it was Clark's turn.

I'm going home tonight - plane is leaving in less than two hours. I don't have time to waste. I decide to be direct and aim for the bulls-eye. "Clark - why have you been hitting your men?"

He glared at me with fiery hatred "Who told you, Major?"

"They all did" I replied "What do you have to say in your behalf?

"They don't pay attention. They do dumb things. They don't know their own jobs. They're lazy."

"So you hit them?"

"It gets their attention." What I took for a sneer crossed his face. "They NEED it sometimes. "

"You're an NCO, Clark."

"Damn right I am."

" Your primary job is to lead men."

He grins, "Yeah, I lead them – out behind the bombing trailer."

"Clark?"

"Yeah?"

"I am writing a report about this"

"To Smith?" Clark leaned back in his chair. "He doesn't care."

"The report will be in SAC headquarters next week. There will be an investigation. I am recommending you be relieved from your duty and investigated for courts martial action. Each man on your crew will report to the Flight Surgeon for a medical review. There will be more."

Clark got up. "Are you through, Major?"

"Yes." I told him "You're dismissed"

I talked to Col. Smith about replacing Clark - he said he couldn't do anything. He was short of men. Clark was his best crew chief. He needed Clark. I had to go. Got an airman to run me down to Base Operations. Barely made my flight.

On the return flight I came back on a C-130. I went up to the flight deck to watch the crew and noticed that the aircraft commander had his eyelids Scotch-taped to his forehead to keep them fully open. I had heard that advanced syphilis could cause a failure of the eyelids - but in an Air Force officer? In the 1970's? But - it *is* Vietnam.

Good to get back. Tonight there's a new girl on the stage at the Officers' Club. Everybody turns and watches as she comes out, we begin clapping and cheering. She begins her routine and slowly strips down. As she progresses, most of us begin to feel a little bit sorry for her. It's obvious she wasn't built for this line of work. We all turn back to our previous conversations.

Later, I glance around the club at all the other men, and wonder if we aren't all a little bit like the "new girl" up on the stage. Maybe it's time for some of us to go look for new jobs too.

# 46
# Peepers

"Thai Food is dangerous." The new report from Pacific Air Force HQ began, "It is contaminated with microbiological organisms and should not be eaten by American Service Personnel." The report concluded by stating that "Consumption of this dangerous food could lead to sickness, be detrimental to the war effort, and could lead to judicial action."

Most of us had eaten some of this food almost every day, and many of us had done so on earlier tours with no adverse reactions. No illnesses were reflected in the healthy and energetic Thais with whom we constantly worked. Some of us thought we could discern a favor being paid by the U.S. government to certain American food corporations. Shipping American food to our troops in Vietnam would be an easy way to get rid of food that could not be sold on a free market!

A number of us ate many meals "downtown". Most of that food had been freshly prepared and featured unfrozen Thai meat and fresh, probably organic produce. But now almost all of "our" food would be placed in a "pipeline" that would slowly bounce and hump its way across the wide Pacific by freighter, heading for its new captive consumers.

A few people recalled similar action throughout Europe occurring after Bob McNamara had taken over the Defense Department. I had been in the Azores when that happened. The immediate result was that the food in the Officers' Club there went from being some of the best in the Atlantic region to the absolute worst that could be found anywhere.

A second result was that the amount of American money received by the Azorean taxis and off-base eating establishments soared. Of course, back then too, we were told that the food off base was not safe to eat, but we already knew better than that.

Now, on the other side of the world, and many years later, Thai taxi numbers were penciled in beside the pay

phones at the Officers' Club, and in time a running commentary was accrued and posted on the walls next to the numbers about the relative merits of different establishments. Club personnel periodically erased this commentary, and from time to time it was painted over. But any waiter in the Officers' Club (all of whom were Thai) could smilingly tell you how to find very good food, and other things as well, off base. Consequently, the Club no longer was a place to gather for supper and perhaps spend an evening, but a place to meet, have a drink, talk with the waiters, and call a taxi.

As far as the sanitary quality of the food in the Thai towns was concerned, there was no way any of us had to measure that. Base veterinarians (responsible for certifying military food) had no way to test the food off base either, except empirically, since we saw some of them eating their evening meals there too.

The produce had an extremely fresh, earthy taste to it; the meat was juicy and usually could be cut with a fork; the bread was unlike any we had ever eaten before and the french-fried potatoes were tough little browned things that exploded with flavor in your mouth as you chewed them. The air in the restaurants was always filled with the aroma of Asian spices, the smell of fresh meat and the sizzle of those fantastic French fries.

Late in February of 1970 a new restaurant called "the Green Coffee House" opened down on the beach. It was Thai owned and operated, and their food was a mix of Thai, Japanese, Chinese, Italian, French and American! A magnificent Filet Mignon could be bought for $1.50. The only thing - was it's spelling: "Feelie me yong."

The rest of the menu was an exciting adventure in working with a newly invented language. All reading of the menu had to be done out loud, because it was an aural language, useless to sight comprehension. One would read the menu out loud to one's self, or to one's companions, slowly. If that didn't work, you would read it out loud quickly.

Several of us had already copied down parts of some menus from all over Asia but The Green Coffee House was a triumph. It began with Fried Porkshops, and then offered Barbed cute dead Porkshops or Bear Be,k ue-dis Spair rl-bisis and Barbe kue dis pair ribs. Another variation was Barbie cute Chicken. One of its bigger sellers was FinneRs switzel, but many swore by the Beep StaRang Evan Off. There was also Rost Beeps, Roagf Orta Stayk and S Teemed Dom,fe Tweth Hamn. For the adventurous they had a Spaynesh oma la Tittie.

The Chinese menu started off with Fish-frashed Frit Ears and then added "Fraid Chickie KanWit Acash Chewed Nut, Chic Koonontop, FryeD Pla Pla Ka Ka Pong, Mongolnian hot Poot, and Girl Leglegg Lapul apusie. The soup menu included split pee soup, grin pee soup and yellow pee soup.

My favorite meal there was Beep with Peepers. The restaurant also served drinks. Two I remember were "Graa Soppers" and Singuh poor Wrasslings.

Eventually it began to dawn on some of us that a few of the restaurants had occasional "help" from the local GI's in the spelling of some of the entrees in their English menus when they were not exactly sure how a certain offering should be spelled.

But anyway, 1970 saw the U.S. Officers' Club dining room patronage shrink to about one-tenth the population of whoever happened to be passing through over any given night, while the Thai eateries were always filled. The most popular place to be in all of this part of Thailand, though, was the Green Coffee House, which was always a place of merriment, joy, conviviality, laughter, extremely good food, and the best fried peepers in the whole wide world.

# 47
# Coonie

When I arrived at our site late in the morning, the computer that was the heart and soul of our bombing system - was sitting in the yard. Coonie had washed it down with the garden hose several hours earlier. Now he was checking it out carefully as he finished another beer.

"Another cleaning, eh?" I commented, trying to appear complacent.

"Yep, It was dirty as hell! How about a beer?" he asked as he opened another one.

"No thanks," I replied, and "I think you really ought to pour that one out - I know you don't want to set a bad example for the military guys."

He grinned as he poured most of it out into his throat, then he dribbled the rest on the grass, rubbed his sandal on it and tossed the can in the nearby trash.

Our computer would bask in the sun another hour before being brought back into the bombing trailer to finish drying under our relentless air conditioning system. Right now it lay on the grass in three parts, one about five feet by eight feet, another probably twelve feet by ten feet, and another about three by eight feet. Each part was mounted on a large electronic "board" and in total it sported some thirty to forty vacuum tubes.

Many of the tubes had aged and lost some of their power, and their electronic characteristics had changed. Our civilian tech rep, known by his nickname "Coonie", had accommodated those problems by installing capacitors or inductors, which were a different size from the original equipment, some of which had even been bought on markets controlled by nations not considered friendly to us.

Normally our computer was positioned deep in the air-conditioned bombing van, wired into its own special place, and mated to our radar system. Together they provide the information and coordination necessary to direct our B-52 strikes against the Vietnamese enemy.

Over the years, these systems had deteriorated significantly. Many of our tech reps, who were the technical representatives of their respective corporate organizations back in the states, had found themselves unable to receive replacement parts for some of this equipment because a major shift away from vacuum tubes was already underway. Diodes and transistors were replacing the tubes and not all of these new items fit in the old electronic boards. Even those that could be incorporated, theoretically, could not really be used because so much of the rest of the system had been "modified" to meet the various deteriation of the basic equipment.

Some of the tech reps here in Vietnam and Thailand, late in the war, also began to resemble their equipment in a number of ways. They too, some of them, had deteriorated significantly and no longer worked according to their original "specs".

Coonie was a good example of that. He appeared to be in the final stages of alcoholism, and was seldom seen without a drink in his hand. Out of respect for our mission perhaps, as well as my orders, he drank only beer when he was on our premises. I would always tell him to pour it out and he would grin and pour it away after one last long drag on the can. It should be clearly understood that he was outside our military chain of command and I could really not order him to do anything other than what was in his contract, but he did so much beyond that original requirement that he really lived in another world, not military, no longer really corporate, but he was totally indispensable. Every site had their own Tech Reps, and while the crewmembers rotated over here and back home, most of the Tech Reps remained with their equipment, sometimes for years.

Of course no one had expected these systems to go on as long as they had. Eventually they became clearly obsolete by almost any method of reckoning, and probably were the very last vacuum tube computers ever used in the Air Force. They were not replaced because the war was obviously ending and the machines still seemed to work. The Tech Reps had been left here to keep these machines still operating. The computers had a lot of problems and so did some of the Tech Reps but they would still deliver a lot of bombs on or very near the target, and in this great jungle that was a small miracle, and it was a reliable one.

I had been to Coonie's "house" a couple of weeks ago. He had invited three of us over for dinner. There were drinks - of course - and then a delicious meal brought in throughout the evening in about six different servings by a pretty, vivacious, happy-looking young Vietnamese woman, whom our tech rep introduced to us as his wife.

After supper we toured his house, all three of the rooms. The "kitchen" was In one corner of one of the rooms. On the floor, was a butane gas stove with two burners, and a large bowl of water.

Now tonight, back at the complex, the computer had been brought in, dried out thoroughly and powered up. It ran well.

The evening was busy and we had many targets. Two were compression runs in which three waves of strikes were brought onto a single target eight minutes apart. Now, new targets were being called into us, emergency targets requested by our ground troops who were experiencing serious problems with enemy forces, all this as bad weather drifted over us.

Until midnight the weather was just another problem but then it turned worse. Electric power was zapping in and out, vanishing in flickers and returning the next second. Shortly before 1:00 a.m. I switched the compound to our diesel generator, but we still had a problem with the switchgear. We were able to stay up but needed some work out in the high voltage area. I wouldn't authorize the work to be done because we would have to power down and certainly drop some missions, and I knew how badly our army troops out there were counting on us to hit these targets. By two in the morning, most of the thunderstorms had passed over but the rain was torrential. We began to lose power significantly now. We were obviously going to drop some missions but I couldn't send anyone out in this dark night with heavy rain falling to work on high voltage equipment.

"Hey - way to go!" Someone shouted in the bombing control room, "He got it! He got it! It's reset!" The power settled down and remained strong and we completed two more compression missions and three other B-52 strikes in the next two hours.

It was an extremely busy night and when it was over, by dawn's light I mentioned to the crew chief, "glad the power stabilized" And he said "yeah, Coonie saved our ass."

"Coonie? What do you mean?"

"Didn't you see him? He came out with all the lightning and thunder and worked in the switchgear in the pouring rain, up to his ankles in water!"

"Coonie? Hell NO - I was in the bomb plot control center talking to the B-52s to keep them from running into each other and plotting and re-plotting all the damn target changes!

"Why do they call you 'Coonie'"?

"I'm a coon-ass", he grinned

"Coon-ass?" I asked - "What the hell is a 'coon-ass'"?

He took a drag on his newly opened beer, "I live on the east side".

"The east side of what?"

Another swig, "The Sabine River"

"Where the hell is the Sabine River?"

"It separates Texas from Louisiana."

"And you're a 'coon-ass'"?

Another swig, "Damn right I am." He grinned.

"What's on the other side of the Sabine River?"

"Texas."

"And they're not coon-asses?"

"Hell NO!"

"What are they?"

He took a really long drag. "They're horses-asses." He grinned like he had just ascended into heaven and it had all been worth it.

# 48
# Coming Home

The Passenger Terminal in Na Kon Phenom Royal Thai Air Force Base, Thailand, is hot and sticky. High ceilings and open windows let the breezes blow through, but the breezes are hot and they're sticky too.

I set my bags in the middle of the floor where an Air Policeman points and I go stand against a wall and wait. I am totally exhausted after two days of constant work and processing off base with no rest or sleep – but now, after six months in Vietnam I'm going home! Getting out of Thailand has not been easy either, with several aircraft malfunctions occurring on the "easy" part of that long trip back.

I walk over to the Amnesty Box, a place where people can put illegal money, guns, drugs, needles or whatever. Anything placed in there will not be held against you. It is a cubicle about six feet square and six feet high. There is a hole a little bigger than a man's head on this side of the box. I look inside. Nothing there. I notice one of the Air Policemen watching me as I go back to my spot on the wall.

A tired, old-looking Staff Sergeant heads over to the amnesty Box and throws a crumpled up empty pack of cigarettes in there as he lights up its last previous occupant. The Air Policeman watches this too.

Another Air Policeman, this one a Tech Sergeant, comes in and gives us a quick briefing.

"Put your bags in the middle of the room and get away from them." He adds: "There is an Amnesty Box in the corner," he points at it, goes over and taps on it. "You may place anything you wish in the box - right here - he puts his hand in the hole, and it will never be held against you – you will walk away free! You'll be back in the States in twelve hours!" He continues, "Items you might want to deposit in the box include –– and these all carry prison terms if you are caught with them." and he reads from a list. Then, "Anyone for the box? Going, going . . . last chance . . . " A long wait. - "Last chance for the Amnesty Box" . . . He looks at each person individually. Then he turns his head to the door, "OK, Bring in the dog!"

The door opens and a young Air Policeman is virtually dragged into the room by a large German shepherd. The dog races at full speed across the bags in the middle of the floor. Suddenly the dog falls, and spins around as if crippled; he leaps on one of the bags and starts pawing viciously at it. His handler pulls him off and another air policeman removes the bag. The dog handler speaks: "O.K. Punji, let 's check the others!" But the dog looks at the rest of the bags in huge disgust and sits down, his gaze returns to the removed bag. The airman and dog leave the room.

The Tech Sergeant goes to the bag, checks the name tag, and called out: "Airman Speed?"

A young man with a very white face raises his hand.

The Tech Sergeant continues: "Speed, put your bag on that table – NOW! The rest of you, have a great trip back and say 'hello' to the Land of the Big BX for us."

We get our bags and as we leave the room, we hear: "Awright, Speed, open your bag, let's have a look!"

The C-130 is incredibly hot, perhaps 160° inside. But we are going home. So we get in smiling and happily strap ourselves into the canvas seats.

The flight to Bangkok is rough. We're at low altitude and bounce hard up and down most of the way. A couple of people get sick and throw up into their burp bags. I try to sleep and read. Not a good combination; when I start to read I doze off, when I try to sleep, I think about the book. It has been a long trip already. I was just off a twelve-hour tour of duty and had been packing and clearing the base for six hours before that, and then another twelve-hour shift before that. The airplane from Udon RTAFB had experienced problems and had to land in NKP. We were put on another plane, and it had problems. It needed a part. Finally, the one we had come in on was repaired and we carried our bags back to it and got on. I was already worn out. We finally reach Bangkok but are late.

We taxi in with the temperature in the aircraft up around 160° again. A few of the passengers start to "moo," like cattle. We are starting to smell like cattle, too. A quick trip to the other side of the base leads us down a long corridor, around a couple of corners and into an air-conditioned building!

Then we are hurried down another corridor onto a great enormous airplane with air conditioning, plush seats, stewardesses and music!

"Please be seated, we will be taking off immediately since the remainder of our passengers have arrived," a female voice with an Asian accent says over the loudspeaker.

Engines start, we taxi and immediately takeoff, sailing low over Bangkok, a city I know well, now headed east, back toward Vietnam. As I look out the window at the jungle below, a woman taps me on the shoulder – "would you care for something to drink?"

"Martini?" I respond.

"How would you like your martini?" She asks.

"Dry martini, please."

She smiles, "Thank you."

I look out the window at the familiar jungles of Thailand and Cambodia. We sail over the Mekong River and into Vietnam.

I sip my martini. Smoke drifts across the face of the jungle, and I can see some of the rings of fire that will protect jungle sites throughout the night which is just beginning.

The olive tastes wonderful. I turn a knob on my armrest and hear a voice speaking over a small set of earphones. I put them on and turn the knob again and hear country music. I listen to a song about Detroit City, and watch a fire deep in the jungle, trailing smoke seaward. I turn the knob again and hear popular music; again, and I hear soul music; again, and Wagner's "Flight of the Valkeries" soars out through the earphones.

I finish my martini, listening to Wagner while picking out explosions six miles below in the jungle. I see the first flares of the evening slowly falling into the jungle. Great columns of smoke pale in the dark, hazy sky and drift far out to sea.

Another tap on the shoulder. "Sir, I'm sorry, but dinner will be another thirty minutes."

"That's OK, don't worry."

"Would you like another martini?"

"Why not? Make it dry."

Later "dinner" arrives. "Sorry sir, all we have left are breakfasts. Seems there is a delegation from Washington up in first class, and they ate more than we expected."

"That's fine, thanks."

I eat a wonderful breakfast.

I see the lights of both Taiwan and Okinawa passing by throughout the night. We descend with a lovely Mt. Fuji setting off our left wing, snowcapped and bright under a full moon, and land in Tokyo at 1:15 a.m. local time. It is warm here and rain is intermittently blowing across the ramp. We quickly board another airplane, one that is much bigger than the last one and which has even more people on it. We take off just before dawn.

Breakfast is served shortly. After that I nap through the short day – the sun is going westward at 800 mph, we're going eastward at 600 mph, so we are going to do a day about every 13 hours or so.

"Lunch" turns out to be breakfast again. Nobody seems to know why.

I nap some more and awaken for the landing in Anchorage, Alaska. It's summer, but still chilly here. We go into the passenger terminal for a few minutes. We see the aurora borealis, smell hamburgers and onions and bacon cooking. But I head back to the airplane again; I won't be late for this trip, not even for a good hamburger.

Airborne again, then there is breakfast again, probably because the sun is coming up again, and we're heading down the long coast heading southeast for California.

Travis AFB is cool, breezy and busy, busy, busy. All the passengers are inquiring about showers. We are told that there are some here but that we have to leave NOW. We are told of a place in San Francisco International Airport where we can get showers for $5, maybe even $3. We are told where to find it. But – our bus is now departing for San Francisco.

It's a tired and bumpy ride to the great airport.

I try to figure how long I have been up. I do know I had been up for almost sixty hours before I got on the airplane in Na Kong Phnom. Then there were two more hours to Bangkok – I think; then four and nine, or twelve, wait, did I forget Tokyo or Alaska? Then there's two more, that's – well, it's much too much to figure.

My watch says 7:00 a. m., but its clearly late afternoon. I am filthy, dirty, and unshaven. I stink, and am shivering – the shivering is from lack of sleep and fatigue. I cram my head up against the window and try to doze off. I am back in the United States of America! Thank God! That's all that counts! I'm **<u>home</u>**!

I notice a pretty young woman in a car that is passing us. She is smiling at us and holding her middle finger up to the occupants of this military bus. Then, I see that her smile is really a sneer. That seems strange, and I wonder what her problem is.

The bus races, leaning from side to side, around the entrances and exits at the airport, and I get off in a rush of cold wind and dirt, and the bus roars off. I have three bags and am totally exhausted. There is nobody to help carry the bags. A skycap walks by and I ask for help. He shouts an obscenity at me, salutes me with his middle finger and tells me to go back to Vietnam and kill more babies and he walks on by. I lift the bags up and carry them all into the terminal. After a long wait I check two bags. Fifty minutes before take off! Time for a breather, and maybe a shower – I've *got* to have a shower!

I locate the showers, and head inside. A young man sits behind a bar filled with towels. Steam comes out of a nearby hallway.

"How much?" I ask him.

He stares at me. "Three dollars, but for you bastards it's five."

"What do you mean?" I respond.

" Are you just back from Nam?" He asks.

"Yes." I say.

"Make it eight dollars."

Thirty-five minutes to gate time.

I pay the eight dollars, lay the clothes out, and then take them all in the shower with me since a couple of young men seem interested in me. They peep in and grin while I'm showering. I throw my expensive bar of soap at one and hit him in the mouth.

Five minutes later, still partly wet, but much cleaner, I leave the shower. "I'll get that guy at the check-in stand!" I think. But it's twenty minutes to gate time. The two young men follow me out into the concourse.

I am amazed at all the hair! It seems as if there must have gone out an edict from a great American king requiring all men to wear their hair long, down their neck, sideburns down to their jaws, and mustaches and beards abound. I realize that I still stand out in my military flattop haircut. My slacks and windbreaker may not be "uniform" but I am still very military because of my haircut and my military briefcase.

That is obvious when a hirsute man wearing a hounds tooth hat with a small bright red feather stares at me and calls me a murderer. Then he clears his throat, purses his lips and spits in my face.

I will kill him. I see myself smashing his face into the concrete and throwing his bloody, faceless, spasmodically jerking body over the railing onto the level far below. I throw my bag down and reach for him. I grab his sleeve and he tears free. He leaps back, ashen faced, and quickly turns and squirms away into the crowd. I have to go back and grab my bag before someone steals it.

Now I am at my gate. Fifteen minutes left. I go into a bar across from the gate and get a beer for five dollars. I realize the sun has set, and it is dark again. How can it be dark again?

After takeoff I am served another breakfast. How many breakfasts in a row does this make? Next time, I vow, I'll write it all down.

We land in Dallas. Change aircraft. It's early morning again; three o'clock, or something like that. People are crying terribly, someone is leaving. It's a young boy in uniform with one stripe. I wonder how old he is. Eighteen? Maybe seventeen? He is fighting back tears, being brave. Several men who are in their forties or fifties are smiling and shaking his hand, welcoming him into manhood even as he leaves their midst. One very old man is crying, over in a corner all by himself. The women are crying. Sleepy children are crying. Then the young man leaves. His mother is crying. He turns around to wave, very proper, very military, stiff upper lip, with a tear creeping down a young cheek. Somehow, I sense an air of death about him. Somehow, I know that he and his mother will never meet again. He waves, stiffly, and quietly says "Bye, Mom, I'll see you soon." Then he turns and marches off. She sits down and stares at him with unbelieving eyes until he is gone. Then she buries her face in her hands and sobs, heavy, deep, racking sobs.

I hope no one spits at him or calls him a murderer.

My aircraft takes off too, different direction. Another breakfast. Finally Chicago for a six-hour layover.

Takeoff again, and another breakfast.

Finally home. And I have figured it out. It's been one hundred and eight hours since I've been to sleep or had food other than a TV breakfast.

The kids are overcome with joy. They have grown a lot. The oldest one is very grown up. They both have very long hair. My little girl doesn't want me to hug her; she is not sure who I am. Our dog smells of me, then goes to his bed and lies down.

Supper is wonderful. The table shakes with the excitement of children eating around me. I am thankful for the deliverance from all the events since we last parted. At last I can relax.

My dog suddenly realizes who I am and comes running and crawls up into my lap wagging his tail and happy. I put my children to bed and hear their prayers again. Thank God. It is so <u>good</u> to be back home again.

I go back in the living room and sit down with my wife and she tells me she wants a separation. She says she has found she can get along without me and the war is not going to end.

My ears are ringing, and then I realize that it is the telephone. It's for me.

"Hey, welcome home!" Says Col. Jordan. "Great to be back, isn't it?"

"Yeah" I say.

"Well, not for long, " he says, "Your orders came in last week."

"Vietnam?" I ask, needlessly.

"Da Nang," replies the colonel. "But Bein Hoa first, and maybe you can get back there later; it's only for six months, anyway – what the hell!"

"When do I leave?"

"Fifteenth – you've got ten days."

"OK, I'll see you tomorrow."

"Tomorrow's Saturday – take the day off" he says. "I'll see you Monday."

"OK, bye." I hang up.

Sunday, when I walk into church, some people seem glad to see me, some look the other way. Two people get up and walk out. One points at me and calls me "Killer!"

The priest says I am a hero.

Eight days to go.

# 49
# Back on Board

I stop in the cafeteria at Travis AFB, California, for coffee and send postcards to my kids. My movements are quick and jerky. I'm already tired, and that's not good.

Soon I will call home for the last time until I get back six months from now.

I walk outside into the hazy sunlight and reflect on my life. This is not the dream I had years ago when I first wore the uniform of my country. Back then I had proudly assumed responsibility to defend this land and its inhabitants, all of whom I considered to be my family. Sixteen years later, I now wonder what would happen to my own family if I were killed in Vietnam. More than that, I find myself wondering if I will have a family to return to when this mess is all over. Somehow, the war has become a special hell for a small group of people and their families. The rest of the people in the United States seem to be hard at work, buying homes, moving forward in careers, putting down roots, building a real life. But some of us in the military seemed pinned to Southeast Asia forever, and we come and go like the rain. This is my third trip. Will there be a fourth? I know people who have been over there five and six times; even eight and nine. Will it ever really end? Will there be anything left?

Once again I have had problems departing. This time I have to pay my own way. My orders to Vietnam did not arrive in time for me to carry them with me. Worse yet, I will have to stop and pick them up en-route. So I have to pass up the 707, nonstop flight from New York to San

Francisco, and go through Shreveport, the headquarters of my organization and pick up my own orders. This means flying to Chicago then through St. Louis, Jackson, and Monroe just to get to Shreveport. After that I will go on to El Paso, Las Vegas, Los Angeles, and finally San Francisco. In order to make the timing right for the trip across the Pacific, I had to leave home at 0300 hours instead of the 1100 otherwise required.

There should be a sergeant to meet me at Shreveport with my orders, but when I arrive, no one is at the reception gate. I only have forty-five minutes, so I run through the small terminal. I find a pay phone and call the Headquarters of my organization.

A tired airman, who is just there in case the phone rings, answers. I ask for Sergeant Whistle and am told he is home. I get his phone number and call and wake him up! It's 0900 hours on a Sunday morning. He forgot I was coming in. He is sorry.

I hang up and call back to the Headquarters and get the telephone number of Colonel Grump, the Group Commander.

After getting more change, I race back to the pay phone then have to wait in a short line. Finally I call the colonel. He blows his stack, then tells me to wait there, he will have Sgt. Whistle get down there ASAP. I tell him my plane leaves in 15 minutes, and he says to go on. He will personally see that they are sent on "Delta Dash" to Travis. I race back to the gate and get on the plane just in time to go with it.

San Francisco International is a mess. The terminal where we deplane is on the "wrong" side of the runway so I have to pay for transit across, and barely make the bus to Travis.

When I get there we have a huge hunt for my orders, but no "Delta Dash" has come in.

Then I am paged over the loudspeakers and go to a desk where I am handed one copy of my orders that have been faxed. The sheet is already turning brown, curling and beginning to tear. I hope it doesn't disintegrate completely before I get to Vietnam.

We land in Hawaii at 9:15 p.m., local time. Small fluffy clouds gleam whitely in the blue-gray night sky as they move quickly by, carried by the trade winds. Palm fronds fly ragged, and flickering torches dance with the wind. I am swept with the smell of the salty sea and tropical orchids and somehow seem washed deeply within.

Just before midnight we take off on an eleven-hour flight, bound for the Philippines. Eight hours later though, after struggling through jet streams all night, we are short of fuel and alter into Agana, Guam. We refuel and take off from Guam at 3:00 a.m. local, and land in Clark Field in the Philippines three hours later at 5:00 a.m. local. An hour and a half later, we are airborne again, this time bound for Saigon.

When I land and walk out into the warm sunlight of Vietnam once again, I feel like I never went home. There is an incredible change of dimension that one goes through between here and there, so when you are in the States, you can't believe there really is a place like Vietnam. When you are over here, the States seem like something you vaguely remember from your early childhood. It's like trying to remember a dream that "unravels" even as you try to recall it. Through unfocused eyes, you seem to watch "Reality" change in front of you. However, it is not the "Reality" out there in front of your eyes which is changing that concerns you, but it is that "Reality" behind your eyes that is troubling. That changes too.

It is obvious that we are pulling out of Vietnam. The Army drawdown is well underway and you can see it taking place. Equipment is now badly in need of maintenance, there are fewer people here now; helicopters are no longer constantly flying over the base. It's much quieter now than it used to be.

Maybe that's why you can sense the presence of the ghosts of war so easily now. It's impossible not to be aware of the force that once was here, a strutting, cocksure, king-of-the-hill — with a chip on its shoulder — don't give a damn insolence of a proud, methodical kill-kill-kill-kill-kill-kill-kill (but with order-and-discipline - yea!) Army that once went anywhere, and could do anything, and always did it with a flourish and a flair. Yes, the sense of a frontier still is here, with a hypnotic narcosis that compels and beckons. You are summoned, initiated, programmed and certified a Grade A Killer — of course you change — you are not the same person you were before, and you will never be that person again. You are anointed and cursed with auras and scars, given memories of death and ancient screams, and you become a god with the soul of a devil.

In spite of all that has happened to our forces over here, a sense of that audacious dare, the disdain and contemptuous confidence still pervades the troops who remain, these few who are left.

No wonder we were so sure we would win.

I am quickly recertified in the Operating Instructions and Rules of Engagement. The onrushing run of military life now sweeps over me, and I take up again where it seems I never really left off.

I climb back on board the war. It has become a disaster, and we are trying to get out of it. It has been a bad war for a long time, now it will get really ugly; the last days of any war are always its worst.

Honor, duty, country? Yes, of course, but there is a dark side to that too. When your country is no longer there with you, and the honor is all yours and your duty is all that is left, then you wonder if there isn't something more worthwhile you and your country could be doing. Maybe it is time for a new dream.

Meanwhile, this war has taken on a soul of its own. It is running on its own power and the people who could stop it are pretending they have more important things to do.

# 50
# The Whisper of the Bicycles

We put our watches and billfolds into the squadron vault, retaining only a few dollars worth of Dong, which was the Vietnamese currency, our dogtags, military I.D and Geneva Convention cards. Colonel Smith, Major Jones and I have decided to make a last visit to Saigon to say goodbye to the great city.

We had been warned not to take any big cameras, especially Canons or Nikons, or anything else that appeared expensive, and absolutely no jewelry; even wedding rings were discouraged. We were told to make sure any camera we might carry would be held so it could be stolen easily if someone wanted to take it. The stories of straps being slashed with machete blades to steal cameras worn around the neck, or hands cut off to take expensive rings or watches were compellingly intense. I took my $35 Olympus TRIP camera and a roll of Plus-X black-and-white film and a roll of Kodachrome slide film. Our Intelligence Section had briefed us there was now a remote possibility of an encounter with Viet Cong in the city.

"How will we know if they're VC?" I asked.

"They may or may not be wearing their black pajamas, but they will be the only young men you will see in town," came the answer.

Jones shifted uneasily, "What action should we take?"

"Look – the war is over – except for a signature or two. They know they won, and they know we're leaving – they are acting pretty cool right now. They are very disciplined and our information tells us that if you ignore them they will ignore you. Whatever you do, just don't go pick a fight!"

So we headed down to the bus stop for our last trip into Saigon.

Saigon is a city of walls. The predominant color is a yellowish beige adobe. We pass under countless trees and I am reminded of Savannah, except there are more trees here. It must have been a beautiful city before the Hondas arrived. Now the city is covered with a dense, oily, blueish haze that smells of Three-in-One machine oil, and our lips taste like they've been sprayed with it.

We did some shopping and stopped in a bar for a San Miguel beer. I tried to talk with the Vietnamese waitresses in my poor college French. They laughed and laughed. One of the young ladies sang me a song in French, and it must have been a bawdy song judging from the laughter. I smiled the smile of wisdom – I think.

We went back out for more pictures and walked along the wide and winding boulevards of Saigon. This part of town reminds me of both Mexico and Madrid, but the French style of brick, stone and wrought iron is predominant here and seems so casually done that it appears as if it must have always been this way.

As in many other places in Asia the merchant shops seem to be owned and managed by Chinese. Most of the owners look fat and sloppy, and go schlepping around in an undershirt and open leather sandals. The bright, quick and neat Vietnamese girls and children work for the Chinese.

There are trees everywhere, even downtown where great canvas awnings stretch over the curbs. Wide sidewalks are filled with families surrounded by merchandise that is mostly junk and which is passionately offered to every passerby. Food is cooking on small charcoal-fired stoves and the smell of onion and spices share the air with incense and Honda oil.

There are women who are eagerly and enthusiastically available for money. We savvy warriors thank them politely and continue on.

And there are people who have come in from outlying areas. Many are pitifully mutilated and begging for

money. Men, women and children who are missing arms or legs or feet, or covered with hideous burns or with no faces, begging for money. Old people, obviously dying, who are begging for money. Women who are nursing babies and offering themselves to you for sex if you will pay them money.

Most of the people on the street though, are storeowners and women are strolling with shopping bags in their hands. Every part of humanity is here except for young men or teen-age boys. In fact we see no men at all except for very young naked men-children, injured men, and very frail old men. Small meek dogs with rib bones protruding lie panting, their quick eyes darting obsequiously about, alternating in interest and fear. "Hello there!" I say to one of them – there is no glint of recognition returning from his eyes. I realize he doesn't recognize English.

It is illegal to carry any American weapons off base, unless under military orders, because the U. S. Government doesn't want the Vietnamese to get access to even one American gun. But in Saigon today, every street corner seems stacked full of M-16s, hand grenades, Colt pistols, even hunting rifles and shotguns. Ammunition is available everywhere. All are for sale. We don't buy any of those, either.

While we shop in a store, one old man spends thirty minutes out on the sidewalk straightening out and then nailing a handful of old rusty tacks into the heel of a ladies shoe which he will later try to sell. One shoe. That's all some people need now.

We cross the street to an outside cafe where we can sit under umbrellas rising from the center of round tables and we enjoy a Japanese beer.

Saigon would be beautiful if it weren't for the Hondas and the crush of refugees. If you want to think back to the prewar writings about Saigon you have to try to ignore the roar of the Hondas, and the smell of hydrocarbons.

Yes, the whisper of the bicycles is gone now, but sometimes you can still smell the wood smoke, and then occasionally there comes an old whiff of fresh mint and flowers and perfume, always with the underlaying body of sandalwood incense rising and falling through the shady streets.

Then the world seems to pause for a moment and you can feel yourself strolling in reverie down these graceful old boulevards. If you listen closely now you can almost hear the haunting strains of accordions playing music from Moulin Rouge drifting in the cool of evening breezes, floating across the parks and over the wide sidewalks and under the awnings. There seems to come a peace that Paris will never know. Then finally you can hear once again the whisper of the bicycles gliding down the boulevards.

Eight teenage boys come around the corner. Five or six of them are dressed in black pajamas. The one in the middle has two revolvers on his belt, and two others carry giant machetes. They walk down the street like kings. We come back to reality quickly. I set my little camera on a table and lean back in my chair, and the boys walk by with only a glance in our direction.

After they pass from view the colonel clears his throat: "Well, gentlemen, I vote we head for the O Club." Jones and I second his motion by standing up. I get my little camera and we all head back to the base.

Goodbye Saigon. Goodbye.

# 51
# Compression

"Congratulations, Major."

"About what?" I replied.

"About being our new commander."

"Commander? Of what?"

"Our new detachment."

" What new detachment?"

"The one in Cambodia."

"Cam-BOD-i-a?"

"Yes sir."

"Sarge, what have you been smoking?"

"Sir, we're going to open a new Skyspot detachment in Cambodia, and you're going to be the commander."

"That's not right, Sarge."

"Yeah, Major, I know it's not *right* – but it's *so*!"

"Where the hell would we even bomb *from* over there?" I asked. "We don't have any bases or compounds or anything else in the whole country."

"We're going to set up a bombing trailer on top of our embassy in Phnom Penh."

"The EMB-bassy?" Now I was concerned about him. "That would violate every rule in all the books ever written!"

"Just you wait and see, sir."

"Sargent Worri, I'm going back stateside next month, and you're going back just before I do."

"No sir, we're going to be extended and sent to Phnom Penh."

"Where in hell did you get such gobbledygook?"

"Lek told me."

"*Lek*?" This was getting worse. "How in the hell would Lek know about anything like this – isn't she your cleaning lady?"

"Well – you know."

"Forget it Sarge." I got my cap and headed for the door. "If your cleaning lady is talking about you going somewhere else, it's just wishful thinking on her part."

That was Wednesday morning.

Friday evening was not exactly TGIF. We were bombing the hell out of a part of the border between southern Laos and Vietnam. Twelve B-52 missions tonight – thirty-six aircraft– will be striking targets in this area during the period of darkness.

One of the attacks will be a "compression strike". Three different flights of three B-52's will hit the same target, each dropping eight minutes after the one before it. The first wave will drop "bunker buster" 500 pound bombs that will collapse the tunnels used by the enemy and there would be survivors wandering about above the ground when the second wave, eight minutes later, will drop Cluster Bomb Units (CBUs) of shrapnel, and the last wave, eight minutes later will drop CBUs of flaming napalm jelly bomblets. With the aircraft releasing their weapons from above 35,000 feet, there will be no sound of their passage above the battlefield

The crew that I had for the night consisted of four airmen and three sergeants, the crew chief was a tech sergeant. He was sharp. The mission director was a captain, a very unhappy pilot who felt he should be flying airplanes through the air instead of standing on the ground in a bombing trailer with a major navigator for a supervisor.

Captain Pout had been heard to comment more than once that "the three most useless things in the Air Force are the runway behind you, the altitude above you, and field-grade navigators." I had first heard that joke almost twenty years ago.

Unfortunately, Capt. Pout was not very good at this job. He would usually hit the release point pretty closely, but too often the aircraft were flying the wrong heading and the bombs would hit far away from their intended target. He seemed to think the Release Point <u>was</u> the target, and of course, the bombs had to fall *from* the Release Point onto the target area. I had to work Pout pretty tightly to get the B-52s to the Initial Point and turned on the right track, then he could do fine. With a Compression Strike, this could result in a huge mess on the ground. We had American forces stationed closely by and they were to move in right after the attack finished. They were going to get a fantastic fireworks display – I wanted to make sure that was all they got from us.

We had a thirty-minute break before the Compression Strike began and I was briefing the crew about the procedures we would follow and how we would handle the coordination problems of transferring from one strike to the next.

As I completed the briefing, the door in the bombing van opened and Lt. Col Bite, the site commander, motioned me to come to the door. I followed him into his office. Lt. Col. Stare, our operations officer, was sitting there.

Bite asked me how things were going and I told him everything was OK. Then he wanted to know if I was looking forward to going home next month and I told him I couldn't wait. "I'll get back, check in at SAC Personnel for my new assignment, and then unpack – can't imagine where I will go, but I'm looking forward to it."

"How would you like to stay in the Combat Evaluation Group?"

"Well, I have enjoyed it – some of it, but I've got to get home and try to put my marriage back together again." I leaned back in the chair. "Maybe I can even get back into missiles."

Col. Bite leaned closer to me. "How would you like to be commander of a detachment?"

"Any time." I replied trying to remember something that seemed familiar but I couldn't put my mental "finger" on where that memory was coming from.

"What if we could have a new site open up?" Col. Stare said quietly.

"New site?"

Col. Bite grinned viciously. "How would you like to go to Cambodia?"

"You're kidding."

"What if you could take a couple of crews, three trailers with full equipment and set up in Phnom Penh – say, on top of the embassy."

"The EM-bassy?"

"Well, that's just an idea. We could maybe go other places – think outside the box, Major – you know."

"Yeah, there is a lot outside 'that box', but some of it is filled with other boxes."

"Yeah, what kind of 'other boxes', Major?"

"Several - like a Geneva Conventions Box, a Nuremburg Trials Box, a War Crimes Box and maybe more than that."

"Col. Bite leaned back. "Well, we were just wondering if maybe we could come up with some thing different."

"That's plenty different."

"IF you were ordered to do something like that - what would you think?" Col Stare asked.

"Go to Phnom Penh and bomb from the embassy?"

"Yeah."

"I wouldn't go."

Col. Bite leaned over the table "You would *refuse* to obey orders, Major?"

"An order like that would not be a legal order."

"On what grounds, Major?"

"It would violate the oath I took when I was sworn in as an officer of the Regular Air Force. Such an order would be detrimental to the Constitution of the United States. We are a nation of laws."

"What *would* you do, if you were ordered to do that?"

"I would write my representatives in Congress – and my senators."

"What state are you from?"

When I told them, Stare said, "That's Senator Shreeknscream's state."

Bite looked at me. "Well, it's just an idea, Major, curious as to what you might think about it."

There was a knock on the door.

"Come in!" shouted Col. Bite.

Sgt. Sharp stuck his head inside. "Major, the first Compression Strike wave is five minutes from the PIP."

"I gotta go." I stood up. "We can talk about this tomorrow."

But I never heard anyone ever speak about it again. We placed all bombs on target that night and a couple of weeks later I rotated home on schedule and was reassigned to a new organization.

More than thirty years later I saw this item in a newspaper article on the web:

*Pacific Stars and Stripes,* Sunday, April 29, 1973, page 1. "Senate investigators disclosed Friday that the United States has been pounding Cambodia with 242 air sorties a day since mid-March, with the fire directed and controlled from a command post located in the U. S. embassy at Phnom Penh."

It went on to explain that the bulk of the attacks were not against the North Vietnamese forces but against Cambodian insurgent forces trying to overthrow the government in Phnom Penh.

An accompanying article written by Sylvana Foa, went on to explain how the bombing from Phnom Penh was even striking parts of the city's environs and how refugees streaming into the city told of complete villages that had been destroyed by the B-52 bombing and relief workers estimated some 1,000 civilians were being killed each week by these strikes. American military personnel acknowledged there were no rules of engagement for this action and the article concluded " . . . a rapidly rising tide of anti-American sentiment has become apparent in Phnom Penh."

Another report published by Yale University:

http://www.yale.edu/cgp/chron.html stated " . . . 50,000 to 150,000 civilian deaths from the bombing. Pol Pot forces use the bombing's killing and destruction as recruitment propaganda and as an excuse for the abandonment of moderate socialist policies in the insurgent zones. "

# 52
# Zero Two Fifteen

The lead navigator walks to the front of the briefing room and speaks: "Eighteen hundred hours, fifteen minutes — in three minutes."

He sits down in the front row. We study our charts and scan the weather information along with intelligence data that is just handed to us. We confer quickly over minor questions.

The coffee is acrid and bitter; it's better just left in its hot paper cup.

"Eighteen-hundred-fifteen — one minute" calls the lead navigator, and silence fills the room as crewmembers align their wristwatches, know as "hack-watches". "Thirty seconds . . . ten seconds . . . five, four, three, two, one, hack!" Snaps are heard throughout the room as watches are restarted, or "hacked". "Fourteen hundred hours, fifteen minutes Zulu; zero-two-fifteen local." The lead navigator sits down.

The briefing officer, a Lt. Colonel, walks to the front of the small stage and after looking at his checklist asks if there is a chaplain present. "No? Then we'll proceed with the briefing. Sgt. Willis has the weather."

But there *is* a chaplain, and he interposes. A tired, old-looking man wearing majors' leaves and dressed in a very wrinkled uniform with large, dark perspiration stains under the armpits walks slowly to the front of the room and lowers his head.

"Almighty God, we ask for a speedy end to this war, we ask that you just send the blessing of your only son to our American servicemen, and especially that you just protect these precious souls present here on their mission tonight. We pray all this in the name of your only son, Jesus Christ, our Lord and Savior, Amen." Then without looking around, he walks out of the briefing room. Eighteen hundred hours, fifteen minutes and forty-five seconds.

"O.K., let's get on with the briefing: Sgt. Willis."

A young woman wearing an Air Force blue uniform walks onto the stage. She dims the lights in the room and places a weather chart on an overhead projector. She speaks in a high girlish, monotone voice.

"You will be in turbulence the entire trip, except for your takeoff here. You can expect moderate to severe turbulence in these areas . . . " pointing on her chart. She continues, now in a higher, almost childlike voice: "You can also expect thunderstorms up to 55,000 feet, maybe higher, just south of your target area. If they move further north over the early morning hours, you may find your target completely covered. These storms should continue developing until they move out to sea." She places another chart on the viewer, "You also may be able to approach the target after diverting a bit to the east; you might want to keep that in mind." She smiles sweetly at us. "Any questions?"

There are no questions, and Sgt. Willis gets her weather charts and leaves for her next briefing.

The briefing officer, standing to one side of the dark stage announces: "Lt. Hayden has intelligence."

A young lieutenant wearing horn-rimmed glasses and brand new fatigues with short sleeves walks heavily to the lectern. He places an overlay on the overhead projector and begins talking.

"This mobile SAM unit that's been down here on the Mekong for the past several days now seems to have been moved again. We recommend you alter your outbound course at least seven miles to the southeast so you will be out of his range." There is some muttering among the crews because that may affect our timing over the target by a minute or two.

Lt. Hayden continues: "Now, listen up!" He peers over the top of his glasses at us. "There are powerful new antiaircraft guns which have just been positioned immediately south of your target."

All of the crewmembers quit scribbling and whispering, and look at the officer.

"These weapons are effective up to 35,000 feet, it is imperative that you cross this area," slapping the tip of his collapsible pointer against figures on the screen, "no *lower* than *37,000 feet*! These weapons are powerful! And they are radar-controlled, so-be-warned!" He points out that the return route is clear of any anticipated problems. "Any questions?"

There is one. Lead pilot speaks: "Weather predicts thunderstorms up to 55,000 feet in that area. Any suggestions?"

"I don't know anything about that. You'll have to play that by ear."

"Weather suggested we might alter to the right and come up on the east side. Any comments?"

"No-no! Do not deviate from your flight path, there will be friendly artillery firing in that area up to 75,000 feet. Don't get involved in that!"

"I'm glad I asked." the lead pilot mutters somewhat sarcastically.

The briefing officer stands up. "That's why we have these briefings! Any more questions?"

Lt. Hayden looks blankly at the crews who look blankly at him.

"I've got another briefing – any more questions?" Hayden gets his chart and stomps out of the room.

The briefing officer flips on the lights and stands at the lectern again.

"O.K., let's see, now. There is a problem with flight lunches but you can get something – your aircraft are parked here." pointing to a chart of the airfield. "Use Charlie channel to contact the command post – there is construction on the east taxiway," pointing again, "not marked well, keep an eye out, even though this is a combat mission flying safety is paramount avoid all thunderstorms by at least twenty nautical miles debriefing will be in T-4279 thirty minutes after landing check the bulletin board crew boxes and schedule before leaving after debriefing put your chairs in order we've got another briefing here in five minutes any questions? Good luck - happy hunting."

We sling our heavy bags over our shoulders, pick up another bag or two and walk out into the sultry black night. It is 2:19 AM. 92° Fahrenheit and the sky smells like rain. Thunder rumbles overhead.

*　　　*　　　*

The B-52 reeks of cordite. It smells like a cap pistol that has just been fired. One hundred and eight 500-pound bombs are loaded on this great black beauty, along with one hundred and seventy-five tons of fuel, and

eight souls will be on board. The great wingtips are heavy with fuel and they droop low toward the ground. The aircraft looks like a gunfighter ready to draw.

Bright lights pierce the hot oppressive darkness, glaring down from high above and you have to squint to see anything clearly. Now and then rain showers sweep across the airfield in windblown sheets. Lightning flashes; more thunder rolls out above the runway. A hot, gusty wind rips through our area and the B-52 moves restlessly like a great monster stirring in its sleep. Our call sign tonight is "Alleycat."

"O.K., let's go do this thing!" The speaker is the pilot, a skinny young lieutenant from Texas, chewing gum fast. He's perhaps 24 years old and is drenched to the skin. His copilot is a younger lieutenant. He's from Ohio, looks very wise and is also drenched. The RN (radar navigator, the guy who will drop the bombs) is an old man, a major, 40 years old or so, ready to retire. He has bright blue eyes, a thin pencil mustache, and is somehow dry.

Inside the B-52, the temperature must be 200°F. There is no air conditioning as we start engines and taxi. Everyone has several short white terry cloth towels that we use to constantly mop our faces. Our flight suits and underwear are drenched with sweat.

We start engines and taxi to the runway and are cleared for takeoff. Carefully we crawl onto the active runway and apply full power. Slowly we inch forward, finally moving a foot or two, then ten feet, and then we feel ourselves being slowly pushed back into our seats. An enormous acceleration increases amazingly; the wing tips lift off the ground, then the wings begin to fly. Some 47 seconds after start of takeoff roll, lift comes to the aircraft and we float briefly, then leap strongly off the runway and fly level for a moment.

"Gear up," calls the pilot.

"Gear coming up!" Responds the copilot.

And the gear comes up with a heavy "Thump! Thump! Thump!" More speed. Flaps come up with a shrieking whine. More speed, and we're bouncing and sliding, skidding to the left, and the left wing falls as the tail comes left. Then the left wing comes up and we leap up again. But the right wing falls and the B-52 drops heavily, falling out of the sky, and then it is lifted up, up, up and up and up, pilots fighting to maintain control. Turbulence begins as a chop, and increases quickly in severity, and then we drop down again into the black night, left wing down, leaning to the left, falling out of the sky, held into our seat only by the belts and shoulder straps. We can feel our wet hair rise within out helmets. Then we're shoved down deeply into our seats as lift returns to the aircraft, and we ride, bucking and bouncing up and down, swaying quickly from side to side as the turbulence abates into a moderate chop. Now we're at 400 knots, and really climbing, finally kicking free of the earth-zone weather we soar into the sky – creatures of the black night in a black airplane, and we smell of sweat and kerosene and gunpowder.

The world is brilliantly lighted as lightning flashes nearby and the airplane takes on a luminescent glow. Radios and intercom go dead; silence seems to embrace the B-52. The pilot and copilot glow with neon blue auras. There's suddenly more turbulence. We drop hard, then lift straight up again and there's more lightning, but the radios return, and the servos click and cycle on, and the generators whine back up to speed.

"Crew this is the aircraft commander. We took a lightning strike, AOK up here; crew report."

A quiet litany of positions follow.

"AC this is gunner, OK back here."

"Spook is OK."

"Nav, RN OK."

And so on. Everybody is OK.

"Jeeze," says the copilot, "did they say that the only good weather we would see on this trip would be at takeoff?"

"How about turning on the goddamn air conditioner?"

"Roger, Gunner, air conditioner coming on."

"AC, nav; prepare to come left to new heading: 047 degrees, in thirty seconds."

"Roger, nav." The pilots reset their N-1 compass heading bezels.

The aircraft is climbing through 25,000 feet now and is above most of the turbulence, except for the thunderstorms that seem to be everywhere.

"AC, nav; standby to alter heading to 047 degrees in 5 seconds . . . three, two, one, mark. New heading 047 degrees."

"Roger that, coming left, 047."

The left wing drops and the aircraft slowly begins its standard rate turn.

The aircraft levels out. "Nav, AC; new heading 047."

"Roger nav, 047."

We sail out over Laos watching as the infamous Skyline Ridge slides far below us. Some firing is visible, aimed our way. We're big airplanes; even at 27,000 feet we look a lot lower than we are.

★ ★ ★

The target is more than seven miles below us, lying beneath great flashing thunderstorms that tower eight miles above it. The area looks like a large city under overcast. Enormous white flashes spread out instantantaneously beneath us at amazing speed. Fighter aircraft and artillery are working the target area over. Nobody knows we're coming yet. Coordinates of Alleycat's strike will be announced over Guard Channel three minutes before our bombs hit the ground. Friendly aircraft will then run like hell. A dozen forest fires can be seen outside of the storm area consuming this rain forest, climbing up over ridgeline after ridgeline. Smoke, ever present, can be occasionally seen drifting across the blazes. Lightning flashes ripple up and down the great storms, and play out on the earth below as the storm in front of us moves across the land like a blind man feeling his way over familiar territory.

I crane my neck trying to see our target. A brilliant red streak rises out of the ground, coming right at us. It

moves with enormous speed and is immediately followed by many others. I think of garden hoses shooting water up at us, but this is burning red water! A flash bulb goes off in front of us, then another and another and another. Small black clouds begin floating in the moonlit sky. Now it seems there are twenty or thirty hoses firing their streams of red water at us and flash bulbs and black smoke are everywhere.

"By God, they *are* beneath us!" mutters the copilot, with his lips pulled back almost to his ears, his teeth shining in the moonlight.

"180 seconds to go." The radar-navigator speaks with a faint country-music twang.

"Roger, RN," says the pilot softly, "you have second station." The radar-navigator is now controlling the flight of the B-52 with the tracking handle of his computer-radar bombing system.

Over the radios we hear an urgent call for action: "Attention all personnel, this is Crown on Guard, there is an Arc Light strike in progress at 18-08N 105-37E; all aircraft evacuate this area IMMEDIATELY! I repeat . . ."

"Roger, pilot, this is RN, I have second station." The aircraft ripples quietly and seems to move imperceptibly.

"120 seconds to go." Two minutes until bomb release. We fly straight into the storm.

Great White Death, indeed it is, and it rises above us and it eagerly reaches out to grab and enfold us.

We fly Great Black Death, penetrating like a lover, and we close together at ten miles every minute.

A dark shadow falls across our flight deck as a thunderstorm moves between us and the moon, and the B-52 ripples with a change in the currents of this high tropical air. The faces of the crewmembers glow red reflecting the light from the instrument panels.

"Sixty seconds." The aircraft moves again, tucking a little to the left.

Some of the flashbulbs can be heard, and some of them seem to be above us now. Hope not.

"Thirty seconds." We now seem to be flying into a great white canyon. The thunderstorm has risen far above us like an enormous Christ of the Andes with its great arms stretched out to receive and destroy us. Great violet crystal rays radiate from it and race up and down its length into and out of the ground. Snow blossoms out of its great white shoulders, and antiaircraft explosions reflect back from its clouds. Our own artillery can be seen off to the right - looks like it's right off our wing. The aircraft shudders with returning turbulence, and it is fishtailing a little. And we fly straight into that Great White Death.

"Fifteen seconds."

Far off to the right, through two other great thunderstorms, lies the ocean, the Gulf of Tonkin. Moonlight shines on its surface. Memories of days by the Florida gulf coast rise in my memory. Some day, I think, some day soon, I'll be back there again. Back on the beach with my kids, camping in our trailer, and the sea will look like that.

"Four, three, two . . . " and as the Radar Navigator punches the release button on the tracking handle, which releases the bombs, "Hack."

The aircraft shudders, and a fast impulsive ripple runs through it as each bomb releases. The B-52 is striking its target, quivering and hunching as if in orgasm, 108 times in 22 seconds.

Now, the right wing drops deeply, pointing at the target, as we enter and leave the high-flung snow of the storm and sweep the night air out of the arms of that great thunderstorm. We sail briefly through its mist as we soar lazily, languidly into a great turn that will take almost three minutes to complete and which will head us home. From far below comes a very faint "fumph-fumph-fumph-fumph-fumph-fumph," cadence five times a second that lasts for more than twenty seconds, a sound that seems to be heard and also not heard. The great thunderstorm lights up like a grotesque, pulsating, neon bonfire.

Mission accomplished.

Two more hours, and we'll be letting down over the South China Sea, ready for twelve hours rest. Then, we'll be back to do the same thing, or a version thereof, tomorrow. Our briefing tomorrow will be zero-four-thirty.

# 53
# Bitter Coffee

The Air Force never had good coffee. It was always rancid, old and bitter. Nonetheless we slowly drank it through nights we thought would never end, on missile tours and ocean flights and bomb runs in Vietnam.

Tonight we're busy up on Monkey Mountain, high up in the fog, way above Da Nang - 0300 hours, bright lights are glaring in the bombing van, servos are whistling, fans humming, static snapping in the air. Smells of ozone, and grease from bearings fill the trailer air and mingle with the bitter smell of old, burnt coffee.

A call from ADVON comes in through the static, bringing coordinates of a new bomb run for later this morning. The B-52s that will be striking this target are already airborne and will contact us in about two hours. The message is encrypted and it comes over a secure phone, and they all begin with a "whoosh" and end with a "whoosh." I decode and plot coordinates of the Pre-Initial Point (PIP), Initial

View of Da Nang from Monkey Mountain

Point (IP), the Release Point, and the Target Area. The PIP is that spot above the earth that the aircrew will navigate to on their own before we take over the bomb run. It is critical that we have the three B-52s running exactly along the line from the IP to the Release Point so their bombs will fall into a rectangular area that covers the target. If the courseline should be as little as two degrees in error, many bombs will be thrown out of the target area even if the aircraft are at the proper point when they release. The weapons that will be dropped are checked on ballistic tables to verify their time of fall and the path that they will "fly" from bomber to target. If there are problems or questions we call ADVON to discuss and clarify those issues.

SAC ADVON (acronym for Strategic Air Command Advanced Liaison, which is pronounced ADD-von) is the Southeast Asia headquarters of the Strategic Air Command, and it controls B-52 bombing missions in Southeast Asia. It is primarily an administrative support area but also makes decisions concerning these bombing missions that are called "Arc Light" strikes.

I plot the new target area rectangle on a map and find it includes a village in South Vietnam that has not yet been designated as "Abandoned." I tell Sgt. Smith, who is the crew leader, to call ADVON and verify the village has been cleared and can be attacked.

"It's a waste of time. " Smith said.

"What do you mean?" I ask him.

"They always say it's cleared." He pours some coffee "Every time – want some coffee, sir?"

"Thanks," I say, pushing my cup in his direction "but the regulations say to verify it with ADVON, so call 'em."

The coffee is bitter. I set the cup down and check my watch. It's fourteen minutes before our next bomb run. I head into the computer room to check the final setup. The plotting board is the point of control on the bomb run. It is located deep in the middle of the radar vans and it receives electronic inputs from computers and radar signals. The "board" itself is actually an easel pad, a 33" by 28" sheet of paper which hangs vertically in front of a fluorescent light box, similar to those used by physicians to examine X-rays. A horizontal "arm" moves up and down in front of this pad, rising and falling vertically, and that "arm" has a pen attached to it that moves horizontally back and forth along it. This combination of vertical and horizontal movement across the pad is essentially the same movement one achieves in the late twentieth century on a computer by using a "mouse."

Earlier the Mission Director had plotted the Release Point and the IP on the sheet, and I had checked, verified and signed for the order from SAC to strike this target. Now it is my responsibility. If anything goes wrong from here on out, it will be my fault.

When our radar and computers are engaged with the aircraft during the bomb run, the pen will touch the pad and mark in ink the track of the aircraft. Aircraft locations will be "pipped" every 30 seconds with the time marked in GMT for a record of the attack.

All looks good. The four crew members and the Mission Director are in position standing in front of the plotting board with their headsets on. We are ready for the bomb run. I put on my headset as our bombers call in.

"Hello Twine, this is Gravel 4-1, flight of three inbound to PIP, ETA 1537Z, copy?" They are on time and look good at this point.

My Mission Director for this attack is a captain who is a pilot. SAC regulations require a field-grade officer with an aeronautical rating of pilot or navigator to supervise all B-52 missions. I am the Senior Mission Director and will monitor the captain's work and give the authorization for release of the bombs.

"Gravel this is Twine, we read you loud and clear, how copy, over?"

Positive identification is completed by having "Gravel" switch beacon settings, then their progress is followed until they reach the PIP.

At this point the Mission Director takes over the bomb run and provides heading and airspeed adjustment information to the lead aircraft. The bombers adjust their airspeed to achieve a groundspeed that will insure weapons fall into the target area rather than fall short or fly long.

The mission proceeds normally, and is a routine run. The "error," plotted is in feet and marked on the sheet that is then torn off, additional comments are added if necessary, it is folded and placed together with other information concerning the bomb run. Tomorrow, administrative personnel will file it as a historical record of the mission. Eventually, it will make its way back to SAC Headquarters where it will remain in a file for seven years.

The "error" is normally very small, although the final results will await reconnaissance photos the next day. Tonight, at 34,000 feet the bombers fly through a wind out of the southwest at 120 knots. While plotting the run, I factored the wind using reports from different altitudes. Those figures become a "vectored average wind." That wind is used to move the Release Point so that the various winds at different altitudes through which the bombs fall will blow them into the target area as they fall. Our "vectored average wind" tonight is from 283°, and blows at 72 knots, or 82.9 mph. That means this wind would blow the falling bombs 82.9 miles every hour they might fall, or 1.38 miles (7,286.4 feet) for every minute they might fall, or 121.44 feet for every second they will fall. Ballistic tables for these weapons indicate that from 34,000 feet they will fall for 28 seconds. I have moved the release point and an Adjusted IP some 3,400 feet in the direction of the reciprocal of 283°, or toward 103°.

That is the point to which we fly the B-52s and where we order them to release their bombs.

It is a precisely accurate, exactly perfect – guess.

I begin setting up the next run and also start preparations for the one to follow it. The coffee is cooler now but seems even more bitter. I drink half and pour the rest out.

"Any word from ADVON?" I ask Sgt. Smith.

"Yes sir, we got clearance . . . the village is deserted," Smith replies, "Just like they always say."

"OK, you got name, time and authentication, right?"

"Yes sir, authentication is "Tango Sierra," coffee?"

"Yeah, why not?"

"Terrible coffee."

"Awful."

The night wears on. It is a busy, twelve-hour long shift with eight B-52 bomb runs, 650 tons of explosives put into target areas, including 324 of those 500-pound bombs on top of one newly deserted village of grass huts.

Later, I open the door of the van and step out to greet the rising sun. The sun was setting when I last came in here. Tonight, as the sun goes down again, I will be back again.

★ ★ ★

Finally, the six-month tour is beginning to approach its end. As part of my processing out of the area I will need to check in at SAC ADVON headquarters. I have never been in there before. I am expecting something like Headquarters SAC, but am disappointed. I talk with one of the controllers on duty, and am offered a cup of coffee.

"Great!" I say, "Thanks."

"No problem." A cup is filled to the brim.

It is the worst coffee I have ever tasted in my life.

"Man, you got worse coffee than we have in Da Nang!" I say.

"Yeah, the coffee is pretty bitter."

A call comes in from a detachment. One of the controllers calls the guy I am talking with.

"Sir, we got a request for clearance to strike an occupied village."

The controller I am talking with pumps his fist in the air and says, "Go *get* 'em!"

He turns to the sergeant and says, "Tell them authentication is TS . . . Tango Sierra."

I take a swig of the bitter coffee and make a face. "Don't you guys check out the coordinates?" I ask him.

"Who cares?" He says with a grin as he scratches his belly. "There ain't no human beings out there!"

We both have another sip of bitter coffee.

# 54
# Babel

Flares explode in the night sky then slowly drift downward, swinging in their parachutes from side to side, falling through their smoke which trails away above them. This is the airbase called Tan Son Nhut outside Saigon. The sound of nearby artillery rumbles occasionally. Overhead, helicopters "fop-fop-fop-fop" as they constantly pass very low over the base.

The Officers' Club is open for business as usual. In its dimly lighted bar, a tower of Pabst beer cans rises out of a low stratus of cigarette smoke. These are drunk fighter jocks, right? No, they're Canadians! Eh wot?

In another corner of the bar, a group of Poles and Hungarians sit quietly, watching all of this with brooding eyes that appear to be uncomprehending. Part of their problem is that they don't speak English. Another is that they are perhaps the first Soviet-bloc armed forces to be members of a United States Officers' Club in over a generation.

There is also a Filipino officer, three more from Indonesia and some South Vietnamese, along with North Vietnamese officers and Viet Cong in the bar tonight. One bartender is Lao and the other is Cambodian.

Tonight the International Peace Commission (IOC) has gained access to the United States Air Force Officers Club. We Americans have been told that we should not even speak to them, and they have all been told not to be seen in our company or talk to us. Sounds pretty tricky – but we're all military officers, disciplined and stoic – used to carrying out orders – there won't be any problems.

When I walked past the cashier's cage at the Officers' Club earlier in the afternoon I overheard a Canadian officer reluctantly putting the American club card into his billfold, with a sigh, and saying in a clipped British accent to the cashier: "But I'm not supposed to have anything 'American' about me!"

The reply was a flat laconic Texas drawl, "Wal Buster, if you ain't a'gotta card, you ain't a'gonna drink!"

"Well, I can't stay the whole time over here without a drink", the Canadian officer said as he turned away from the cashier, "after all we're just here to help you Yanks get yer arse out of this crack you've wedged it into!"

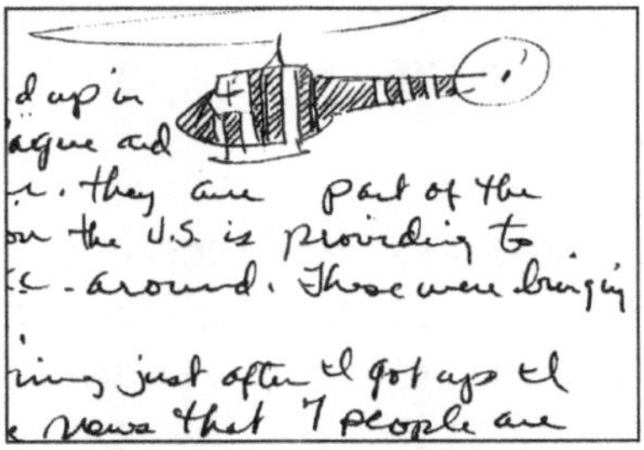


Later, eight or ten helicopters landed near the center of the base. They were all American choppers, still dressed in their normal jungle camouflage but now sporting brand new white stripes, or bands that encircle their fuselage and which signify they are on an IOC mission. They are part of the transportation the U.S. is providing to carry members of the IOC around. Two of the helicopters unloaded Canadians, three had Austrians, all with red stars on their shoulders, and one helicopter was loaded with Viet Cong, clad in their black pajamas.

Now, later that same evening the sun has set and red clouds drift by under a red heaven. At 9:00 p.m. we are being profligate with our flares. Periodically our big guns rumble, as they will throughout the night. Possibly it's all a show for those who don't speak English.

As the evening turns into night we run out of Pabst beer, which is the only beer available, probably due to some corporate influence back in Washington.

More beer is found. It is brought in and served warm, because there is no ice available. It is hard to tell who made the beer because the name seems to have been scrubbed away. It looks like the label printed on the can has worn thin. Someone figures out the name had once been "Schlitz". Worse, it is not pop-top. It is the old fashioned steel can that requires a "church-key" to open. Worse yet, there are no "church-keys" in the entire club. So we are forced to cut our way in with pocketknives. There are a few injuries. A Hungarian Lieutenant stands up brandishing a huge bayonet above his head and he is greeted with a great cheer.

The beer is terrible. It tastes awful. Everyone wonders where it was found. We haven't seen this type of can in years! And what has happened to the can to begin with?

"You know where the Yanks found this stuff?" A Polish-sounding voice cries out in a high-pitched shout.

"Well, it's just American beer!" An Asian accented voice in the crowd ventures.

"Yow, what the 'ell do you expect?" Yells someone else, with a strong Cockney accent. "Yer en Huh-merica now!'

"Ghod!" The first voice responds. "It's leftover beer from that other mess'n Korea!"

"Oh NO!" Uproar and grumbling follow, then a stentorian English voice calls out.

"Yah, the label ha been 'blit'rated w' naval jelly!"

"Boooo!" A stomping of feet is heard and a sound of hissing rises in the club.

Well, let the record reflect that an ad hoc multinational, multilingual task force was assembled to collect funds of different currencies from those present and then proceed off base to buy beer.

Soon, real beer is available and appreciatively being consumed. Singh-ha, Kirin, and of course, Heineken. Singing breaks out. A multilingual peacekeeping arm of the UN is exuberantly pursuing common goals and striving earnestly toward world peace.

It is suggested by someone that we commandeer a helicopter for the beer runs. A great cheer goes up!

The jukebox strikes up a song about a city in Michigan. We all sing along with different words and strange accents: "Well . . . I spent last night . . . in Saigon City . . . "

But – wait! This could be dangerous. Aren't these the bad guys?

Or was that us?

Wot th'ell, the war is over – we're goin 'ome!

# 55
# The Day the Domino Fell

Tuesday 23 January, 1973. Tan Son Nhut, South Vietnam. If I were a Greek poet inclined along the lines of tragedy, I would have to write of this Great War now ending.

Better yet, it would have to be a play; a long, writhing and torturous enactment filled with hideous and haunted creatures. In the last act I would appease the Gods of War by sacrificing all the great players in the name of Hatred and Vengeance. They would all be together in that final act. Ho Chi Minh would be there and so would General Giap. JFK would have a cameo roll and would be there too, along with Goldwater and Nixon. They would all have their parts to play, and then go down into the underworld, each gibbering in his own self-righteous way.

The bit players would be composed of SAM gunners and B-52 crewmembers.

The main chorus, standing on elevated benches around the back of the stage would be composed of the U. S. Congress, singing their great anthem "I Am Still Playing Dumb on Purpose."

In the end, of course, all the players would devour each other and then as the war ended, the gods would demand one last, magnificently worthy sacrifice. Then they would snatch a surprised - and not-yet-ready-to-go - Lyndon Johnson and drag him down screaming into the underworld.

Finally satisfied, they would retire for a while from the affairs of man. I can almost hear their muted voices departing into the realms below: "Come LBJ, after you have suffered sufficiently, we will make you one of us! Then we'll all come back again . . . ho-ho-ho!" And their voices would fade into the crevice, which would close above them leaving a final plume of smoke to gasp with a hiss into the world.

Wednesday, 24 January 1973. "LBJ IS DEAD!" All over MACV headquarters lay copies of today's military newspaper, The Pacific Stars and Stripes, with three-inch high headlines telling the news.

On the morning radio broadcast we hear that President Nixon will address the nation today at 1100 (Saigon time). Before that he will talk with his cabinet and leaders of congress. There is an air of expectation that is very strong over here in MACV HQ. Nobody knows for sure what the details will be as far as Cambodia and Laos are concerned, or the timing of the withdrawal, but there is a feeling of finality, and a cautious, expectant waiting, a feeling of subdued celebration. Every twenty minutes the military radio station runs a thirty-second bit with "Hail to the Chief" and announces that Nixon will address the nation at 1100 hours and that all radio stations in Vietnam will carry it.

Same day, 1230 hours. So, the war is to end at 0800 hours Sunday morning. MACV has gone from an almost Christmas Eve electricity to the quietness of a Sunday afternoon. A general feeling of peace is here now, but it seems like the aftermath of a big football game. It's over. And we lost. Much work will have to be done to put the pieces back together again and move us all out of Vietnam but nothing is being done by anybody right now.

Later. 1500 hours. I stand outside MACV Headquarters and make a picture of the flag at half-mast for LBJ. It is unreal – so quiet – no one is around, there is no movement of anything, anywhere. Sounds seem far away and muted, the smell of grass lingers on the air; fluffy little clouds slowly float over the earth as if nothing has changed for the past ten million years. All is still, very still. But everything has already changed dramatically from this morning.

Saturday 27 January 1973. Tan Son Nhut Airbase, South Vietnam. Fifteen minutes until midnight. At this very

moment, the agreement to end the American involvement in the Vietnam war is being signed in Paris.

Outside, however, the sky is burning. Flares are falling through black clouds of smoke all around the base. The sky is filled with fire. The sound of our artillery is continuous, like thunder – no, more like a heavy "thump" like a big rug is shaken - "thump-thump-thump-thump-thump-thump" ... on and on. And we have been rattled and shaken four times since 10:00 p.m. by Arc Light strikes (B-52 missions) nearby, one of which caused buildings on Tan Son Nhut to sway and things inside them to rattle and fall off shelves. The artillery firings seem very close and continue long into the early hours of the morning.

Sunday 28 January 1973. Tan Son Nhut Airbase, South Vietnam. This is it. The day the war ends. The domino shall finally fall. At 6:30 a.m., one and one-half hours before the cease-fire goes into effect, I am awakened as my bed and room are violently shaken. The window is rattling in its frame. "Boom-boom!" "Boom-boom!" A double noise, hollow-sounding, not so much like something exploding as it is like something very heavy hitting the ground. I think of an old wooden case full of cola bottles that might have fallen from a roof to the sidewalk - two of them falling right together. The explosions continue, intensifying and getting closer; then suddenly there is silence.

On the telephone poles outside, the base loudspeaker system, known as "Giant Voice", can be heard but it is muffled and cannot be understood. Immediately thereafter, the base sirens rise in a piercing wail. I get my little pocket radio and turn it to "Lone Star" the base "civil defense" FM station.

"This is Radio Lone Star, 101.4 on your FM dial. Tan Son Nhut Air Base is under attack. All personnel take cover; I repeat . . ." Then the loudspeaker kicks in again: "This is Giant Voice, This is Giant Voice! Tan Son Nhut is under rocket and artillery attack. Alert Status is Red. All personnel take cover immediately; I repeat. . . "

6:40 a.m. "Boom-boom!" "Boom-boom!" I feel the shock waves from more mortars hitting close by. Immediately the sirens sound again. Lone Star broadcasts its statement every minute. Then there is a new sound: "Fop-fop-fop-fop!" All over the place, helicopters, barely airborne, are racing at great speed across Tan Son Nhut just above the rooftops. Giant Voice comes up again informing us that the Red Alert was now "Option One" and that nonessential personnel were to take cover and remain there until further notice. It added that the Security Police would not assemble for shift change at 0700 hours.

6:50 a.m. The sirens sound again, and almost immediately a very faint "boom-boom!" boom-boom!" can be heard. Now there is a new sound, that of the big rug being shaken. Our artillery has gotten coordinates and is coughing into life. First, one gun sounds, about half-a-minute later a second fires, another ten seconds and a third gun sounds, and then a fourth and a fifth. Then the firings merge into a constant sound until they increase to become a hollow, unbroken roar like that of a great waterfall nearby.

7:00 a.m. The AFVN news speaks of the great happiness in the United States over the cease-fire. A few megacycles up the FM band, "Lone Star" continues: "Tan Son Nhut is under attack! All personnel take cover! Take cover!" The artillery attack by our own forces intensifies and the sky is filled with helicopters.

8:00 a.m. The AFVN reads Nixon's proclamation about one minute of quiet for thanksgiving at the movement of the cease-fire, and the station is quiet for one minute. Lone Star is not. I tune my radio back to it: "Tan Son Nhut is under attack! All personnel take cover! Take cover!" Neither are our big guns or helicopters quiet. The place is roaring and vibrating with heavy sounds.

Back to the other frequency where I hear now how happy the US is and how peace has come to Vietnam.

Back to Lone Star: "Tan Son Nhut is under attack! Tan Son Nhut is under attack! All personnel take cover! Take cover!"

Back to the other frequency where I hear about the wonderful ceremony that is taking place at this moment in Vietnam. "Right now, at this moment, at Tan Son Nhut Air Base, in Vietnam, a great ceremony of peace is being conducted at the base chapel."

My quarters are right across from the base chapel. I go to the window in my door and look across the street. The base chapel is deserted. The siren on the pole by the chapel is starting up again.

The radio continues. ". . . And now peace will come to this entire region . . .."

0815 hours. Giant Voice announces that we are now on Yellow Alert. So I take off my flak jacket and go outside on a flawless Sunday morning. Clean, beautiful, fresh. Rubber plants are blooming their perfect little wheel-like white petals accenting the low clouds, which lazily float by. The roar of our artillery which had been absolutely

constant for almost two hours continues without letup until 0830 hours when all firing ceased instantly.
The rest of the day is quiet.

Monday 29 January 1993. Tan Son Nhut Airbase, South Vietnam

The IOC Peace Team is evident today. Indonesians are everywhere. Today, in front of MACV headquarters there is an American staff car with a large white flag of truce, or surrender, on its fender, and a small Canadian flag under that.

Walking down the halls of MACV headquarters about 11:00 a.m., I hear someone ahead of me whistling very loudly the tune of "Joy" from Beethoven's great Ninth Symphony. Ironic! I think to myself. There really hasn't been very much joy of any kind over here for a long time. There certainly isn't any joy over the peace treaty and cease-fire because we feel that we gave away far too much. So, the enthusiasm has been very restrained – officially. A BOQ full of Forward Air Controllers got drunk last night and tore up their quarters in a futile remembrance of their close friends and buddies who had been shot down and lost. Among the staff, skepticism and resignation is conveyed on long sighs. But still, we are out! The matter of whether we approve or disapprove no longer matters because it is over. We are through in Vietnam. That thought is slowly forming in our minds and beings. The Domino has fallen – and it turns out that we military people were it. There is no joy here.

Yet, the unknown whistler has kept on whistling and it is becoming louder and louder, to the point where it is almost embarrassing. Like many others, I too am looking to see who is doing it, but can't locate him. Then someone else joins him! And then another, and another! Finally, I too join in, and then others also. And the halls of MACV headquarters ring and resonate to a choir of whistlers marching without cadence to Beethoven's "Joy."

Now, finally Lord – a moment of grace.

# 56
# Doom Pussy

The first time I saw the Doom Pussy it was crouched on a mantel staring at the open door. Subdued light played over its smooth silver-gray ceramic body and above its mystical smile the dawn of apocalypse glinted from its emerald-green eyes.

Squadron patches had been hung above and all around the bar, here at the Officers' Club in Da Nang. And painted on the wall behind the bar was a mural of a Vietnamese hillside with an F-4 flying down through the area shooting people who were trying to run. Below the picture was a title: "Yea, though I fly through the Valley of the Shadow of Death, I will fear no evil – 'cause I'm the meanest son-of-a-bitch in the valley!"

I arrived on an Army Caribou, a U-21, landing at 0915 on 8 Jan, 1973. Da Nang was first visible as a tall black column of smoke. We could see flames leaping 200 feet or more into the sky. We taxied in and shut down in front of base operations. Everybody but us had a rifle or pistol. All the conversation was about the rocket attack at 0820.

Later though, we were to find out that the U.S. Navy had bombed the fuel tanks at Da Nang by mistake.

The next morning I joined up with several sergeants for our trip up Monkey Mountain to our radar site. The truck was a 2 1/2 ton stake bed with a canvas cover. Three of us rode up front, I manned the right side window; one sergeant got in the back. He brought in with him a number of large rocks and pieces of concrete, each of which probably weighed between 20 and 40 pounds. Since they appeared to be obviously trash, I asked Sergeant Jones about it and he said "That's in case anyone tries to climb in the back of the truck when we drive through town . . . Smith wants to have some 'business cards' to 'hand out.'"

We picked up the rest of the crew for the trip up the mountain and Jones brought in a mean looking rifle.

"What's that?" I asked

"Grease gun," Jones said as he started the truck engine.

"What's it for?"

"This your first trip to Da Nang, sir?"

"Yes, how'd you know?

"Oh, just curious."

We rolled out of the motor pool and slowly drove off Da Nang Air Force Base. The country was filled with people. I noticed a couple of young one-armed women carrying babies, a number of little boys on crutches, some with one leg missing.

We drove through the edge of what appeared to be a city.

"Get ready to roll the window up if I call for it," Jones said.

About half way through the town we had to slow down as a woman on a bicycle with a little baby behind her slowed down in the road ahead of us.

"A'Right!" Shouted Jones, " We're being attacked. . . look out for the cowboys!"

He stuck his head out the window. "Smith!" He called toward the back of the truck. "Watch out!"

The woman with the baby slowed down and I noticed a young man wearing a straw hat and flip-flops and carrying a machete coming into view on a motor scooter.

"Roll up the damn window!" Jones shouted. He turned the truck quickly to the left to try to pass the woman, but she turned and stayed in front. Jones turned violently to the right, almost running over the guy on our right, but he had just moved closer to us and was now joined by another scooter with two guys on it and who rode right behind him. Two other scooters closed in on our left side. This was obviously a carefully practiced maneuver. The woman turned again and stayed in front us.

One of the guys on the back of the scooter was reaching for our truck door handle and the woman with the bicycle was going slower and slower, still right in front of us.

Jones was downshifting the truck ready to stop. Then he gunned it and ran one of the "cowboys" into the side of the road where he collided with a fruit stand and then he passed the woman who was still trying to get in front of him knocking her and the baby down into the road, as we got free of them.

The trip took on a somber tone and we proceeded in silence, driving up the mountain on an asphalt road that was cracked in many places, worn and gutted all over. It varied in width from one-car wide to areas where it would accommodate three or four vehicles. I had noticed that the mountain on which our radar site was located was actually named "Marble Mountain," so I asked why everybody called it "Monkey Mountain."

"Well, let me TELL you . . ." Sergeant Taylor replied emphatically. " . . . Right up here . . . couple more curves . . . there's an overlook . . ." He started looking through the windshield at the jungle as the trees formed a canopy over the road. "About six months ago, Sergeant Wells and me was driving up here. He stopped the jeep and I got out to take a leak, and a damn monkey came out of the bushes and gibbered and danced and started putting on a big show, the most amazing thing I ever saw. It was really funny. Then I heard Wells shouting: 'Let's Go - LET'S GO!' I looked and saw a whole bunch of these monkeys galloping at full speed from another direction. I jumped in the Jeep, and the monkey who had been dancing for me jumped in with me – he was as big as I am. I shot him with my .38 just as he grabbed me and we barely got away . . ." He looked carefully at the jungle, now close to the truck. "... now I go to the bathroom *before* I make this trip." The "monkeys", I found out later, were really members of the baboon family and thought to be dangerous if encountered in a pack.

We passed out of the jungle and worked our way back and forth along a ridge that looked down on the jungle on one side and onto the ocean and Da Nang on the other.

Finally we reached the radar site that was built into a large bunker on top of Monkey Mountain. We called in at a telephone on a pole outside identifying ourselves. The gate opened and we passed into the compound.

When we parked, Smith climbed out of the back of the truck and said he had "handed out" two or three "business cards" going through town.

That was the first time I saw Da Nang.

The second time I went there, the Officer's Club was not in good shape. There was still a Doom Pussy but it was not the real thing, just a poorly thrown ceramic imitation. That was when I ran into Marshall, a pilot with whom I had flown a number of times in the past. I hadn't seen him in years. He looked terrible. We talked for a minute. I had to go, my airplane was leaving. He got my arm, wouldn't let go. Told me he was flying C-123s and had just come off of a series of runs in and out of fields out in the jungle carrying troops into combat positions. The last group he took in, he said, were all kids who had just gotten over to Vietnam.

"I made a bad approach, bounding up and down in the updrafts and I made a hard landing . . . almost let it get out of control and nearly ran into the goddamn jungle . . . barely stopped and got turned around while the troops got out and the platoon on the ground loaded us back up again . . . I had to go down to the cargo area to help get the load put in so the weight would be even . . . some of the bodies were not . . . in bags . . . we got blood and . . . parts . . . pieces . . . all over the place . . . one of the kids was crying and wanted to talk to ME - he grabbed my arm and was trying to tell me something - we started getting hit by small arms fire . . . I had to PULL my arm away from him. I climbed back up on the flight deck and got the hell out of there."

Marshall sat down, slumping into his chair and looked down towards the floor.

"I gotta go, Marshall . . ." I said " . . . it's good to see you . . . I gotta go."

He took my hand in his, holding it tightly and looked up at me as the smell of smoke from fires outside drifted into the room.

"We got back here . . . taxied to the loading point . . ." his eyes were red ". . . new guys . . . just got in from the states last night" his voice got real high "first night in 'Nam . . . they were kids . . . just boys . . . they followed their sergeant on and saw all the bodies and . . . blood . . . and pieces . . . and . . . " he shook his head slowly ". . . they all had their lips pulled way back, some were crying . . . you could see their teeth they were so scared. Marshall buried his face in his hands. "One kid fainted . . . the sergeant made them take the bodies and . . . the pieces . . . out of the cargo area . . . wash it down with a hose . . . we took off . . . the cargo area where they sat . . . going into combat, smelled like hell – it smelled like . . . death . . . I made a terrible landing and the kids jumped out . . . one of them had wet his pants . . . God, going into combat like that . . . and then . . . their first job . . . load bodies and . . . parts . . . of the guys they were relieving, in our cargo bay . . . then we took off . . ." Marshall started crying quietly, his face all wrinkled up. I pulled my hand out of his.

I had to go, my flight was leaving. I never saw him again.

The last time I saw Da Nang was during my third tour over there, very late in the war after peace negotiations were pretty well finalized. Our withdrawal was well underway and the truce teams had begun arriving at

MACVHQ. I remember pausing at a wooden bridge over a klong in Da Nang City under palm trees, looking at the people, so many of them in pain, and on crutches, missing a leg and sometimes an arm, some badly burned. There was a feeling in the air that you could almost touch: "Charlie's Coming!"

The Officer's Club was a disaster. Water was running from broken faucets, the front door was gone. A Doom Pussy was still there but missing its head and shoulders. The picture behind the bar was also still there but a devil's head protruded out of the F-4 cockpit and the words "HAH! HAH! HAH!" had been smeared in red, like it was blood, and maybe it was, across the picture. The squadron patches had been ripped out and many were still lying on the floor. Some had been burnt, some urinated on.

We had to get down to the flight line, get on our airplane.

It was time to go.

# 57

# Simple Things

Snow fell on our southern mountains last night and it was carried by some wind, and between the two of them our National Public Radio station was off the air this morning. By noon the snow ended and the afternoon brings sunshine and warmth, and the winter day becomes mild and gentle.

I scan the radio dial looking for news while making sandwiches. One country music station is playing the "Green, Green Grass of Home." I listen for a moment then resume my search and when I can't find any news I turn the radio off. But that song stays in my mind.

I slice the buns thinking *how long ago was that nightmare, really?* My last trip over there was 1973, more than thirty years ago. *It has been a long time.* Horseradish mustard is spread over the buns, *Yes, it was a long time ago; let's forget about it, it was just one of those things.* I get onion slices and bell pepper out of the refrigerator and begin chopping them.

As I turn back to the refrigerator for cheese, I glance out the kitchen door and look across the peaceful valley at the beautiful mountains. What a wonderful winter day, and what great pleasure to savor the simple things of life.

I smell the fragrance of newly sliced cheddar cheese. Simple things of life, yes, the smell of cheese and mild winter days, like the green, green grass of home, and being in the presence of those you love.

"Hey," my wife calls from the living room "there's more to decorating the tree than just putting it in the stand!" And she peeps around the corner of the room, smiling sweetly at me.

"I'll be back but I have get this done too." And I return the smile as I lay a slice of tomato on the cheese, which now lies on the bun.

*And they'll all come to see me . . .* I think of McNamara and his admission in 1995 that he and President Johnson knew the war was lost as early as 1965, and that we fought all the rest of it, the big part of it, those last seven years, killing 50,000 more American troops and more than a million Vietnamese to try to "save the presidency." All that to try to save Johnson and then Nixon from disgrace.

I chop cilantro, listening to the Christmas music now coming out of the living room, "Oh Come, All Ye Faithful." Those guys who died over there, most of them probably knew that song, it's one you learn pretty early in life.

*What have I learned since I came back from there?* After divorce and remarriage, it was mostly simple things: watching your kids graduate from school, playing baseball with them, holding hands with your wife, watching plays at school, talking with your children. Sharing simple things with your grandchildren. Like joy. "Joy to the world! The Lord is come!" Fresh green lettuce is put on top of the tomatoes and jalapeno peppers are sliced and added.

*Why must there be four gray walls in that other song?* That's not simple. I slice olives and look for oregano. *Yes, why does there have to be four gray walls?*

Well, sometimes that's the way it turns out when the truth gets too complicated to be told straight.

Our dogs bark at something that can't be seen, then lose interest in that and stretch out in the sun. The cat is on the deck railing, licking her paws. *They'll all come to see me . . . well, perhaps not all.* For a moment I wonder how many dogs and cats had lain in the sun, long, lonely days, a third of a century ago now, trying to recall the familiar face or the voice of a kid, their dearest companion, whose face had been stomped out in the mud of a faraway Vietnamese jungle, but who still somehow, seemed very near to them, where they might sometimes strongly feel his presence but who was just *barely* out of their reach.

Meanwhile, "New Strategies for Victory" followed each other in ghastly parade, marching like good soldiers, out of the Oval Office, marching to graveyards, every one. But dogs and cats are not really important, not in the grand scale of battles and kingdoms and presidencies. They are also simple things, and cannot stand in the way of important people or of Necessary Lies or the slow turning of the earth. So they slowly turned along with the earth, fading, day by day into oblivion.

Women sit rocking, out on these mountain porches, smiling at their husbands, and their children, and now their grandchildren. Do they remember those young men, kids really, who would have been their husbands and who would have fathered their children and shared their life with them - if they had come back from Vietnam? I know they haven't forgotten them. Those women didn't go over there, that's true, but a part of them didn't ever come back from over there either. And I wonder if they ever think of how it might have been.

And there are the parents - now gone perhaps, or maybe just simply forgotten. Old people they are today, cheated out of children and grandchildren, who live in a strange world of emotions in which even joy, when it comes to them, comes with sighs and a sad smile on its face.

So now that is over – all but the memories and the dreams. And I like the dreams best of all. Oh yes, I still remember what it was like to be young and to fly and fight for my country. In those days, before McNamara, Johnson and Nixon, it seemed easy to know what was wrong and what was right. We thought the bad guys were all "over there" somewhere, and we military men went over there to carry the fight to them and straighten them out.

But Vietnam was different. It was a war that began as a president's lie which the politicians turned into the nation's war. Somehow, it all wound up in the end being just the military's peculiar little problem.

Eventually, we learned again, one more time, that peace does not come through the waging of war; defense is one thing, but war only creates more war. Peace can only come from the waging of peace. And that's another of those simple things of life.

www.ingramcontent.com/pod-product-compliance
Lightning Source LLC
Chambersburg PA
CBHW031613160426
43196CB00006B/121
*9780965554657*